Claire Macdonald and her husband run Kinloch Lodge Hotel on the Isle of Skye, which is also the family home for them and their four children. Claire is a well-known exponent of Scottish cooking and travels widely, lecturing and demonstrating recipes.

Also by Claire Macdonald

SEASONAL COOKING
SWEET THINGS
MORE SEASONAL COOKING
SUPPERS

and published by Corgi Books

Celebrations

Claire Macdonald
of Macdonald

CORGI BOOKS

CELEBRATIONS
A CORGI BOOK : 0 552 99436 7

Originally published in Great Britain by
Bantam Press, a division of Transworld Publishers Ltd

PRINTING HISTORY
Bantam Press edition published 1989
Corgi edition published 1991
Corgi edition reprinted 1992
Corgi edition reprinted 1994
Corgi edition reprinted 1995
Corgi edition reprinted 1996

This book was set in 11/12 Baskerville by
Photoprint, Torquay, Devon.

Corgi Books are published by Transworld Publishers Ltd,
61– 63 Uxbridge Road, London W5 5SA,
in Australia by Transworld Publishers (Australia) Pty Ltd,
15– 25 Helles Avenue, Moorebank, NSW 2170,
and in New Zealand by Transworld Publishers (NZ) Ltd,
3 William Pickering Drive, Albany, Auckland.

Printed and bound in Great Britain by
Cox & Wyman Ltd, Reading, Berkshire

Contents

Acknowledgements

I have a great many people to thank for helping me with this book, chiefly Kate Parkin, until recently of Bantam Press; Kate has become such a friend over the past few years, and she is infinitely supportive and encouraging. With Kate work seems like fun. I would also like to thank Sue Atkinson, who took the photographs. Sue, Kate and I worked very hard whilst doing the photographs and in spite of storm force winds and driving rain during the week of photographing, we even achieved an outside picnic shot – no mean feat, considering the Hebridean weather conditions, I can tell you! I would also like to thank Annette Stephen, from the bottom of my heart, for all her hard work during the photography session, and at all other times in our lives generally. It is thanks to Annette that I ever get anything done at all in my life, because she does for me all the things which take up time as well as setting me a good example by beavering away in the background. I want to thank dear Pete (Peter Macpherson) for all his work, help and encouragement, and also Millie MacLure and Sharon Dowie, both indispensable members of our team here at Kinloch.

I want to thank my friends, all of them, but in particular Minty Dallmeyer, Char Donaldson, and Caroline Fox (in diplomatic alphabetic order!) and my dear cousin, Judith Coleridge. Thanks too to my sisters, Camilla Westwood and Olivia Milburn. Last but not least, I would like to dedicate this book to darling Gog, and to my four fantastic children, Alexandra, Isabella, Meriel and Hugo, who put up with a vague and dotty mum and they often can't think why I'm endlessly typing or on the phone – as Meriel said to me one day, 'Mummy, your name is on the cover of this book,' and when I told her that was because I had written it, she began to comprehend just what I was doing at the typewriter! So, a big thank you and hugs all round.

Introduction

I do love an excuse for a party, and luckily life is punctuated throughout the year by genuine reasons to indulge the desire to entertain; some of these are annual events like Christmas, New Year, Easter, birthdays, anniversaries, and some are the once-in-a-lifetime events such as Christenings, Confirmation or First Communion, Silver or Golden Wedding Anniversaries. Living where we do, in the Isle of Skye, off the north-west coast of Scotland, one rarely invites friends for lunch or dinner, whatever the occasion. Much more usually the invitation is for at least a couple of nights' duration – as far as I'm concerned, the longer the better! I love having family and friends to stay – but there is one great proviso to this, and that is, that over twenty years of married life, fifteen of them living here in Skye, I've realized ever increasingly that *my* amount of enjoyment in entertaining lies in the work and preparation put in before my guests arrive. That is where I hope this book will be useful to you. It is written for those of us who have very little or no help in the kitchen, and so the menus and recipes are planned and thought out to involve the minimum of last-minute preparation, and with as much as possible being made, prepared ahead, in some cases frozen, to allow you, the hostess (or host), the maximum time to spend with your family and friends. My advice is to decide on everything to be eaten for each meal (breakfast included)

9

throughout the duration of a visit. I make a menu list, and stick it on the fridge door, with, beside it, an almost equally important list to remind me of what to take out of the freezer and when! The menus are also designed for the great number of people who say to me that they just can never decide what to cook when; the menus are intended to be a guideline only, you can, of course, exchange recipes for various occasions throughout the book, the suggestions are there only to save you thinking for yourself – and hopefully to inspire you! They follow a pattern that I have used myself on so many occasions, truly a case of experience. For example, for the chapter on Easter, I have planned roast smoked pork loin for dinner on Maundy Thursday, advising you to cook more than you need, so that you can have it thinly sliced to serve with scrambled eggs with crumbled goat's cheese in it for Brunch on Easter Saturday. Thankfully, brunch is becoming a far more widely recognized meal in this country – it has been so for a long time in the United States. Brunch means that if your guests get up rather late you avoid having two meals, breakfast and lunch within a short space of time, instead, able to enjoy a leisurely and delicious meal and then have a long time to go for a walk or sit and read or play games till it's time for a cup of tea – and something delectably cake or biscuit orientated to eat with it! That's the thing about entertaining over a space of a few days, it seems (or should seem) like a holiday for everyone under the roof – host and hostess included.

There is a chapter with suggestions for Picnic and Barbecue entertaining – both forms of entertaining which I love. There are several occasions which call for picnics or picnic food more elaborate than the cold sausage and chicken drumstick variety, and they are great fun to plan for – and to eat! As for barbecues, well, I just love them, because however smart they are in their food content, they have an unavoidable air of informality.

Within the book there is a brief chapter on funerals; don't for one minute think that I consider them a Celebration, but they *do* occur in every family's life at some time or another, and however expected the demise of the member of the family, there is very little time and warning between death and funeral to plan. As a great many people attending the funeral of a friend often travel some distance to do so, they naturally require some sustenance following the service. This is not nearly so sad an event as might be supposed, because it is an inescapable fact that a sort of euphoria descends immediately following the service and funeral, but food there has to be. In this chapter I suggest cold weather food and food for warmer weather which is simple (no one attending such an event comes in anticipation of a gastronomic treat), straightforward to prepare, and which will be able to be either kept warm while everyone is at the service, or which can be left all ready to be eaten immediately on return. I hope it helps not to have to rack brains as to what to cook for such an occasion, when it occurs. Another chapter contains Festival Food – as so many cities throughout Britain host festivals, there is often a real dilemma as to what to eat during the festival evenings, when keen festival-goers return, peckish, from an evening of culture. The same food, of course, is perfect for after theatre or cinema eating anywhere and at any time, festival or no.

The biggest chapter in the book is the one on Christmas and New Year; these have to be planned for together, and as far in advance as is possible. Such is my love of this particular time of year with its celebrations, that my anticipation begins round about the end of June! But almost more than any other time of the year, Christmas and New Year planning is vital, because there is just so much going on, especially if you, like us, have a number of children in the family with countless stockings to fill (everyone under the roof gets a stocking here),

11

numerous presents to wrap, and all the other thousand and one things to try not to forget during the month of December and leading up to January. Personally, I always feel that December should have six weeks in the month – four of them being before Christmas, and an extra one between Christmas and New Year. However, hopefully, if you follow one or two of my suggested menus you will be able to forget the food side of life, once Christmas arrives, and be able to enjoy each day every bit as much as those staying with you. I have given three possible main courses for Christmas, all with stuffings and accompaniments which can be made three or four weeks in advance and frozen. Much of the other food suggested for eating around Christmas and New Year can be frozen, all ready to be just lifted from the freezer and thawed, before being reheated ready to serve to your family and friends.

There are a couple of small chapters, one with a few recipes for alternative main courses to substitute wherever necessary should you be entertaining non-meat eaters, and the other small chapter with ideas for Sunday night suppers, should you have guests staying until Monday morning. Although I love people to stay for as long as possible, somehow Sunday evening supper catches me at my all-time culinary low! So I hope those of you who feel the same way will find inspiration in the half dozen suggestions.

I just hope that the contents of this book are a real help to all who read it – entertaining *should* be fun, and guests should never be made to feel that they are a nuisance just because they are there and have to be fed and entertained. I'm sure that if the prospective hostess reads within there will never be any reason for her to feel even remotely martyred. Good luck, and good entertaining!

TWO CHRISTENING LUNCHES FOR TEN

—————⁕⁕⁕⁕⁕—————

Cheese and anchovy triangles
Spicy meatballs
Spicy tomato sauce

Cold poached salmon
Lemon, cucumber and chive mayonnaise
New potatoes with dill
Tomato, melon and applemint salad
Mixed green salad
OR
Venison ragoût with chestnuts, port and orange
Glazed celeriac, parsnips and carrots
Mousseline potatoes
Rich lime pie with crystallized lime slices
Chocolate and coffee iced profiteroles
Lemon christening cake

Christening Lunch

Whether you have your baby's christening within weeks of birth or at a few months old, you will still be short of time, due to the inevitable and unavoidable demands of an infant. I think the second baby is the worst – for the first one at least there is no-one to consider besides yourselves and it; with the second you have not only the new arrival but also the predecessor to contend with! Our children all seemed to be christened within six or seven weeks of birth, and for our second daughter's christening I felt numb with exhaustion. In the days running up to the event we had several mishaps via the antics of Alexandra, our eldest, then two-and-a-half. She flooded a bathroom while I was getting ready to ice the christening cake, and then, when I went to investigate the possible cause of water cascading down the larder walls, she went into the kitchen, saw the marzipanned cake, and couldn't resist taking a mouthful from the top and side, until then as neatly edged as I could make it. I had to turn the cake upside down and start again, filling in with a chunk of marzipan the bite-sized hole, like a master plasterer. I vented my wrath on her bottom.

The important thing to remember about a christening lunch is that it has to be carefully planned so that the food can be made and frozen, or at least be prepared, several days in advance without spoiling. Also, if, as is most usual, the service takes place in the morning, you want to be able to leave everything ready for you and your guests to come home to, and spare yourself any further slaving away in the kitchen. I suggest two menus; one, for warm weather, consists of *Cold poached salmon*, with *Lemon, cucumber and chive mayonnaise*, accompanied by *New potatoes cooked with dill*, *Tomato, melon and applemint salad*, and a mixed green salad; for cold weather, my suggested main course is *Venison ragoût with chestnuts, port and orange* – a warm and rich casserole which can be made two or three days in advance and kept, covered, in a fridge. With the venison, I would serve *Mousseline potatoes*, and *Glazed celeriac, parsnips and carrots*.

In my planning I dispense with an actual first course as I think two dishes which can be eaten in the fingers with a drink, on return from church, are much better. Whatever the weather, *Cheese and anchovy triangles* and *Spicy meatballs* served with a tomato sauce dip are both tasty. The triangles, meatballs and tomato dip can be made the previous day – or, in the case of the *Cheese and anchovy triangles*, they can be made several weeks ahead and frozen, then just warmed through to serve.

Two puddings which can be enjoyed in warm or cold weather are *Rich lime pie with crystallized lime slices*, and *Chocolate and coffee iced profiteroles*. For a christening cake we tend to think of a rich fruit cake, and for a first baby there is usually the top tier of the wedding cake which has been kept for just this occasion. If you like a fruit cake I can think of none better than the Christmas cake recipe on pages 266–8. But for a break with tradition why not try a pale cake, flavoured with lemon and simply white-iced? I am not a very proficient cake icer so, for me, the simpler the better, but a white icing with tiny rosettes piped around the top edge and the base of the cake looks surprisingly neat. And in the centre of the cake a small silver or glass vase or container with a few fresh wild or garden flowers, depending on the time of year, looks simple and suitable.

Cheese and anchovy triangles

Makes about 60 triangles

These can be made as far in advance as you like and
frozen. Thaw them for a couple of hours at room
temperature and warm them in a cool oven to serve.

---

8 oz/250 g chilled butter
8 oz/250 g plain flour
8 oz/250 g grated Cheddar
  cheese

2 rounded tsp mustard
  powder
a dash of Tabasco
Anchovy paste – you can buy
  this from good
  delicatessens, or use
  Patum Peperium
  (Gentlemen's Relish)

Cut the butter into bits and put into a food processor
together with the flour, grated cheese, mustard powder
and Tabasco. Whiz till the mixture forms a ball. Then
dust a work surface with flour, and take about a third of
the dough. Form it into two long strips, and roll these to
a thickness of about ¼ in/5 mm with a floured rolling
pin. If you form the dough into the strips with your
floured hands before rolling it, it is much easier – it is
such a rich dough it tends to stick to a rolling pin if you
try to roll it from the first. Spread each neat strip with a
thin layer of anchovy paste. Cut each strip into triangles,
each about an inch/2.5 cm across. Using a palette knife,
put the cheese pastry triangles onto a baking tray. Bake
in a hot oven – 450°F/230°C/Gas 8/top right oven in a 4-
door Aga – for 10 minutes (take care, they burn easily).
When they are cooked, let the triangles cool for a minute
on the baking tray before carefully lifting them off, with a

palette knife, onto a wire cooling rack. When they are quite cold, store them in an airtight tin, for a few days, or freeze them in the tin.

Spicy meatballs

Makes 50–60 meatballs

These meatballs can be served cold, or you can reheat them in a moderate oven for 15 minutes while your guests are removing their coats on return from church. Serve them on an ashet or serving plate with a bowl of the *Spicy tomato sauce* (see below) in the middle of the plate, and an eggcup of toothpicks to spear the meatballs and dip them to avoid messy fingers.

---

2 lb/1 kg lean beef, minced
1 medium onion, skinned and chopped very finely
2 oz/50 g fresh white or brown breadcrumbs
2 tbsp chopped parsley
½ tsp salt, and freshly ground black pepper

1 rounded tsp medium curry powder
1 large egg, beaten
1 dstsp mango chutney, avoiding any pieces of mango
about 2 oz/50 g plain flour
oil for frying (I use sunflower)

In a food processor whiz together well the minced beef, finely chopped onion, breadcrumbs, parsley, salt, pepper and curry powder, beaten egg and chutney. Form the mixture into little balls, each about 1 in/2.5 cm across, and roll each in flour. Put them on a baking tray, cover them with clingfilm and keep them in the fridge till you are ready to cook them. Fry them preferably in a non-stick frying pan, then you need only a smear of oil in the frying pan. Make sure they are browned all over; they need about 10 minutes' cooking time.

Spicy tomato sauce

Serves 10–12

This can either be made two or three days in advance and kept in a covered container in the fridge, or it can be frozen. Thaw overnight. The spiciness in the sauce comes from the horseradish.

---

4 tbsp oil (I use sunflower)
2 medium onions, skinned and chopped
1 stick of celery, washed and chopped
2 carrots, peeled and chopped
2 × 15 oz/450 g tins of tomatoes

1 garlic clove, peeled and chopped
2 tsp grated horseradish – you can buy this in delicatessens or good supermarkets
salt and freshly ground black pepper
½ tsp sugar

Heat the oil in a saucepan and add the chopped onions. Cook for about 5 minutes, stirring occasionally, then add the chopped celery and carrots. Cook for a further few minutes, then add the tomatoes, chopped garlic, and horseradish. Season with salt, pepper and sugar, and simmer the sauce gently for 35–40 minutes. Cool, then liquidize. You can serve this sauce as a cold dip for the spicy meatballs, or you can reheat it and serve warm, if you prefer. Personally, I rather like the sauce cold with the hot meatballs.

19

Cold poached salmon

Serves 20

The great thing to remember about salmon is that it is a very rich fish and therefore very filling; it always surprises me how far a fairly small amount goes. Having said that, there are so many delicious things to do with leftover salmon, it is almost worthwhile deliberately cooking more than you need, just to have some to make into kedgeree, or salmon fishcakes, or just to eat cold with mayonnaise. It makes a most convenient main course, as it has to be cooked the previous day. The *Lemon, cucumber and chive mayonnaise* can also be made the previous day – or the lemony mayonnaise can be made several days ahead and the diced cucumber added to it the previous day.

11–12 lb/4.5–5 kg salmon
1 pt/600 ml dry white wine
2 onions, skinned and cut in quarters

handful of parsley
several peppercorns
2 tsp rock salt

Cooking a salmon to be eaten cold is far and away easiest done in a fish kettle. Few households have a fish kettle as part of their kitchen equipment, but it is surprisingly easy to borrow one. A salmon weighing about 11–12 lb/ 4.5–5 kg is adequate for 20 guests. Put the fish into the fish kettle and cover it with cold water. Add a pint/600 ml of dry white wine, 2 onions, skinned and each cut in quarters, a good handful of parsley stalks, several peppercorns, and two teaspoons of rock salt. Put the fish kettle onto a moderate heat and let the water come up to the boil. When it is boiling, let it bubble for one minute, then take the kettle off the heat and let the fish sit in the liquid till it is cold. No matter how small or large the fish, this way of cooking it will produce a perfectly cooked salmon, because the larger the fish, the longer the water will take to come to the boil, and afterwards to cool around it. When the fish is cold – probably having sat overnight – carefully lift it out of the liquid, using two fish slices, and onto a large serving dish. Ease the skin off one side, and carefully remove the head and tail if they weren't taken off before cooking. Then, using the two fish slices again, turn the fish over and take the skin off the other side. Mop up any liquid round the fish with absorbent kitchen paper.

To decorate the fish, lay a thin line of finely sliced cucumber down the middle, lengthwise. Or cover the entire surface of the fish with overlapping fine slices of cucumber. But if this is left for any length of time the cucumber curls up as it dries out, so carefully brush it with sunflower oil all over or, if you prefer, with a thin layer of aspic. Cover the fish with a muslin cloth while you are at the church, which you can whip off on your return. Tuck bunches of parsley round the base of the fish, if you feel it looks rather naked on its serving plate.

Lemon, cucumber and chive mayonnaise

Serves 10

This is an excellent sauce to go with the salmon. It tastes good, the diced cucumber gives a satisfying contrasting crunch, and it looks attractive, flecked with the snipped chives.

This amount should be made twice over, to serve 20 guests.

---

1 large egg and 1 large egg yolk
1 tsp salt and plenty of freshly ground pepper
2 tsp caster sugar
grated rind and juice of 1 lemon
1 rounded tsp mustard powder

½ pt/300 ml oil (I use sunflower)
3 tbsp white wine vinegar
2 tbsp snipped chives
½ cucumber, peeled, cut in half lengthwise, deseeded, and the flesh diced finely

---

Put into a food processor or liquidizer the whole egg, the yolk, salt, pepper, sugar, the grated rind of the lemon and the mustard powder. Whiz. Then, still whizzing, add the oil drop by drop to start with, then in a thin trickle. Whiz in the lemon juice and the wine vinegar and, if you feel the mayonnaise is too stiff, two or three tablespoons of very hot water, to let it down. Stir in the snipped chives – don't think they will break down in the food processor or liquidizer, they just don't, they twist themselves round the blades. The day before the christening, peel, deseed and dice the cucumber, and stir it through the mayonnaise.

New potatoes with dill

Dill is one of my favourite herbs, and it goes very well with new potatoes – and with salmon. I think that all herbs (with the exception of sage) go together very well, and mixing chopped dill with the new potatoes leaves you free to use mint in the melon and tomato salad.

Allow 3–4 average-sized new potatoes per person, more if they are small. Scrub them – in Scotland new potatoes are always cooked unpeeled, which is so much better than scraping off their tasty skins. Put them into a large saucepan with a teaspoonful of salt. Cover with boiling water from a kettle, and simmer till they are tender when stuck with a knife. Drain well, steam dry, and turn into a warmed serving dish. Dot with bits of butter and sprinkle a tablespoon of chopped dill over them. Mix into the potatoes, along with the melting butter. Cover the dish and keep it warm till you are ready to serve.

In a covered dish, these potatoes will keep warm in a low oven for over an hour without spoiling. In fact, this gives the flavour of the dill a really good chance to get into the potatoes.

Tomato, melon and applemint salad

Serves 20

This is one of my favourite salads, the flavours seem to go so well together. You can skin, deseed and slice the tomatoes, and put them into the serving dish the previous day to the christening, and you can cut the melon into the chunks – but keep the melon in a separate dish to the tomatoes, as melon juice accumulates to a surprising extent, and it has to be drained off before the melon and tomatoes are combined. Applemint is just so much nicer than the more usual spearmint, so chop about 2 tablespoonfuls the day before and mix all three ingredients together on your return from church – this won't take a minute – and dress the salad with *French dressing* at the last minute before serving.

---

12 medium tomatoes, skinned, halved, deseeded, and each half cut in 6 wedges

5 good juicy melons – 4, if they are large
2 tbsp chopped applemint

FOR THE FRENCH DRESSING

1 tsp salt
1 rounded tsp caster sugar
about 15 grinds of black pepper

1 tsp mustard powder
¼ pt/150 ml oil (sunflower or olive)
2 tbsp wine vinegar – more, if you like a sharper flavour

Shake all the dressing ingredients together well, in a screw-topped jar. This dressing can be made a week ahead and kept in the fridge. Give the jar a good shake to mix up the ingredients before dressing the salad.

Serve a mixed green salad also, to accompany the salmon, potatoes and mayonnaise.

Venison ragoût with chestnuts, port and orange

Serves 20

This is a perfect dish for a chilly weather christening lunch because it both tastes good and is convenient in that, like all casseroles, it benefits from being made a day or two in advance. On the other hand, you can make it several weeks ahead and freeze it (it freezes beautifully). If you can't get venison, you could substitute beef, but venison is now very widely available, and can be found in the butchery departments of many good supermarkets. As venison is so much better for you than beef, it is worth seeking it out. If you find this amount daunting, divide and make it in two or three batches.

---

8 lb/3.5 kg venison, cut in chunks about 1½ in/ 3.5 cm in size

5 rounded tbsp plain flour

1 tsp salt and lots of freshly ground black pepper

oil in which to brown the meat (I use sunflower oil), about 3 tbsp to start with

1 pt/600 ml port

2 slightly rounded tbsp redcurrant jelly

6 onions, skinned and sliced finely

3 pt/1.75 L vegetable stock – made by simmering together the skins and interiors of vegetables such as onions, celery, carrots, leeks and cauliflower with parsley, rock salt and peppercorns, for an hour

grated rinds and juice of 3 oranges

2 × 15 oz/450 g tins of whole chestnuts in brine, unsweetened

---

Start by coating the chunks of venison in the flour, seasoned with salt and pepper. Heat the oil in a very large saucepan (a jam pan) or casserole, and brown the meat, in small amounts at a time so as not to lower the temperature in the pan – which would let the juices run from the meat and therefore stew to a greyish hue rather than browning nicely and sealing in its flavour. Add more oil to the pan as you think necessary. As the meat browns, keep it warm on a dish in a low oven. While the meat is browning, measure the port and redcurrant jelly into a saucepan, and melt the jelly in the port over a moderate heat. Set to one side. When all the meat is browned, add some more oil, lower the heat a bit under the pan or casserole, and add the finely sliced onions. Cook them for about 10 minutes, stirring occasionally so that they cook evenly. Then dust in 2 tablespoonfuls of the seasoned flour, cook for a further minute, before gradually adding the strained vegetable stock, stirring continuously till the sauce boils. Stir in the grated orange rinds and juice, the port and redcurrant jelly, and the chestnuts. Replace the meat in the casserole or stew pan, and cover with a lid. Cook in a moderate oven – 350°F/180°C/Gas 4/bottom right oven in a 4-door Aga – for 2 hours. Cool completely, and either keep in a cold larder or fridge, or freeze it.

On the day of the christening, give the casserole a further 1½ hours, simmering in a moderate oven – if you are putting it in the oven from the fridge, put it in 2 hours before you intend to serve it, to let it come to simmering point. If it is in a dish covered with foil, it will need a longer cooking time, because foil is such a rotten conductor of heat it takes ages for the contents of what it is covering to come to simmering point.

Glazed celeriac, parsnips and carrots

Serves 20

The flavours of these root vegetables, especially when combined as they are in this dish, seem to enhance and complement the venison more than any other vegetables I can think of. It is also a convenient dish, because it can be cooking gently while you are at the christening service, and will be ready to eat when you get home.

---

3 oz/75 g butter and 3 tbsp sunflower oil

2 medium-sized celeriac, peeled, and cut in fat julienne strips, about ½ in/1 cm wide

10 medium-sized carrots, peeled and cut in flat, even-sized, julienne strips

10 parsnips, peeled and cut in fat julienne strips

1 tsp sugar

1 pt/600 ml chicken stock

salt and freshly ground black pepper

In a heavy casserole, melt the butter and heat the oil. Add the prepared vegetables, and sprinkle on the sugar. Cook over a moderate heat for 5 minutes or so, stirring from time to time, so that the vegetables all get coated in the butter and oil. Pour in the stock, season with salt and pepper and let the stock come to simmering point, then cover the casserole with a lid and put it into a low oven – 250°F/125°C/Gas 1/top left oven in a 4-door Aga – and leave for 1–1½ hours. When you get back from church stick the point of a knife into a piece of carrot (the vegetable of the three which takes longest to cook) and test to see if it is tender; if it feels too firm for your liking, put the casserole into a moderate oven – 350°F/180°C/Gas 4/bottom right oven in a 4-door Aga – for about 20 minutes.

Mousseline potatoes

Serves 20

These are just mashed potatoes beaten with an electric beater, with chicken stock, cream and parsley beaten into them. They are light and fluffy, and a perfect accompaniment to the rich venison casserole.

The potatoes can be cooked, mashed and beaten, left in a low oven while you are in church, then beaten again with the cream and parsley on your return before being put into serving dishes for lunch.

---

30 medium-sized potatoes, peeled and cut in half (these can be peeled up to three days before the christening day, and kept in a bowl of cold water, providing the water is changed each day)
1 tsp salt

4 oz/100 g butter
1 pt/600 ml chicken stock
½ pt/300 ml single cream, warmed in a saucepan
3 tbsp chopped parsley
salt and freshly ground black pepper

To cook the potatoes, put them into a large pan with cold water to cover and the salt. Bring to the boil, and simmer till the potatoes are tender when pierced with a knife. Drain them well, and steam them over heat to remove the last of the water. Mash them very well, beating in the butter. Beat in the chicken stock, then cover the pan and place the potatoes in a very low oven. Before serving beat the potatoes again, very well, and beat in the warmed cream, and the chopped parsley. Season with salt and freshly ground black pepper to your taste, and put into warmed serving dishes.

Rich lime pie with crystallized lime slices

Serves 10

This is sharp and fresh-tasting, and can be made a day in advance – indeed, the pastry can be made and baked two or three days in advance, but I wouldn't advise you to make and bake the filling more than a day ahead. The crystallized lime slices can be made two or three days ahead, and kept on a bakewell paper-lined tray till you are ready to arrange them around the edges of the pies.

FOR THE PASTRY

5 oz/150 g plain flour
1 oz/25 g icing sugar

*a few drops of vanilla
    essence*
*4 oz/100 g butter, hard from
    the fridge, cut in bits*

FOR THE FILLING

*4 oz/100 g butter, cut in
    pieces*
8 oz/250 g caster sugar

5 large eggs, beaten
*grated rinds and juice of
    4–6 limes*

Put the flour, icing sugar and vanilla essence into a food processor with the butter, and whiz till the mixture resembles fine crumbs. Pat around the sides and base of a 9-in/23-cm flan dish, and put the dish into the fridge for at least half an hour, preferably longer, then bake it in a moderate oven – 350°F/180°C/Gas 4/bottom right oven in a 4-door Aga – for 20–25 minutes, until the pastry is pale golden. Take the pastry case out of the oven.

Meanwhile, make the filling. Into a heatproof bowl

put the butter cut in pieces, and the caster sugar, sieve in the beaten eggs and add the grated lime rinds (*not* the juice – yet). Put the bowl over a saucepan of simmering water, and stir till the butter has melted and the sugar dissolved. Then take the bowl off the heat, and stir in the lime juice. Pour this carefully into the pastry case, put it into a moderate oven – 350°F/180°C/Gas 4/bottom right oven in a 4-door Aga – and cook till the filling is just set, 15–20 minutes, but stop the cooking before the filling turns in colour. Shake the flan dish gently to see whether there is any wobble in the filling – if there is, give it a further few minutes' cooking time. Take it out of the oven, and cool.

Crystallized lime slices

How many limes you will need for the two pies depends on how thinly you can slice yours, but I can do it from 4 limes, 2 for each pie.

Into a wide shallow saucepan (you could use a frying pan) measure two parts granulated sugar to one part water; it is easiest to do this in a measuring jug. Over a gentle-to-moderate heat gently shake the pan from time to time till the sugar has dissolved completely in the water – don't let the liquid boil till the sugar has dissolved. Then boil fast till the liquid clears – it will be quite cloudy at first. When the sugar syrup is clear, put in the finely sliced limes, and lower the heat so that the syrup is barely simmering. If you let the syrup boil fast, the slices tend to disintegrate. Cook, with the syrup just moving, for 1½–2 hours. And if, as I once did, you overheat and overcook the slices, just think of them as caramelized rather than crystallized, they taste delicious either way! Arrange them around the edges of the pies on the smooth, pale lime filling.

Chocolate and coffee iced profiteroles

Serves 20

As the guests at christenings tend to include a wide range of ages, it is as well to provide food for all tastes, and these profiteroles appeal to everyone, young and old alike. They are a good contrast to the *Rich lime pie*, and the profiteroles (or you may decide to pipe the mixture into éclair shapes) can be made several weeks in advance and frozen, then just popped into an oven to heat through and refresh them, before they are iced and filled with whipped cream.

---

1 pt/600 ml water
8 oz/250 g butter, cut in
small pieces

10 oz/275 g plain flour,
sieved twice
6 large eggs, beaten

Put the water and cut-up butter into a saucepan over a gentle-to-moderate heat, and melt the butter in the water, taking care not to let the water boil before the butter has melted. Sieve the flour into a bowl then sieve again. As soon as the first rolling bubbles appear in the butter-and-water mixture, whoosh in the twice-sieved flour all at once and, with a wooden spoon, beat like mad till the mixture comes away from the sides of the saucepan. Then let the mixture cool for about 10 minutes, before adding the beaten eggs a little at a time, beating really well between each addition (I find a hand-held electric beater ideal for this). When all the eggs are added, rinse two baking trays with cold water – this is so that, as the profiteroles (or éclairs) cook, the steam which rises from the dampened baking trays helps them to rise too. Pipe small profiteroles the size of a 10-pence piece evenly onto the baking trays. Or, if you prefer, using a plain piping nozzle, pipe small 2-in/5-cm long shapes,

31

cutting the choux mixture off at the required length with scissors dipped in water to prevent it from sticking to the scissor blades. With a damp finger (dip it in water first), gently press the surface of the eclair down if there should be any points sticking up from where you cut it. Bake the profiteroles or éclairs in a hot oven – 425°F/220°C/Gas 7/ top right oven in a 4-door Aga – for 20–25 minutes, till they are golden and quite firm – swap the trays around half way through the cooking. Ease them off the baking trays with a palette knife, and cool them on wire cooling racks. When the profiteroles or éclairs are quite cold pack them into tins and freeze them – freezing them in tins protects them should anything drop on them in the freezer. Come the christening, ice the profiteroles or éclairs with *Chocolate and coffee icing* (see below).

Chocolate and coffee icing

If you have frozen the profiteroles, thaw them for about 3 hours at room temperature, then bake them for a few minutes in a moderate oven – 350°F/180°C/Gas 4/ bottom right oven in a 4-door Aga – cool them and ice them. You can do this the day before the christening, but I'm afraid you can't fill them till the morning of the christening lunch, as otherwise the profiteroles go soggy.

---

12 oz/350 g icing sugar, sieved
1 rounded tbsp cocoa powder, sieved
2 tsp coffee granules dissolved in 1 tbsp boiling water

3 oz/75 g butter
¼ pt/150 ml water
3 oz/75 g granulated sugar
1 pt/600 ml double cream

Take two mixing bowls, and sieve 6 oz/175 g icing sugar into each. Into one of these sieve a rounded tablespoon of cocoa powder, for the chocolate icing. Stir the dissolved coffee granules into the second bowl, for the coffee icing.

Put the butter, water and granulated sugar into a small saucepan and melt the butter and dissolve the sugar over a moderate heat, then boil the liquid fast for 3–5 minutes. Pour half the liquid into each bowl of icing sugar, and beat each well till the icing cools and thickens. Ice half the quantity of profiteroles or éclairs with the chocolate and half with the coffee icing.

On the morning of the christening lunch, fill each profiterole with whipped cream – you can whip the cream the previous day and keep it in a covered bowl in the fridge. The easiest way to fill them is to pipe the whipped cream, poking a hole in the side of each profiterole or éclair with the piping nozzle. Arrange them alternately on a large ashet or serving plate, or a pretty tray, and leave them ready, alongside the lime tarts.

Lemon christening cake

This is a suggestion for an alternative to the more usual fruit christening cake. Although I am a great traditional-ist, I don't think we should feel bound by tradition, and I am all in favour of a change in flavour for christening – or wedding – cakes. This recipe makes a large, 10-in/25-cm diameter cake with two layers. As the cake isn't an integral part of the christening lunch, your guests will want to eat only a small piece of cake with their coffee.

FOR THE CAKE

10 oz/275 g butter
10 oz/275 g caster sugar
6 large eggs, beaten

10 oz/275 g self-raising
  flour, sieved
grated rind and juice of
  2 lemons

FOR THE BUTTERCREAM FILLING

6 oz/175 g unsalted butter
6 oz/175 g icing sugar,
  sieved

grated rind of 1 lemon

Butter two 10-in/25-cm round cake tins, and line the base of each with a disc of bakewell paper (siliconized greaseproof paper).

Beat the butter well, gradually beating in the caster sugar, and continue until the mixture is soft, pale and fluffy. Beat in the eggs, alternately with spoonfuls of sieved self-raising flour. Lastly, beat in the lemon rinds and juice. Divide the mixture between the two prepared cake tins, and bake in a moderate oven – 350°F/180°C/ Gas 4/bottom right oven in a 4-door Aga – for 30–35 minutes, or till the cake is just coming away from the sides of the tins. Take the cakes out of the oven, cool for a few minutes in their tins, then turn them onto wire cooling racks to cool completely.

To make the buttercream filling, beat together the butter, sieved icing sugar and grated lemon rind, beating till the buttercream is soft and fluffy. Spread it evenly over the surface of one of the cooled cakes, on a pretty serving dish or tray, and carefully put the remaining cake on top of the buttercream-covered one.

Icing for the christening cake

This is a royal icing, which is more substantial than a glacé icing, and also more suitable for the simple decoration which you are going to pipe around the top and bottom of the cake. You can make the cake two or three days in advance, and ice it the day before the christening.

---

2 egg whites
1 lb/500 g icing sugar,
   sieved

juice of ½ lemon

Beat the egg whites till frothy, then beat in, with a wooden spoon, the sieved icing sugar. Beat well, and beat in the lemon juice. Have ready a deep jug of very hot or near-boiling water, and a large spatula, to dip into the hot water and smooth the surface of the cake. Spread the icing over the cake, smoothing it carefully around the sides – but only smooth where it is absolutely necessary, one can feel tempted to go on and on to get a more even surface. Leave the cake for a few hours, then, with a small fluted piping nozzle and a steady hand, work your way round the top edge, piping small blobs of an even size next to each other. Don't hurry as you work. Then pipe the same decoration around the base of the cake. Leave to dry.

On the morning of the christening put a small, light vase of fresh or wild flowers in the centre of the cake to finish off the simple decoration. By the way, if the cake should not be sufficiently solid to support the vase you use, put a wooden stake under it, through the cake. It will, however, be strong enough to support a *light* vase or container.

PRE-CONFIRMATION
DINNER FOR EIGHT

❧⸲⸱⸲❧

Mushroom-stuffed red peppers with tomato sauce
Poached fillets of halibut with sorrel and lime sauce
Mousseline potatoes
Glazed carrots
Coffee jelly with chocolate Chantilly cream
Chocolate oatmeal biscuits

Pre-Confirmation Dinner

Usually, confirmations take place in the month of May. They are another milestone in life, and on a slightly frivolous note, a good chance for old friends, in the form of godparents, to get together again. As I write, we are approaching our second daughter's, Isabella's, confirmation. She will be confirmed at her school, Kilgraston, at Bridge of Earn, and so sadly we won't be entertaining our old friends at home but in a restaurant. However, were we to be at home, the following menus, for dinner the night before confirmation, and lunch after the service, are just what I would be cooking.

Mushroom-stuffed red peppers with tomato sauce

Serves 8

This first course can be prepared in the morning, ready to bake for serving hot for dinner, and its accompanying tomato sauce may be frozen. Once baked, the stuffed peppers will keep hot without spoiling for up to half an hour. They are also delicious served cold, as an accompaniment to barbecued food.

Because the main course is fish, you can afford to be generous and serve two halves of pepper per guest without fear of overfilling them.

| 8 red peppers | 5 tbsp olive oil |

FOR THE STUFFING

4 tbsp olive oil	2 oz/50 g breadcrumbs
1 onion, skinned and	(I use brown granary
chopped finely	bread)
1 garlic clove, skinned and	½ tsp thyme
chopped finely	salt and freshly ground
1½ lb/750 g mushrooms,	black pepper
wiped (no need to skin	
them) and sliced thinly	

First make the mushroom stuffing. Heat the 4 table-spoons of olive oil in a wide saucepan or frying pan and add the chopped onion. Cook gently till soft and transparent, about 5 minutes, then add the chopped garlic. Stir in the mushrooms, over a fairly high heat which will prevent the mushrooms from shrinking and oozing their juices. Stir in the breadcrumbs and the thyme, and season with salt and freshly ground black pepper. Cook till the crumbs brown, then take the pan off the heat. Meanwhile, cut each pepper in half lengthways, remove the seeds and trim off the stalks. Put the olive oil in a large shallow baking dish, and coat the pepper halves well, inside and out, with it. Using a spoon, stuff the peppers with the mushroom filling. Bake in a moderate oven – 350°F/180°C/Gas 4/bottom right oven in a 4-door Aga – for 1½–1¾ hours, till the pepper halves are very soft.

Serve the peppers with *Tomato sauce* (see below). This can be made and frozen, or made and kept in the fridge for 2–3 days.

Tomato sauce

Serves 8

---

2 tbsp olive oil
1 onion, skinned and
   chopped finely
1 stick of celery, washed and
   diced finely
1 large garlic clove, skinned
   and chopped finely

1 × 15 oz/450 g tin of
   tomatoes
1 tbsp pesto (optional) or
   ½ tsp dried basil
½ tsp sugar
salt and freshly ground
   black pepper to taste

Heat the olive oil, add the chopped onion and cook for about 5 minutes till the onion is soft and transparent, then add the diced celery and chopped garlic and cook for a further few minutes. Liquidize the tinned tomatoes, and stir them with the pesto or basil, sugar, salt and pepper into the onions and celery and simmer, with the pan uncovered, for 35–40 minutes. Serve hot, warm, or cold, with the stuffed peppers.

Poached fillets of halibut with sorrel and lime sauce

Serves 8

I love firm-fleshed white fish, and these pieces of filleted halibut can be cooked in minutes while you clear away the first-course plates. You can make the flavoured fish and vegetable stock (*court bouillon*) in the morning, strain it into a roasting tin and keep it almost simmering on the heat, all ready to slip the pieces of fish into. They need only minutes of cooking, and the sorrel and lime sauce is one of my favourites for serving with fish. It tastes delicious and looks very attractive.

---

8 pieces fillet of halibut
    about 4–5 oz/100–135 g
    each

FOR THE COURT BOUILLON

Some halibut skin and bones (ask your fishmonger) or 8 oz/250 g cod or haddock
2 pt/1.2 L water
1 pt/600 ml dry white wine
2 onions, skinned and halved

1 stick of celery
a handful of parsley
a few black peppercorns and 1 tsp rock salt

Put all the ingredients for the *court bouillon* into a large saucepan and bring to the boil. Simmer gently for an hour, then strain, and pour the liquor into a deep roasting tin, ready to heat up and poach the fish. Before you and your guests sit down to dinner, reboil the liquor in the roasting tin, and keep it barely simmering on one side of the cooker. When the first course is finished, slip the 8 pieces of filleted halibut into the water, and cook them, barely simmering, for 2–3 minutes. Lift them out with a fish slice, and put them onto a warmed serving dish, mopping up any liquid with kitchen paper.

Sorrel and lime sauce

Sorrel is sauce- (or soup-) enhancing because it keeps its bright fresh colour and flavour however long it is kept hot, unlike parsley which assumes a brownish hue if kept hot for too long. The lime goes particularly well with the sorrel in this delicious sauce.

---

a good handful of sorrel
    leaves (stripped of their
    stalks)
2 oz/50 g butter
grated rinds and juice of
    3 limes
1 rounded tsp plain flour

½ pt/300 ml milk and cream
    mixed or single cream
4 large egg yolks
1 tsp Dijon mustard
a pinch of salt, and freshly
    ground black pepper

Put the above ingredients, *except for the lime juice,* into a food processor or liquidizer and whiz till smooth, then pour into a heatproof bowl. Put the bowl in a roasting tin with simmering water coming halfway up the sides of the bowl, and put the tin over a gentle-to-moderate heat. With a balloon whisk, stir the mixture – not continuously but from time to time – till it thickens; this will take about half an hour. (If you have a microwave oven I believe you can cook it in that.) When the sauce has thickened (you can get it to this stage before your guests have a pre-dinner drink) take the bowl and roasting tin of water off the heat, and then replace the tin on the heat while you cook the halibut. Then stir in the squeezed juice of the 3 limes. Serve the sauce in a sauceboat, or poured or spooned over each piece of fish.

Serve with *Mousseline potatoes* (see page 158), and the glazed carrots with grated lemon.

Coffee and Tia Maria jelly with chocolate Chantilly cream

Serves 8

The coffee jelly can be made a day or two in advance, and the dark chocolate for the cream grated and kept in a covered bowl in the fridge. The biscuits can be made three or four days ahead and stored in an airtight container, so all that remains to do before dinner is to turn out the jelly, whip the Chantilly cream and fold in the grated chocolate. Heap this in the centre of the jelly ring and put the accompanying *Chocolate oatmeal biscuits* (see below) on a plate. Simple!

FOR THE COFFEE JELLY

¼ pt/150 ml Tia Maria
  and water mixed
  (mostly *Tia Maria!*)
2 sachets powdered
  gelatine –
  approximately
  1 oz/25 g

1¼ pt/750 ml very good
  strong hot Italian-roast
  coffee (good de-
  caffeinated is fine),
  freshly made

FOR THE CHOCOLATE CHANTILLY CREAM

½ pt/300 ml double cream
1 large egg white
2 oz/50 g caster sugar

½ tsp vanilla essence
4 oz/100 g good dark
  chocolate, grated (this
  is easiest done in the
  grater of a food
  processor)

Put the Tia Maria and water mixed into a saucepan, sprinkle over the gelatine, then heat gently till the gelatine dissolves – you will need to stir it, because in the thick liqueur it tends to sit on the bottom. When it is dissolved, stir it into the hot coffee (which I like to make in a cafetière). Pour into a ring mould and leave to set in the refrigerator.

Whip the cream together with the egg white. Whip in the caster sugar and vanilla essence, and fold in the grated chocolate. Pile into the centre of the turned-out coffee and Tia Maria jelly ring.

Chocolate oatmeal biscuits

Makes 12–14 biscuits

---

4 oz/100 g softened butter
3 oz/75 g caster sugar
4 oz/100 g plain flour

1 oz/25 g cocoa powder (not drinking chocolate!)
1 oz/25 g medium oatmeal
a few drops of vanilla essence

Put the butter into a bowl and beat till smooth, then beat in the caster sugar. Sieve in the flour and cocoa and work in the oatmeal and vanilla essence. You will now have a fairly stiff dough. Roll it out, and cut into 2-in/5-cm circles. Put them on a greased baking tray, and bake in a moderate oven – 350°F/180°C/Gas 4/bottom right oven in a 4-door Aga – for 12–15 minutes (check after 12), take them out of the oven, cool for a moment on the tray, then carefully lift them onto a wire cooling rack, with a palette knife. When cold, store in an airtight container.

CONFIRMATION LUNCH
FOR TEN

*Cold roast leg of lamb, flavoured with garlic
and rosemary
with Spiced apricot sauce*
OR
*Cold roast duck with grapefruit,
orange and honey jelly*
New potato salad with chives
Avocado, tomato and pistachio salad
Chocolate, apple and toasted almond cake
Blackcurrant and applemint mousse

Confirmation Lunch

Here is a suggested lunch menu to be eaten after the confirmation ceremony. It is a cold menu, so that it can all be left ready to eat when you get back from the church following the ceremony. There is a choice of two main courses, one being a *Cold roast leg of lamb, flavoured with garlic and rosemary*, and accompanied by *Spiced apricot sauce*. The alternative is *Cold roast duck with grapefruit, orange and honey jelly*. The salads are a *New potato salad with chives*, where the hot, cooked new potatoes are tossed in a chive vinaigrette, an *Avocado, tomato and pistachio salad*, and a mixed green salad.

For pudding, there is *Chocolate, apple and toasted almond cake*, and *Blackcurrant applemint mousse*.

Cold roast leg of lamb, flavoured with garlic and rosemary

1 leg of lamb weighing about 6 lb/2.75 kg	*butter*
2–3 garlic cloves, peeled	*salt and pepper*
	dried rosemary

Trim off as much fat from the lamb as you can. Push the point of a sharp knife into the lamb in several places, and push slivers of peeled garlic cloves into these slits in the meat. Rub butter all over the leg of lamb, grind some salt

45

and pepper over it, and sprinkle over some rosemary. Roast in a hot oven – 425°F/220°C/Gas 7/top right oven in a 4-door Aga – for 15 minutes to the lb/½ kg weight of the lamb. Take it out of the oven and let it cool completely – ideally, and most conveniently, overnight. Then, on the morning of the confirmation, carve the lamb and arrange it neatly on an ashet or serving plate. Serve the *Spiced apricot sauce* (see below) separately.

Spiced apricot sauce

Serves 10

This delicious sauce is good with cold roast lamb, as here, or it is equally good with hot roast lamb. The spice in it is cumin seed, full of flavour but not at all hot in the fiery sense, so don't be put off by the word 'spiced'.

---

4 tbsp sunflower oil
2 medium onions, skinned and chopped
1 garlic clove, skinned and chopped
2 tsp cumin seed (not ground, which has much less flavour than the whole seed)

12 oz/350 g dried apricots, snipped in half with scissors
1 pt/600 ml chicken or vegetable stock
salt and freshly ground black pepper

Heat the oil in a saucepan and add the onions. Cook for about 5 minutes, stirring occasionally to prevent them sticking and to make sure that the onions cook evenly. Add the chopped garlic, cook for a minute or two, then add the cumin. Cook for a couple of minutes before adding the snipped dried apricots, and stir in the stock. Simmer gently till the apricots are plumped up and soft –

about 30–35 minutes, adding a little more liquid if they boil too fast and the liquid reduces so much that the apricots are in danger of sticking to the bottom of the saucepan. When the apricots are cooked, take the pan off the heat, cool and liquidize the sauce, and add salt and pepper to your taste.

Cold roast duck with grapefruit, orange and honey jelly

Serves 10

The flavour of cold roast duck is perfectly complemented by the orange, grapefruit and honey jelly. It is a most delicious main course dish.

---

5 ducks, each weighing about 4 lb/1.75 kg

3 onions, skinned and halved
chopped parsley for garnish

FOR THE JELLY

4 oranges
3 grapefruit
1 pt/600 ml red wine vinegar
4 tbsp thick honey
1½ pt/1 L chicken or duck stock – you can make duck stock using the giblets and carrots, onions, celery and water, boiled together for 1–1½ hours, then cooled and strained

4 rounded tbsp arrowroot – arrowroot thickens while leaving the sauce clear, and as it cools it becomes jelly-like. If you have difficulty buying arrowroot, you will always get it in a chemist's
salt and freshly ground black pepper to taste
chopped parsley

To roast the ducks, put half a skinned onion in each duck, put the ducks into two roasting tins, and roast them in a hot oven – 400°F/200°C/Gas 6/top right oven in a 4-door Aga – for 2 hours, switching around the position of the roasting tins during cooking. Take them out of the oven, leave to cool completely, then cut the meat from the carcasses in pieces as neatly as you can. Remove the legs, and leave them whole.

Next make the fruit jelly. Pare the rind from 3 of the oranges and 2 of the grapefruit – this is easiest done using a potato peeler. Shred the rind into fine slivers, of as even a size as possible. Put the slivers of rind into a saucepan and cover with cold water. Bring to the boil, and simmer gently for 10 minutes. Drain under cold water, shake dry in a sieve, and set to one side. Using a serrated knife, cut all the pith off all the oranges and all the grapefruit. Cut in towards the centre of each fruit, removing segments without pith. Keep the segments to one side, in a bowl.

Put the wine vinegar and honey together in a saucepan, bring to the boil, and boil fast until well reduced to a caramelly syrup. Pour the stock into the reduced vinegar and honey, as well as any juices which have collected round the citrus segments. Boil fast for 5 minutes. Slake the arrowroot with a little water in a small bowl, pour in a little of the hot stock, mix well, then stir this arrowroot mixture into the hot liquid in the saucepan. Stir till the sauce comes to the boil, let it simmer for a minute or so, then take the saucepan off the heat, check the seasoning, and let cool completely. When it is quite cold, stir in the shredded rinds.

You can make the jelly up to this point a day or two in advance, but don't stir in the grapefruit and the orange segments or the duck till just before you are going to arrange it all on an ashet or serving plate. Sprinkle with chopped parsley.

New potato salad with chives

Serves 10

This simple new potato salad goes so well both with the lamb and the duck. The potatoes are scrubbed, boiled in their skins, then drained, and mixed with a chive vinaigrette while they are still very hot – that way they absorb the flavours of the vinaigrette much more.

3–4 average-sized new
potatoes per person – more
if the potatoes are
marble-sized

FOR THE CHIVE VINAIGRETTE

½ tsp salt and plenty of
freshly ground black
pepper
½ tsp caster sugar
1 tsp mustard powder

2 tbsp wine vinegar (white
or red)
4 tbsp olive oil or sunflower
oil
2 tbsp snipped chives

Put the scrubbed potatoes into a saucepan with a teaspoonful of rock salt, and cover them with boiling water. Simmer till the potatoes are tender.

Mix all the ingredients for the vinaigrette well together, toss gently with the potato salad and dish up onto a serving dish.

Avocado, tomato and pistachio salad

Serves 10

The nuts add a good contrasting crunch to this salad, and their delicious saltiness gives an edge to the smooth avocado and the tomatoes. When the avocados have been skinned and sliced, toss them gently in lemon juice to prevent them from discolouring. I think the fault a lot of people fall into when making a salad without lettuce or another green vegetable to provide bulk, is to not be generous enough; in this salad there really is enough for your guests to enjoy it as a proper salad rather than a small spoonful on the side of their plates.

---

10 large tomatoes and
    20 cherry tomatoes
5 avocados

juice of ½ lemon
2 oz/50 g shelled pistachios

FOR THE VINAIGRETTE

½ tsp salt, and plenty of
    freshly ground black
    pepper
½ tsp caster sugar

1 tsp mustard powder
2 tbsp wine vinegar (white
    or red)
4 tbsp olive or sunflower oil

Start by skinning the 10 large tomatoes. Stick a fork into each and dip it into a saucepan of simmering water just until the skin starts to peel off the surface – about 5 seconds, depending on the tomato's ripeness. Peel the skin off each and slice them as thinly as you can. Carefully peel the skin off the avocados, which is easiest done if you first score the avocado in quarters. Cut each in half, and flick out the stone. Cut each half in half, and slice as evenly as possible. Carefully mix in the lemon juice, so as not to break up the slices.

Make the vinaigrette by shaking together all the ingredients in a screw-topped jar.

Before going to church, gently mix together the tomato slices, the avocado slices and the cherry tomatoes. Sprinkle over the pistachio nuts, and drizzle the shaken vinaigrette over all in the serving dish. Cover with a cloth or clingfilm till your return from the service, when you want to serve lunch.

Chocolate, apple and toasted almond cake

Serves 10

This cake consists of two rectangular layers of rich dark chocolate cake – which is simply a chocolate roulade mixture made of chocolate, eggs and sugar – sandwiched together with a lightly cinnamon-flavoured purée of apples folded into whipped cream. It has a covering of the same apple and cream mixture on top, and toasted almonds strewn over the surface. The combined flavours of dark chocolate, apples and toasted almonds are very good.

FOR THE CAKE

6 large eggs
8 oz/250 g caster sugar

10 oz/275 g dark
   chocolate

FOR THE APPLE PURÉE

2 lb/1 kg good eating apples
   (not *dreary Golden
   Delicious*, use Cox's or
   Granny Smiths)
1 tsp powdered cinnamon
1 oz/25 g butter

½ pt/300 ml double cream
2 oz/50 g soft brown sugar
3 oz/75 g flaked almonds,
   toasted till golden brown

Separate the egg yolks from the whites, and beat the yolks very well, gradually adding the caster sugar. Break the chocolate into a bowl and put the bowl over a saucepan of nearly simmering water, but take care not to let the bottom of the bowl touch the water. When the chocolate has melted, beat it into the egg yolk and sugar mixture. Whisk the whites till very stiff and, using a large metal spoon, fold the whisked whites quickly and thoroughly into the chocolate mixture.

Line two baking trays measuring approximately 10 × 12 in/25 × 30 cm with bakewell paper (siliconized greaseproof paper) and divide the chocolate mixture between the two tins. Bake in a moderate oven – 350°F/ 180°C/Gas 4/bottom right oven in a 4-door Aga – for 20–25 minutes, then take them out of the oven, cover with a damp tea towel and leave the two cakes to cool completely. Meanwhile, make the apple purée.

Peel, core and chop the apples, and put them into a saucepan with the cinnamon, butter, and 2 tablespoons of water. Cook over a gentle heat till you can squash the bits of apple against the sides of the pan with a wooden spoon. Cool.

Whip the double cream with the sugar and fold into the cold apple purée. Put one of the cakes onto a serving dish or a pretty tray, and spread half the apple and cream mixture evenly over it. Put the other cake on top, and spread the remaining apple cream over it. Strew the toasted flaked almonds over the surface.

You can make the cakes and freeze them to save time, and the apple purée also freezes very well, but don't make and assemble the cake and then freeze it; it would become soggy as it thawed.

Blackcurrant and applemint mousse

Serves 10

This deliciously fresh and tangy mousse combines the flavours of blackcurrant and applemint, but if it is too early in the year for you to get applemint you can use pared lemon rind instead. Lemon brings out the flavour of all fruits, and it is particularly good in this recipe. The mousse can be made two days in advance and kept, covered with clingfilm, in the fridge, but try to remember to take it out of the fridge an hour or so before lunch, to let it get to room temperature. By doing this you prevent the gelatine from being too rubbery, and the texture of the mousse relaxes.

4 tbsp cold water
1 sachet powdered gelatine
   (approximately ½ oz/
   15 g)
1½ lb/750 g blackcurrants

2 handfuls of applemint
   (applemint has a much
   superior flavour to the
   more usual spearmint) or
   pared rind of 2 lemons
5 large eggs, separated
6 oz/150 g caster sugar
½ pt/300 ml double cream,
   whipped

Put the 4 tablespoons cold water in a small saucepan, sprinkle over the gelatine, leave it for 5 minutes to become spongy, then dissolve over gentle heat, taking care not to let it boil.

Cook the blackcurrants with the applemint or lemon rind till the juices run and the currants are soft. Liquidize and then sieve them – you have to sieve the liquidized purée as it's the only way to remove the woody pips. Let it cool.

Beat the egg yolks, gradually adding the sugar, and continue beating till the mixture is very thick and pale. Fold in the appleminty (or lemony) blackcurrant purée, and the dissolved gelatine. Fold in the whipped cream. Whisk the egg whites till they are very stiff, and, using a large metal spoon, fold them quickly and thoroughly into the blackcurrant mixture. Pour into a glass or china serving bowl, cover with clingfilm, and put the bowl in the fridge. Decorate the surface, if you like, with whipped cream.

CAKES AND TEATIME GOODIES

Brides' slices
Orange and ginger cake
Chocolate and coconut squares
Marmalade gingerbread
Ginger biscuits
Iced apricot biscuits
Date and orange squares

Cakes and Teatime Goodies

Having people to stay, whether family or friends, often includes children. Even if it doesn't, teatime is never the same without something to eat with a cup of tea. Being away for the weekend or for a holiday means that you are meant to indulge yourself to a certain extent, and we always stock up the biscuit tins with cake or biscuits of some description. Annette Stephen, who ostensibly looks after the children but is actually indispensable in every way, bakes for the guests' teas as well as our own, and she turns out tray after tray of mouthwatering cakes, biscuits and slices of this and that. Several of the following recipes are hers.

Brides' Slices

These are the most delicious slices. With their rich pastry base, middle of dried fruit, layer of easy homemade marzipan and a thin glacé icing they are quite perfect for those who love the heavenly combination of fruit and marzipan. They are one of Annette's more calorific numbers, but worth every calorie. They are also quite filling, so you (even I!) can't manage to eat more than one slice (well, maybe one and a half).

FOR THE PASTRY

5 oz/150 g chilled butter cut
  in pieces
7 oz/200 g plain flour

1 oz/25 g icing sugar
a few drops of vanilla
  essence

FOR THE FILLING

10 rich tea biscuits or
  ginger snaps, crushed
  to crumbs
4 oz/100 g softened butter
6 oz/175 g caster sugar

3 large eggs
1½ tsp mixed spice
1½ lb/750 g currants
4 oz/100 g glacé cherries,
  chopped

FOR THE MARZIPAN

1 lb/500 g ground
  almonds
8 oz/250 g caster sugar
8 oz/250 g icing sugar

2 eggs
juice of 1 lemon

Put the cut-up butter, flour, icing sugar and vanilla essence into a food processor and whiz until the mixture resembles breadcrumbs. Pat into the base of a baking tin measuring 14 × 10 in/35 × 25 cm and about 1½ in/4 cm deep.

To make the filling, put the biscuits into a polythene bag and crush them with a rolling pin. Beat the butter, gradually adding the sugar and beating till light and fluffy. Beat in one of the eggs; beat really well, then beat in the others, one by one. Mix in the crushed biscuits, mixed spice, currants and chopped cherries, and spread this mixture over the pastry in the tin. Bake in a moderate oven – 350°F/180°C/Gas 4/bottom right oven in a 4-door Aga – till firm on top – 30–35 minutes. Take the cake out of the oven and let it cool in the tin. Meanwhile make the marzipan.

Put all the ingredients for the marzipan into a food processor and whiz together well. Spread the marzipan over the cooled surface of the fruit cake. Ice with *Glacé icing* (see below).

Glacé icing

Cover the top of the cake with this thin glacé icing: mix 3 rounded tablespoons sieved icing sugar to just-pouring consistency with a tiny amount of near-boiling water. Let the icing set, then, with a sharp knife, cut the cake in its tin into neat slices or squares, and store them in an airtight container.

Orange and ginger cake

This orange and ginger cake is very light, and when cooked it has a mixture of orange juice and granulated sugar with bits of chopped ginger in it poured over the surface. As this sets, it forms a sugary crust.

FOR THE CAKE

5 oz/150g butter
5 oz/150 g caster sugar
3 large eggs

grated rind of 2 oranges
5 oz/150 g self-raising flour
1 rounded tsp ground ginger

FOR THE ORANGE AND GINGER CRUST

grated rind and juice of
  1 orange
3 oz/75 g granulated
  sugar

4 pieces preserved ginger,
  chopped finely

Butter a springform cake tin about 8 in/25 cm in diameter, and line the base with a disc of bakewell paper (siliconized greaseproof paper).

Beat the butter well, gradually adding the sugar and beating until the mixture is pale and fluffy. Beat in one egg, the grated orange rind, then beat in the flour and ginger, sieved together, alternately with the other two eggs (by alternating you avoid any curdling of the mixture). If it does curdle a bit, it will come together with the beating in of the dry ingredients – and don't worry, it won't affect the cake. Put the cake mixture into the prepared tin, and bake in a moderate oven – 350°F/180°C/Gas 4/bottom right oven in a 4-door Aga – for 35–40 minutes. The cake is cooked when you stick a skewer in the middle and it comes out clean. Take the cake out of the oven.

To make the topping, mix together the orange rind and juice, sugar and chopped ginger and pour this over the surface of the cake.

Chocolate and coconut squares

These are really like chocolate brownies, squidgy squares of chocolate cake with a soft coconut top. As I love the combination of chocolate and coconut, I find these very hard to resist.

---

4 oz/100 g butter
4 oz/100 g good dark
  chocolate
10 oz/275 g soft light brown
  sugar
4 large eggs, beaten

a few drops of vanilla
  essence
1½ oz/40 g cocoa powder
  (not drinking chocolate)
8 oz/250 g self-raising flour,
  sieved

FOR THE COCONUT TOP

2 large egg whites
2 oz/50 g caster sugar

6 oz/175 g desiccated
  coconut

Line a baking tin measuring about 12 × 14 in/30 × 35 cm with bakewell paper (siliconized greaseproof paper).

Put the butter and the dark chocolate, broken up, into a saucepan over gentle heat till the butter and chocolate have melted. Stir in the sugar, beaten eggs, vanilla essence, cocoa and sieved flour, mixing all together well. Pour into the lined baking tin, smooth the surface, and bake in a moderate oven – 350°F/180°C/Gas 4/bottom right oven in a 4-door Aga – for 10 minutes.

As the cake cooks, make the coconut top. Whisk the 2 egg whites until they are stiff, then whisk in the caster sugar a spoonful at a time. Fold the coconut into the meringue, and spread it over the top of the chocolate mixture after its initial 10 minutes' cooking, then replace the tin in the oven and cook for a further 15 minutes.

Take it out of the oven and leave to cool in the tin. Mark into squares and store in an airtight container.

Marmalade gingerbread

Have you ever eaten marmalade on buttered ginger-bread? It is so good that I thought of including marmalade in my recipe for gingerbread, and I loved it. I love the bits of orange peel from the marmalade mixed through the gingerbread, and they go well with the raisins and chopped ginger which I like to put in gingerbread anyway.

You can either make this in a 2 lb/1 kg loaf or terrine tin, or in a round cake tin about 8–9 in/20–23 cm in diameter, whichever you prefer.

½ pt/300 ml milk
2 tsp bicarbonate of soda
8 oz/250 g butter
8 oz/250 g marmalade
8 oz/250 g soft dark brown sugar
12 oz/350 g plain flour

1 rounded tbsp ground ginger
2 tsp powdered cinnamon
2 large eggs, beaten
4 oz/100 g raisins
6–8 pieces preserved ginger, chopped

Butter the cake or loaf tin, and line the base with a disc of bakewell paper (siliconized greaseproof paper) if it's a round tin, or line the narrow ends and the base of a loaf tin.

Warm the milk and bicarbonate of soda together and set aside. Melt together the butter, marmalade and soft dark brown sugar. Sieve together the flour, ginger and cinnamon and mix into the melted butter mixture with the beaten eggs, mixing well. Mix in the warm milk and

bicarb mixture, beating all really wel.
the raisins and chopped ginger. Put this
prepared tin, and bake in a gentle oven -
Gas 2½/bottom of the bottom right oven of
– for 1½ hours. Cool in the tin.

Ginger biscuits

These crisp biscuits are very simple to make and very
good to eat.

---

6 oz/175 g chilled butter, cut   6 oz/175 g self-raising flour
   in pieces   2 rounded tsp ground ginger
6 oz/175 g caster sugar

Put all the ingredients into a food processor and whiz till
the mixture forms a ball. Take walnut-sized lumps of
dough and roll each into a small ball. Put them on a
baking tray, and with the palm of your hand flatten each
slightly. Bake in a low oven – 250°F/130°C/Gas 1/top left
oven in a 4-door Aga – for 1–1½ hours. The biscuits
should lift easily off the tray with a palette knife. Cool,
and store in an airtight container.

Iced apricot biscuits

These cake-like biscuits are cooked in a baking tin and
cut into squares while warm. The 'icing' goes on them
before they are cooked, and is baked in with the biscuit
mixture.

FOR THE BISCUITS

4 oz/100 g softened butter
6 oz/175 g caster sugar
2 large eggs, beaten

½ tsp vanilla essence
8 oz/250 g plain flour, sieved
1 tsp baking powder, sieved
4 oz/100 g dried apricots,
   snipped into bits

FOR THE ICING

1 large egg white
6 oz/175 g demerara sugar

½ tsp vanilla essence

Butter a baking tin measuring approximately 10 × 12 in/
25 × 30 cm.

Beat the butter, gradually adding the sugar, and
beating till the combination is light and fluffy. Beat in the
eggs and vanilla, then mix in the sieved flour and baking
powder, and the pieces of apricot. Spread over the greased
baking tin.

To make the icing, whisk the egg white till very stiff,
then mix in the demerara sugar and vanilla essence, and
spread this over the apricot mixture in the tin. Bake in a
moderate oven – 325°F/170°C/Gas 3/bottom of the
bottom right oven in a 4-door Aga – for 30 minutes. Cool
in the tin, but cut into squares while the iced biscuits are
still warm. Store, when quite cold, in an airtight
container.

Date and orange squares

If you ignore the butter in this recipe, these squares make
really very healthy eating. They are an oat and sugar

mixture, with a filling made of dates cooked with orange juice to form a near-purée. I think we originally got this recipe off the back of either a packet of porridge oats or a container of dates. I can't remember which and it was many years ago, but the recipe lives on!

---

8 oz/250 g chopped dates
½ pt/300 ml orange juice
8 oz/250 g porridge oats
6 oz/175 g self-raising flour

6 oz/175 g soft brown sugar
  (light or dark)
1 tsp bicarbonate of soda
6 oz/175 g butter, melted

Butter a baking tin about 8 in/25 cm across and 1 in/2.5 cm deep and line it with bakewell paper (siliconized greaseproof paper).

Put the chopped dates and the orange juice into a saucepan and simmer till the liquid has been absorbed into the dates, and it has turned into a thick mixture.

Mix together the oats, flour, brown sugar and bicarbonate of soda and mix in the melted butter. Spread half of this mixture in the lined baking tin. Spread the orange-flavoured date purée over, and cover with the remaining oat mixture. Bake for 40–45 minutes in a moderate oven – 350°F/180°C/Gas 4/bottom right oven in a 4-door Aga. Cut into squares while still warm.

SPECIAL ANNIVERSARY DINNER FOR TWO

———— ⟨⟨⟨∙∙∙⟩⟩⟩ ————

Goat's cheese and hazelnut soufflé
Marinated pigeon breasts with port sauce
Baked matchstick potatoes and onions
Steamed cauliflower with fried parsley and breadcrumbs
Coffee and praline iced cream with chocolate sauce

Anniversaries

Although many people consider that an anniversary should be celebrated with dinner in a special restaurant, it is just as much fun to have a special dinner at home, just the two of you. It is seldom – if ever – that a couple cooks dinner-party food for themselves, usually it is kept for entertaining others, so, just occasionally – and an anniversary is surely such an occasion – it is great fun to make a special dinner. On this evening above all, I don't advocate food which necessitates you leaping up after each course to cook the next one so the menu I have in mind will give you all the time you want to relax, reminisce and enjoy the food and wine. For a first course there is *Goat's cheese and hazelnut soufflé*; this is followed by *Marinated pigeon breasts with port sauce*, accompanied by *Baked matchstick potatoes and onions,* and *Steamed cauliflower with fried breadcrumbs and parsley.* For dessert, you have *Coffee and praline iced cream with chocolate sauce.*

Throughout married life there are milestones of special anniversaries (actually, these days, with endless divorces, each anniversary should be a noteworthy milestone) and the first one is the twenty-fifth, the Silver Wedding Anniversary. Following that is the Golden Anniversary, and for these I give you ideas for a buffet lunch party – lunch rather than dinner, because by the time a couple reach their Golden Anniversary they are obviously getting on in years, and a gathering of friends may well include some from afar who won't want to travel long distances at night. The other good reason for having a lunchtime celebration is that as people grow older, they prefer to eat more in the middle of the day rather than at night.

Special Anniversary Dinner for Two

Goat's cheese and hazelnut soufflé

Serves 2

This soufflé – like all soufflés – can be prepared, with the egg whites whisked and folded into the mixture and the dish covered with clingfilm, three or four hours before you want to cook it. The soufflé mixture comes to no harm, and rises as beautifully as if you had whisked the egg whites at the last minute, as I always used to do until this invaluable tip was given to me by my great friend Char Donaldson.

---

1 tbsp ground hazelnuts
1 oz/25 g butter, plus a little
   for greasing
1 oz/25 g flour
¼ pt/150 ml milk

salt and freshly ground
   black pepper
3 or 4 gratings of nutmeg
2 large eggs, separated
3 oz/75 g goat's cheese,
   crumbled
optional sauce to serve
   (see below)

Butter a round ovenproof dish or a soufflé dish of about 1 pint/600 ml capacity. Dust it with the ground hazelnuts.

Melt the butter in a small saucepan and stir in the

flour, let it cook for a couple of minutes, then stir in the milk. Stir till the sauce boils, then season with salt, pepper and nutmeg. Take the pan off the heat and beat in the egg yolks, one at a time. Stir in the crumbled cheese, stirring till it melts. Whisk the egg whites till they are very stiff, and with a large metal spoon, fold them quickly and throughly through the cheese mixture. Pour into the prepared dish, cover the dish with clingfilm, and leave. When you think you're almost ready to eat, pop the dish into a hot oven – 420°F/220°C/Gas 7/top right oven in a 4-door Aga – and bake for 25 minutes. Eat immediately.

If you like, and I do, you can serve this simple sauce with the soufflé: just warm 4 tablespoons of double cream in a saucepan with a tablespoon of snipped chives, and serve it around each helping of soufflé.

Marinated pigeon breasts
with port sauce

Serves 2

---

2 pigeons, breasts removed | 1 tbsp sunflower oil
1 oz/25 g butter

FOR THE MARINADE

2 tbsp olive oil
1 onion, skinned and sliced
1 stick of celery, chopped

a small bunch of parsley,
   chopped
2 garlic cloves, skinned and
   chopped
1/4 pt/150 ml red wine

FOR THE SAUCE

about 1/2 tbsp flour
2 juniper berries, crushed
   (I use a rolling pin)
1/4 pt/150 ml strained
   pigeon stock
   (see below)

1/4 pt/150 ml port
2 slightly rounded tsp
   redcurrant jelly
salt and freshly ground
   black pepper

First prepare the marinade. Heat the oil and add the
sliced onion, chopped celery, parsley and garlic. Cook for
a few minutes, then pour in the red wine. Simmer for 3–4
minutes, then take the marinade off the heat and let it
cool. Put the pigeon breasts into a dish and pour the cold
marinade over them. Leave for several hours or overnight in a cool place.

Make stock with the 2 pigeon carcasses. Put them into a saucepan and cover them with cold water. Add two onions, skinned and cut in half, a stick of celery, a few black peppercorns and a teaspoon of salt. Simmer for 1 hour, then strain the stock.

Heat the oil and melt the butter together in a saucepan. When it is hot, brown the pigeon breasts on each side, cooking them for 2–3 minutes. How long you cook the pigeon breasts depends on how well done you like them; some people like them very rare, personally I like to eat them just tinged with pink, no redder. Take the breasts out of the pan and put them on a dish to keep warm while you make the sauce.

For the sauce, add the flour to the fat in the pan together with the crushed juniper berries. Cook for a minute or two then, stirring all the time, add the stock and port, stirring till the sauce boils. Add the redcurrant jelly, and stir till it melts, season to your taste with salt and pepper. Pour this sauce over the pigeon breasts in the dish, cover, and keep warm in a low oven till you are ready to eat. To serve, slice the breasts lengthways, in half, or, if you prefer, in three pieces so that they fan out on each plate. Spoon the sauce or gravy over them.

Baked matchstick potatoes and onions

Serves 2

These go very well with the pigeon breasts in their port sauce, and they can be prepared in the morning. Cook them for as long as possible, 2½–3 hours in a low-to-moderate oven; they should be brown and crispy on top.

3 medium-sized potatoes	milk
1 onion	salt and freshly ground
2 oz/50 g butter, hard from	black pepper
the fridge	

Butter a shallow ovenproof dish. Peel the potatoes and skin the onion. Carefully slice the potatoes across as thinly as you can, then slice them again into matchsticks. Slice the onion too as thinly as possible. Arrange the vegetables in layers alternately in the dish, dotting with some of the butter about halfway. Pour in enough milk to come level with the top layer. Dot the surface with the remaining butter, add seasoning, and bake in a moderate oven – 325°F/170°C/Gas 3/bottom of the bottom right oven in a 4-door Aga – for 2½–3 hours. The vegetables can keep warm in a cooler oven very well.

Steamed cauliflower with fried parsley and breadcrumbs

Serves 2

½ medium-sized cauliflower	1 oz/25 g butter
1 oz/25 g brown	2 tbsps oil (I use sunflower)
breadcrumbs	salt and freshly ground
small bunch of parsley	black pepper

Half a medium-sized cauliflower should be enough for two people, and by steaming it till the stalk is tender you will find its flavour quite intense in comparison with cauliflower cooked in water.

For the breadcrumb and parsley mixture, whiz together in a food processor or liquidizer the brown breadcrumbs and a small bunch of parsley.

In a frying pan (preferably a non-stick one, then you need to use less oil and butter) melt the butter and heat the sunflower oil till they are hot. Fry the breadcrumb and parsley mixture, seasoning it with salt and freshly ground black pepper, and turning it over as it cooks so that the crumbs brown and crisp evenly. When it is browned, keep it warm in a dish lined with several thicknesses of kitchen paper, and sprinkle it liberally over the cauliflower on each plate as you dish up.

Coffee and praline iced cream with chocolate sauce

Serves 6

This simple and most delicious iced cream can be made as early as you like – it obviously has to be made the day before at the latest, to give it time to freeze. The following recipe will make more than you both can eat, but it is so useful to have it in the freezer for another time.

FOR THE ICED CREAM

1 tbsp coffee granules	*4 oz/100 g icing sugar,*
3 tbsp boiling water	*sieved*
4 large eggs, separated	*½ pt/300 ml double*
	cream, whipped

FOR THE PRALINE

3 oz/75 g granulated sugar   *2 oz/50 g flaked almonds*

Start by making the praline. Put the granulated sugar and flaked almonds into a saucepan over a moderate heat. Let the sugar melt slowly – don't be tempted to hurry it, as once the sugar burns the bitter taste cannot be overcome and the only solution then is to start again. As the sugar begins to melt and turn colour – and nothing will appear to happen for a while – shake the pan from time to time so that it melts evenly. Butter a baking sheet and when the sugar is all melted to a rich golden brown colour, pour it onto the buttered sheet. Let it grow quite cold, then cover it with greaseproof paper and bash it with a rolling pin till it is sufficiently fine. You can also pulverize it in a food processor, it makes an awful noise but it does the trick! Store in an airtight container.

For the iced cream, make the small amount of strong coffee by dissolving the granules in 3 tablespoons of boiling water. Whiz the egg yolks and pour in the nearly boiling coffee as you do so. Whiz till the yolks are thicker – 3–4 minutes.

With clean whisks, whisk the egg whites, and when they are stiff, gradually add the sieved icing sugar, a spoonful at a time. Whisk till the sugar is all incorporated. Fold the whipped cream into the egg yolk and coffee mixture, and fold the crushed praline into this mixture. Using a large metal spoon, fold the meringue mixture into the coffee and praline combination, folding them together thoroughly so as not to leave any little pockets of meringue. Put the mixture into a container with a lid, and freeze it.

Take the container of iced cream out of the freezer as you start your main course, and leave it at room temperature. That way it will be easier to spoon out. (By the way, with this recipe there is no need to whip the iced cream halfway through its freezing time.) Serve with *Chocolate sauce* (see below).

Chocolate sauce

This too can be made ahead, several days if you like, as it keeps very well in a screw-topped jar in the fridge. Reheat it to serve with the iced cream.

---

6 oz/175 g soft brown sugar
¼ pt/150 ml water
3 tbsp golden syrup
(dip your spoon in hot
water first, that way the
syrup slips easily off the
spoon)

3 slightly rounded tbsp cocoa
powder, sieved
1 tsp vanilla essence

Put all the ingredients into a saucepan to melt and dissolve, then boil hard for 4–5 minutes.

GOLDEN WEDDING CELEBRATION FOR TWENTY-FIVE

⁓⦿⦿⦿⁓

Mixed fish and shellfish in dill sauce
Basmati rice with parsley
Chicken in pimento mayonnaise
New potato and herb salad
Orange and avocado salad
Tomato jelly rings with watercress and crispy bacon
Coffee and almond meringue
Raspberry and lemon parfait
Dark chocolate terrine with coffee sauce

Golden Wedding Celebration

This will invariably involve a number of people, because by the time a couple reaches their Golden Wedding anniversary they have accumulated a lot of family as well as a lifetime of friends, so the planning for this special anniversary could well be on a fairly large scale. I think the ideal food for this occasion would be served buffet-style, with members of the family or hired staff to help the guests to the food. Then the guests would take their plates to tables, each with its seating plan and everyone with a placecard.

One thing to consider with older people is that they may find food which demands much chewing a nuisance – barbecued beef, for instance, would have no place on this menu! I would suggest a choice of two main courses, one a chicken dish in a pimento sauce, the other a fish and shellfish combination in a dill-flavoured sauce, served with rice. Three interesting salads: one a new potato salad full of chopped herbs (parsley and dill); another an arranged salad of orange and avocado which both looks attractive and is easy to eat; and the third, set tomato jellies with watercress and crispy bacon bound together with cream cheese.

For puddings I suggest a choice of three, and the ones I have chosen have the added advantage that they all taste good together, should any guest decide on some of each! I would serve champagne before lunch, wine with the meal, and a glass of Beaumes de Venise or Sauternes with coffee and the inevitable speech which will follow lunch.

Mixed fish and shellfish in dill sauce with rice

Serves 25

---

5 lb/2.25 kg salmon
4 lb/1.75 kg halibut (or turbot or monkfish, also firm-fleshed white fish)

2 lb/1 kg (shelled weight) prawns or Morecambe Bay shrimps if you can get them
24 scallops

FOR THE COURT BOUILLON

3 pt/1.75 L water
fish skins and bones
1 pt/600 ml dry white wine
a handful of parsley stalks
2 onions, skinned and halved

4 sticks of celery, washed and chopped
½ bulb of fennel
a small handful of black peppercorns
2 tsp rock salt

Put all the ingredients for the *court bouillon* into a saucepan and bring to simmering point. Simmer gently, with the saucepan covered, for about 40 minutes, then take pan off the heat. Let the liquid cool completely, then strain.

Fillet the salmon (or ask your fishmonger to do this for you) and skin it, and the halibut or other fish. Cut the fish into bite-sized chunks. Trim the dark tube off each scallop, and cut each scallop in half. Reheat the *court bouillon* to a simmer, and poach small amounts of the fish and shellfish for no more than 30 seconds in the simmering liquid – fish cooks very quickly and is ruined if overcooked. By cooking the fish in small amounts, you avoid undercooking some pieces and overcooking others. Remove the fish with a slotted spoon from the cooking liquor and leave to cool. Serve with *Dill sauce* (see below).

Dill sauce

Serves 10–12

This is a mayonnaise-type sauce, well flavoured with dill, a herb which I love to combine with all fish as well as the salmon with which it is more usually associated.

Make the following amount twice, to serve 25.

1 large egg, plus 1 large egg yolk	*½ pt/300 ml oil (I use sunflower oil)*
½ tsp salt	*4 tbsp wine vinegar, more if you like*
1 rounded tsp mustard powder	*¼ pt/150 ml near-boiling water*
freshly ground black pepper	
1 rounded tsp caster sugar	*3 tbsp dill weed*

Put the egg and extra yolk into a food processor or liquidizer with the salt, mustard powder, freshly ground black pepper and caster sugar, and whiz, gradually adding the oil – drop by drop at first, then in a very thin trickle. The mayonnaise should be very thick. Whiz in the wine vinegar and the dill, and lastly, with the machine still running, the hot water. This will thin down the sauce so that you can more easily mix the cooled fish through the sauce.

Make the sauce twice, pour it into a very large bowl (or divide the fish and mix in two lots) and carefully mix the fish into the sauce. Arrange on two large ashets or serving plates.

Basmati rice with parsley

Allow 1½ oz/40 g rice per person, and cook it till tender in boiling salted water. When it is cooked, rinse it under running cold water, to remove any excess starch. Drain well, then stir through 5–6 tablespoons of chopped parsley. Arrange the rice around the edges of the fish in its dill sauce – the green-flecked rice looks attractive beside the green-sauce-coated fish. Cut lemon wedges and press them face down into the rice, as a garnish.

Chicken in pimento mayonnaise

Serves 25

This dish, of cooked chicken cut into bite-sized pieces and coated with a rosy-coloured sauce, which looks attractive and tastes so good with the flavour combination of pimento and garlic (although you can leave out the garlic altogether if you like), makes an ideal dish for a large party. Serve with the *Basmati rice with parsley* above.

5 chickens, weighing about
   3½ lb/1.5 kg each
4 onions, skinned and halved
4 sticks of celery, washed
   and cut in half

4 leeks, washed and halved
   (leave the green bits on,
   they flavour the stock)
a handful of parsley
a small handful of black
   peppercorns
2 tsp rock salt
finely shredded lettuce for
   garnish

Put the chickens into a large pan (or two, if you don't possess one which will hold all 5 chickens) and cover with cold water. Add the vegetables, parsley, pepper and salt, and bring to simmering point. Simmer gently until each chicken, when stuck in the thigh with a sharp knife, runs with clear juices not even faintly tinged with pink – about 1½ hours' simmering. Take the pan off the heat and let the chickens cool completely in the liquid, which will ensure that the flesh stays moist and succulent. (Keep the delicious stock to reboil with the chicken carcasses after you've stripped the meat from them, then strain the stock and make soup or freeze it.) Strip the meat from the chickens, cutting the larger bits into neat pieces. Put the cut-up chicken into a large bowl. Mix with *Pimento mayonnaise* and serve as described below.

Pimento mayonnaise

Make the following recipe twice, to serve 25.

81

1 large egg and 1 large egg
   yolk
½ tsp salt
freshly ground black pepper
1 tsp caster sugar
1 rounded tsp mustard
   powder
½ pt/300 ml sunflower oil

1 garlic clove, skinned and
   chopped
4 tbsp wine vinegar, more if
   you like a sharper flavour
2 red peppers
¼ pt/150 ml boiling water

First of all, make the basic mayonnaise using the ingredients above (except for the red peppers, of course, and the boiling water) and following the method for the dill sauce on page 79.

Grill the red peppers till the skin chars and then put them into a polythene bag for several minutes – you can then peel off the skin more easily. (This invaluable tip was given to me by my mother.) Cut each in half and remove the seeds, then put the skinned peppers into a liquidizer or food processor, together with the boiling water and whiz till smooth. Whiz this red pepper purée into the mayonnaise sauce. Mix the sauce into the pieces of chicken so that all is thoroughly coated. Arrange on large ashets or serving dishes, piling it up, and surround it with finely shredded lettuce (Iceberg is ideal).

New potato and herb salad

Mixed herbs in a small amount of vinaigrette tossed with hot, just-cooked new potatoes make a potato salad which goes very well with both the chicken and with the fish dishes. You can make this the day before the party, and keep it in a cool place. Use as many fresh herbs as you can get – bar sage, they all go together so well – but if you can get only parsley and chives, just use them liberally.

Allow 2–3 new potatoes per person – this sounds mean but it is a fact that at buffet parties guests eat less than at a smaller, totally sit-down occasion.

FOR THE VINAIGRETTE

1 tsp caster sugar	*¼ pt/150 ml sunflower oil*
½ tsp salt	*1–2 tbsp wine vinegar*
plenty of freshly ground	*4 rounded tbsp chopped*
black pepper	*mixed herbs – such as*
½ tsp mustard powder	*parsley, chives, chervil,*
	dill, mint

Scrub the new potatoes (which can be done 2 days ahead) but leave their skins on. If the potatoes are uneven in size, cut up the larger ones so that they are more or less the same size as the smallest potatoes. Put them into saucepans with a teaspoon of salt in each, and cover them with boiling water. Boil till the potatoes are tender, and drain well.

Shake together all the ingredients for the vinaigrette so that they are thoroughly mixed, and mix them and the mixed chopped herbs (which don't need to be very finely chopped) into the hot, cooked new potatoes. Arrange on serving dishes.

Orange and avocado salad

Serves 25

This is an arranged salad, where alternate pieces of sliced avocado and pithless orange segments create a cartwheel effect on a large flat dish – or two, depending on what size they are. A small amount of vinaigrette is drizzled over the arrangement, and two or three table-spoons of snipped chives sprinkled liberally over, their colour contrasting nicely with the orange and pale green of the avocado and oranges, and the flavour of the chives adding that vital taste which makes this salad so delicious. Avocados are still a slightly special item, and so do be generous. The only drawback to this salad is that it has to be made the day of the party, but the avocados can be sliced and brushed with lemon juice 2–3 hours in advance, and they won't discolour.

---

25 oranges	*vinaigrette dressing (see*
15 avocados, preferably	*page 83)*
smooth-skinned	*2–3 tbsp chives, snipped*

Peel the 25 oranges (you really will need all these); be patient as you slice off their skin with a serrated knife, and slice in towards the centre of each, removing segments but leaving behind the tough white pith.

Next prepare the avocados. These are easier to slice if they are the smooth-skinned green ones, rather than the smaller dark knobbly skinned variety. With a small sharp knife, cut each avocado in quarters, peel off the skin – it should come off easily if the avocados are ripe – and slice each quarter into 3 long slices.

Make up the same amount of vinaigrette as for the *New potato and herb salad* on page 83, mix well, and pour it sparsely over the arranged sliced avocados and oranges. Sprinkle liberally with snipped chives.

Tomato jelly rings, with watercress and crispy bacon

Serves 25, to fill three ring moulds about 9 in/23 cm diameter

These look nice on the buffet table, and taste delicious. They are made from a mixture of fresh tomato purée (made by liquidizing tomatoes then sieving them) which is then liquidized again, this time with garlic, cream cheese and dissolved gelatine, to set the purée. Turned out from their ring moulds, and with a filling of watercress and crispy bacon dressed in a thin cream cheese coating, they enhance any buffet table.

FOR THE TOMATO JELLY

18–20 tomatoes, depending on their size

½ pt/300 ml water or chicken stock

6 sachets powdered gelatine (approximately 3 oz/75 g)

1 pt/600 ml orange juice (preferably freshly squeezed but you can use canned)

3 garlic cloves, skinned and chopped finely (or less, if you prefer a less pronounced flavour)

salt and freshly ground black pepper

1 lb/450 g cream cheese (2 large packets of Philadelphia)

FOR THE FILLING

8 oz/250 g cream cheese
milk
1½ lb/750g thinly sliced smoked streaky bacon

6 handfuls of watercress – or 3 punnets from Marks and Spencer

---

Liquidize, then sieve, the tomatoes – you will need just about 2½ pt/1.4 L purée. Sprinkle the powdered gelatine over the water or chicken stock, then warm gently over a low heat until dissolved completely.

In a food processor or liquidizer, in two or three sessions, combine the tomato purée, orange juice, finely chopped garlic and dissolved gelatine. Season with salt and pepper, whiz, and add the cream cheese. Pour into a large bowl to mix everything – when making it in two or three lots you can never be quite sure that the seasoning or gelatine or ratio of orange to tomato juice is even, so it's as well to mix the whole mixture before dividing it between the three ring moulds. Leave to set – you can make this 2 or 3 days in advance. Turn out to serve, and fill the centre with the following filling:

In a food processor, whiz the cream cheese to the thickness of pouring cream by letting it down with milk till it reaches the right consistency. Grill the bacon till it is evenly crisp. Drain well on kitchen paper, then break into bits. Tear up the watercress, put it into a bowl and mix in the broken bits of bacon. Mix in the thin cream-cheesey dressing and divide this combination between the centres of the three moulds.

Coffee and almond meringue

Serves 10–12

This pudding satisfies my love for meringue, especially when it is flavoured with coffee and has toasted flaked almonds scattered over its whipped coffee-cream covering. For 25, make the following amount twice over.

FOR THE MERINGUE

5 large egg whites   *10 oz/275 g caster sugar*

FOR THE FILLING AND COVERING

1 pt/600 ml double cream
1 tbsp coffee granules
*   dissolved in 3 tbsp*
*   boiling water then cooled*
*   completely*

2 tbsp coffee liqueur, such as
*   Tia Maria or Kahlua*
3 oz/75 g flaked almonds,
*   toasted till pale brown*

To make the meringue rounds, line two baking trays with bakewell paper (siliconized greaseproof paper) and mark two large circles by tracing round the base of a 10 in/25 cm round cake tin.

Whisk the egg whites till they are very stiff then, still whisking, add the sugar a spoonful at a time, whisking till the sugar is all incorporated. Divide the meringue mixture evenly between the two marked circles, smooth over, and put the baking tins into a moderate oven – 350°F/180°C/Gas 4/bottom right oven in a 4-door Aga – for 5 minutes, then lower the heat to 225°F/110°C/Gas ¼/top left oven in a 4-door Aga – and bake for a further 2½ hours. When the circles lift easily off the bakewell paper they are cooked. Cool them.

For the filling, whip the cream, gradually adding the cold coffee and the liqueur. Put half the cream on one layer of meringue, put the other on top. Cover with the remaining cream, and sprinkle the nuts neatly around the edge.

Raspberry and lemon parfait

Serves 25

Much as I loathe the word, a parfait seems to be a cream-less mousse, and therefore a very useful part of our menu. After a fairly rich lunch, it is something of a relief to have a dessert without one rich ingredient, and this parfait has a light texture and an intense flavour of raspberries enhanced by lemon. You may use frozen raspberries when you can't get fresh, so this isn't exactly a seasonal pudding.

If you find it daunting and haven't got the necessary number of large bowls to whisk large quantities of egg whites etc., divide the ingredients in half, and make the parfait in two goes.

---

4 lb/1.75 kg raspberries
pared rind of 3 lemons (I use
  a potato peeler to avoid
  getting any pith)
1½ sachets gelatine
  (approximately 1½ oz/
  40 g)

juice of 2 lemons
12 large eggs, separated
12 oz/350 g caster sugar

To start with, put the raspberries and pared lemon rinds into a saucepan and cover with a lid. Heat till the juices run from the raspberries. Meanwhile, sprinkle the gelatine over the lemon juice, leave to sponge up, then heat gently until the gelatine dissolves completely. Take the pan off the heat; leave to cool. Liquidize the raspberries and lemon rind together with the dissolved gelatine and lemon juice. Sieve the purée – this is the only way to get rid of the woody pips.

Whisk the egg yolks, gradually adding the sugar, and continue whisking till the mixture is very thick and pale. Fold in the raspberry and lemon purée. When it has set enough to coat thickly the back of a spoon, whisk the egg whites till very stiff, and, with a large metal spoon, fold them thoroughly through the raspberry mixture. Pour into glass or china serving bowls and decorate with fresh raspberries.

Dark chocolate terrine with coffee sauce

Serves 10–12

This is an ideal buffet pudding, easy to serve and irresistible for those who, like me, are complete chocolate addicts. This is very densely chocolatey, and the slightly bitter coffee sauce goes so well with it – much nicer than whipped cream.

Make the following amount twice, to pour into a 2–3 lb loaf tin or terrine.

½ pt/300 ml water and Tia Maria or Kahlua (coffee liqueur), mixed half and half
1½ sachets gelatine (approximately 1½ oz/ 40 g)

2 lb/1 kg good dark chocolate
1½ pt/1 L single cream
8 egg yolks

Sprinkle the gelatine over the mixed water and coffee liqueur, then warm gently till the gelatine dissolves.

Line the base and narrow ends of the terrine or loaf tin

with a strip of bakewell paper (siliconized greaseproof paper). Break the dark chocolate into the bowl of a food processor, and put the single cream into a saucepan. Heat the cream to scalding point, and pour onto the chocolate. Put the lid back on the processor, cover the lid with a teatowel, and whiz till the chocolate and cream form a smooth mixture. Whiz in the egg yolks, one by one, and the dissolved gelatine and water/liqueur mixture. Pour the chocolate into the lined terrine or loaf tin and leave to set.

To turn out, dip the terrine for a count of barely 10 in a bowl of warm (*not* very hot) water, slip a knife dampened in warm water down the long sides, and turn onto a serving plate. Remove the tin, and peel off the paper. Serve with the *Coffee sauce* (see below).

Coffee sauce

Serves 25

1½ pt/1 L single cream	1 tsp cornflour, sieved
2 tbsp coffee granules	4 oz/100 g caster sugar (the
8 egg yolks	sauce isn't meant to be too
	sweet)

Put the cream into a saucepan and heat it; when hot, sprinkle on the instant coffee granules. In a bowl, beat the yolks well with the sieved cornflour, gradually adding the caster sugar. Pour a little of the hot cream onto the egg yolks, mix well, and pour this back into the pan with the rest of the cream. Over a gentle heat, stir till the sauce coats the back of the spoon thickly enough so that when you trace a path down the back of the spoon with your finger the path remains. (This will be about the consistency of pouring cream.) Take the pan off the heat. Wring out a piece of greaseproof paper in cold water, and press it down over the surface of the sauce, to prevent it from getting a skin as it cools.

MEATLESS MAIN COURSES
FOR EIGHT

Three-cheese and pepper roulade
Spinach, tomato and cheese lasagne
Mushroom-stuffed crêpes with cheese and nutmeg sauce
Vegetable gougère
Spinach roulade with egg and mushroom filling
Asparagus and mushroom gratin

Meatless Main Courses

Here are half a dozen substitute main courses for those who prefer not to eat meat.

Three-cheese and pepper roulade

Serves 8

This cold roulade consists of a *roux* made from well-flavoured milk – don't try to skip the flavouring of the milk, it is all-important to the end result – and cheese. The filling is of peppers sliced in thin strips (I like to use red and yellow peppers only, because I don't much like green peppers) and cooked with finely chopped garlic in olive oil till soft, then bound with cream cheese let down with milk until it's of a spreadable consistency. There is freshly grated Parmesan round the outside of the roulade, hence the three cheeses in the recipe title.

FOR THE FLAVOURED MILK

1 pt/600 ml milk
1 onion, skinned and halved
1 stick of celery, washed and
  cut in half

a few black peppercorns
1 tsp rock salt
a handful of parsley

FOR THE ROULADE

2 oz/50 g butter
2 oz/50 g flour
the strained flavoured milk
4 oz/100 g Cheddar cheese,
  grated
5 large eggs

salt and freshly ground
  black pepper
freshly grated nutmeg
freshly grated Parmesan
  cheese
chopped parsley for garnish
  (optional)

FOR THE FILLING

4–5 tbsp olive oil
2 red and 2 yellow peppers,
  halved, deseeded and
  sliced in thin strips
1 large garlic clove, skinned
  and chopped very finely

8 oz/250 g cream cheese
  (such as Philadelphia)
  let down in a food
  processor with milk to a
  thick cream consistency
salt and freshly ground
  black pepper

Put the milk and other ingredients into a saucepan and heat to scalding, then take the pan off the heat and let the milk absorb the flavours for an hour. Strain, throwing away the flavourings.

Next make the roulade. First, line a baking tray with bakewell paper (siliconized greaseproof paper). Melt the butter in a saucepan and stir in the flour. Cook for a couple of minutes then, stirring continuously, add the flavoured milk, stirring till the sauce boils. Take the pan off the heat, and stir in the grated cheese. Beat in 1 whole egg, then the yolks of the remaining 4 eggs one at a time. Season to taste with salt, freshly ground pepper and grated nutmeg. Whisk the egg whites, and with a large metal spoon fold them quickly and thoroughly into the sauce. Pour this mixture onto the lined baking tray, and bake in a moderate oven – 350°F/180°C/Gas 4/bottom right oven of a 4-door Aga – for 20–25 minutes. Take it out of the oven, cover with a piece of bakewell paper and then with a damp teatowel (this saves you having to wash the teatowel afterwards!). Leave to cool completely.

Meanwhile, make the roulade filling. Heat the olive oil in a wide saucepan or frying pan and cook the sliced peppers and finely chopped garlic till the peppers are very soft – this will take 20 minutes or more, and they will collapse in size as they soften, so don't be alarmed if initially there looks to be far too much pepper! When ready, leave to cool.

Put the thick cream cheese mixture into a bowl, season with salt and pepper, and mix the cooled cooked peppers into the cream cheese.

To roll up the roulade, lay a fresh piece of bakewell paper on a table or work surface, and sprinkle liberally with freshly grated Parmesan cheese (try not to use the prepackaged stuff, which tastes and smells disgusting). Take the teatowel and paper off the top of the roulade, take the shorter ends in either hand, and flip it over face down onto the Parmesan. Carefully peel the paper off the back of the roulade, tearing it in strips parallel to the roulade – that way you need have no fear of tearing the roulade itself. Cover the roulade with the cream cheese and pepper mixture and roll it up, then slip the roulade on to a serving dish. Sprinkle, if you like, with chopped parsley, and serve in slices.

Spinach, tomato and cheese lasagne

Serves 8

This is delicious, and it freezes well. The lasagne which doesn't need pre-boiling is such a boon, but you do have to remember not to make the sauces too thick, otherwise you end up with a very stodgy dish. The lasagne needs to be able to absorb a lot of liquid as it cooks.

12 oz/350 g green lasagne –
the ready-to-bake variety

FOR THE TOMATO SAUCE

3 tbsp olive oil
1 onion, skinned and
chopped finely
1 stick celery, washed and
sliced very finely
1 carrot, peeled and chopped
finely
1 garlic clove, skinned and
chopped finely
1 × 15 oz/450 g tin of
tomatoes, liquidized
¼ pt/150 ml red wine
½ tsp sugar
salt and freshly ground
black pepper

FOR THE SPINACH AND CHEESE SAUCE

3 oz/75 g butter
2 tbsp sunflower oil
1 onion, skinned and
chopped finely
3 oz/75 g flour
1 rounded tsp mustard
powder
2 pt/1.2 L milk
8 oz/250 g grated Cheddar
cheese – but keep 2 oz/
50 g aside for sprinkling
over the top of the finished
lasagne
salt and freshly ground
black pepper
freshly grated nutmeg
1 lb/500 g frozen spinach,
thawed, well drained,
and puréed in the food
processor

Start by making the tomato sauce. Heat the olive oil in a saucepan and add the chopped onion, celery and carrot. Cook for 5–7 minutes, stirring occasionally to prevent the mixture burning. Add the finely chopped garlic, cook for a few minutes, then pour in the liquidized tomatoes and the red wine. Season with the sugar, salt and pepper. Simmer, with the pan uncovered, for 20–30 minutes.

Make the spinach and cheese sauce by melting the butter and heating the oil together in a saucepan and adding the finely chopped onion. Cook for about 5 minutes, then stir in the flour. Cook for a further couple of minutes before stirring in the mustard powder, and the milk, then stir continuously until the sauce boils. Take the pan off the heat, stir in 6 oz/175 g of the grated cheese, and season to your taste with salt, pepper and nutmeg. Stir in the puréed spinach.

In an ovenproof dish put a layer of spinach and cheese sauce, a layer of tomato sauce, then a layer of lasagne, and continue till the dish is filled, ending with a layer of either tomato or spinach and cheese sauce, not the lasagne. Sprinkle the surface with the reserved 2 oz/50 g of grated cheese. Bake in a moderate oven – 350°F/180°C/Gas 4/bottom right oven in a 4-door Aga – for 40–45 minutes, till the sauce is bubbling and when you stick a knife into the centre it feels soft.

Mushroom-stuffed crêpes with cheese and nutmeg sauce

Serves 6–8
(allow 3 crêpes per person for a main course, 2 for a first course)

This dish freezes well, and it tastes very good too.

FOR THE CRÊPES

6 oz/175 g plain flour
3 large eggs
1 oz/25 g butter, melted
salt and freshly ground
    black pepper

a handful of parsley
freshly grated nutmeg
¾ pt/750 ml milk and water
    mixed (two-thirds milk,
    one-third water)

FOR THE MUSHROOM STUFFING

3 oz/75 g butter
1 tbsp sunflower oil
1 onion, skinned and
    chopped finely
2 lb/1 kg mushrooms,
    wiped, stalks removed
    and caps chopped

1 garlic clove, skinned and
    chopped very finely
2 oz/50 g fresh brown
    breadcrumbs
salt and freshly ground
    black pepper
1 tbsp finely chopped parsley

FOR THE CHEESE AND NUTMEG SAUCE

2 oz/50 g butter
2 oz/50 g flour
just over 1 pt/600 ml milk
salt and freshly ground
    black pepper

freshly grated nutmeg
6 oz/175 g grated Cheddar
    cheese – but keep 2 oz/
    50 g aside to sprinkle over
    the finished dish

Put the flour, eggs, melted butter, seasonings and parsley into a liquidizer or food processor and whiz, then, still whizzing, gradually add the milk and water, whizzing till the batter is smooth. Leave for at least 30 minutes before making up into crêpes – you can leave the batter overnight, giving it a good stir with a fork or whisk in the morning before making up into crêpes.

If you have two crêpe or omelette pans the task of making the crêpes will be much quicker. Melt a small knob of butter in the pan till foaming, then, swirling the pan with your left hand (if you are right-handed) pour in a small amount of batter to cover the bottom of the pan thinly and evenly. Cook for a few minutes, then, using a small palette knife and your fingers, turn the crêpe over and cook on the other side. Continue till the batter is all used up, and put a disc-shaped piece of bakewell paper between each crêpe as it's made, which will prevent them from sticking together. Set aside, covered, until required.

Next, make the mushroom stuffing. Melt the butter and heat the oil in a saucepan or frying pan and add the finely chopped onion. Cook gently for 5 minutes, then add the chopped mushrooms and garlic and cook – over a high heat but without burning the mushrooms – until soft. Stir in the breadcrumbs, and season with salt and pepper. Cook for several minutes, then take the pan off the heat and stir in the chopped parsley.

Make the cheese sauce by first melting the butter and stirring in the flour. Let the mixture cook for a couple of minutes then add the milk and cook, stirring all the time, till the sauce boils. Then take the pan off the heat and stir in 4 oz/100 g of the grated cheese, and seasonings to taste.

Divide the mushroom stuffing mixture evenly between the crêpes, folding the sides of each stuffed crêpe under to form a parcel. Arrange them in a buttered, shallow, ovenproof dish. Pour the cheese sauce over and sprinkle with the remaining grated cheese. Bake the crêpes in a moderate oven – 350°F/180°C/Gas 4/bottom right oven in a 4-door Aga – till the sauce bubbles – 15–20 minutes.

Vegetable gougère

Serves 8

You can use any combination of vegetables you like in this recipe. Here I have chosen a selection of root vegetables: leeks, carrots, parsnips, onions and turnips in a parsley sauce. The crisp gougère surround goes so well with the vegetables in their sauce.

FOR THE GOUGÈRE

¾ pt/450 ml cold water
7 oz/200 g butter cut in pieces
9 oz/260 g plain flour, sieved twice
1 oz/25 g mustard powder, sieved twice

a few drops of Tabasco
5 eggs, beaten
8 oz/225 g grated Cheddar cheese

FOR THE FILLING

2–3 carrots (2 if large, 3 if small), peeled and sliced thinly
2 parsnips, peeled and sliced thinly
½ turnip, peeled and diced
3 oz/75 g butter
1 tbsp sunflower oil
2 onions, skinned and chopped finely
1 garlic clove, skinned and chopped finely

2 leeks, washed, trimmed and sliced thinly
2 oz/50 g flour
1½ pt/1 L milk
salt and freshly ground black pepper
grated nutmeg
3 tbsp chopped parsley

Put the water and pieces of butter into a saucepan over a moderate heat till the butter melts in the water – take care not to let the water boil before the butter has all melted. As soon as the liquid rolls to a boil take the pan off the heat and whoosh in the twice-sieved flour and mustard powder and, using a wooden spoon, beat the mixture hard till it comes away from the sides of the pan. Leave it for 10 minutes then beat in the beaten eggs a little at a time – I use an electric whisk for this. Beat in 6 oz/175 g of the grated cheese and the Tabasco.

Butter a shallow ovenproof dish and spoon the cheese choux pastry round the sides and in a thin layer over the bottom of the dish. Sprinkle over the remaining grated cheese. Bake in a hot oven – 400°F/200°C/Gas 6/top right oven in a 4-door Aga for about 20 minutes.

To make the filling, steam the carrots, parsnips and turnip till tender. Next, melt the butter and heat the oil together in a saucepan, and add the finely chopped onions, garlic and sliced leeks. Cook over a moderate heat for 10–15 minutes, until soft. Stir in the flour, cook for a minute or two, then stir in the milk, and continue stirring till the sauce boils. Season to taste with salt, pepper and nutmeg, and stir in the steamed vegetables.

Just before serving stir the chopped parsley into the sauce and vegetables, and pour them into the middle of the cooked gougère. Serve immediately – the choux pastry will start to deflate if it sits for too long.

Spinach roulade with egg and mushroom filling

Serves 8

This can be served hot or cold.

2 lb/1 kg frozen spinach,
    thawed and thoroughly
    drained
5 large eggs, separated

1 oz/25 g butter
salt and freshly ground
    black pepper
freshly grated nutmeg

FOR THE FILLING

3 oz/75 g butter
1 garlic clove, skinned and
    chopped finely
8 oz/250 g mushrooms,
    wiped and sliced
3 oz/75g plain flour

1¼ pt/750 ml milk
salt and freshly ground
    black pepper
4 hardboiled eggs, chopped

Line a baking tray with bakewell paper (siliconized greaseproof paper).

Put the thawed and drained spinach into a food processor and whiz, adding the egg yolks one by one, and then the ounce of butter. Season to taste with salt, pepper and a pinch of nutmeg. Whisk the egg whites till very stiff and, using a large metal spoon, fold them thoroughly into the spinach mixture. Pour this onto the bakewell paper-lined tin, and bake in a moderate oven – 350°F/180°C/Gas 4/bottom right oven in a 4-door Aga – for 20–25 minutes, till firm to the touch.

While the spinach roulade is cooking, make the filling. Melt the butter and add the finely chopped garlic. When the butter is very hot, but not burning, add the sliced mushrooms and cook them for a couple of minutes over as high a heat as possible. Stir in the flour, cook for a further minute, then gradually add the milk, stirring continuously till the sauce boils. If the sauce seems thick to you don't worry, it needs to be so as not to run out of the roulade when it's rolled up. Season with salt and pepper. Stir the chopped hardboiled eggs into the sauce.

To roll up the roulade, lay a piece of bakewell paper onto a table or work surface. Take the short ends of the roulade paper in each hand and flip it over face down on the paper. Carefully tear off the paper from the back of the cooked roulade, tearing it in strips parallel to the roulade to prevent the roulade tearing with the paper. Cover the roulade with the egg and mushroom sauce filling, roll it up, and slip it onto a serving plate. This roulade will keep warm quite satisfactorily in a low oven for up to 20 minutes.

Asparagus and mushroom gratin

Serves 8

This is rather a rich main course, so I would plan for a fairly light, simple first course and pudding to precede and follow it. I like to serve it with plain boiled brown or basmati rice.

---

1 lb/500 g mushrooms, wiped and sliced	a good pinch of thyme
2 oz/50 g butter	juice of ½ lemon
1 tbsp sunflower oil	salt and freshly ground black pepper
8 oz/250 g asparagus, trimmed, and cut in 1 in/ 2.5 cm pieces	2 oz/50 g fine breadcrumbs (white or brown)
1 pt/600 ml double cream	2 tbsp chopped parsley
12 oz/350 g grated Cheddar cheese	

Start by cooking the sliced mushrooms: melt the butter and heat the oil together in a wide saucepan or frying pan, heating till it is very hot. Cook the sliced mushrooms in small amounts till almost browned then take them out of the pan with a slotted spoon, and keep to one side. Steam the asparagus until just tender and set aside also.

Put the cream, 8 oz/250 g of the grated cheese, and the thyme into a saucepan and heat over a gentle-to-moderate heat. When the cheese has melted in the cream take the pan off the heat, and stir in the lemon juice, salt and pepper.

Stir the steamed asparagus and cooked mushrooms into the rich sauce. Pour it into a wide, fairly shallow ovenproof dish, mix the rest of the grated cheese with the crumbs and parsley and sprinkle over evenly. Put under a hot grill till the crumbs brown.

FUNERAL LUNCH FOR 12

— ⁓◦⁓ —

Steak, kidney and beer casserole
Root vegetable ragoût
OR
Cold chicken in a curried mayonnaise
Rice, grape and almond salad

Lemon and blackcurrant pudding

Funerals

Whilst not exactly qualifying as a celebration, funerals are a fact of life for all families, at some time or another, and they do have to be considered. There is such a short time between a death and a funeral, and inevitably there are family and friends who travel from afar to be at a funeral and who will need sustenance following the service. Strange as it may seem, an odd feeling of euphoria prevails following a funeral, and a funeral lunch (because that is the most likely meal, for reasons of allowing guests travelling time to get to the service and home again afterwards) isn't the gloomy affair one might suppose it to be. I am giving you suggestions for a summertime lunch, and also a menu for cold weather. If you have the time and inclination to make one, a good pudding is *Lemon and blackcurrant pudding* – easy, delicious, and ideal for any time of the year, with frozen blackcurrants always being available. But if a pudding is the last straw, cheese, biscuits and fruit to follow the main course is quite enough – no-one is going to expect a gastronomic treat on such an occasion.

The main thing to take into consideration when planning food to follow a funeral is that you should be able to leave it slowly cooking in the oven without spoiling – and it must be warming, comforting food if it is chilly weather, or alternatively, food which can be left, covered, all ready to eat on your return from the church or crematorium if it is warmer weather. To sum up, the criterion for such a meal must be simplicity.

Steak, kidney and beer casserole

Serves 12

This is very comforting food on a chilly day, funeral or not. A casserole is so much easier to leave simmering very gently in a warm oven than a steak and kidney pie, where the pastry would dry out. The beer in this recipe complements the steak and kidney very well, and forms a delicious rich gravy, enhanced by grainy mustard.

---

4 tbsp flour
salt and plenty of freshly ground black pepper
5 lb/2.25 kg lean steak, trimmed and cut into 1–1½ in/2.5–4 cm chunks
2 lb/1 kg ox kidney, trimmed and cut in large, even-sized chunks

6 tbsp oil, and more as required (I use sunflower)
3 medium onions, skinned and chopped finely
2 cans (1 pt/600 ml) beer
2 tsp grainy mustard
1½ pt/1 L water

Mix the salt and pepper into the flour in a dish, and roll in it the trimmed chunks of steak; set to one side. Mix the cut-up kidney into the rest of the flour, but keep the steak and kidney separate. (I say this because the steak will take longer to brown than the kidney.)

Heat 3 tablespoons of the oil in a large, heavy casserole-type saucepan, and brown the steak, a little at a time, removing it as it is ready to a dish to keep warm as you brown the rest. Brown the kidney last.

Add more oil to the casserole, and the finely chopped onions. Cook the onions over a moderate heat, stirring occasionally, for about 5 minutes, till they are soft and transparent-looking. Stir in any remaining seasoned flour, scraping the bottom of the casserole, then stir in the beer and the water. Stir till the sauce boils, then replace the steak and kidney in the casserole, let the liquid come back to simmering point, and cover with a lid. Cook in a moderate oven – 350°F/180°C/Gas 4/ bottom right oven in a 4-door Aga – for 1 hour. Take the casserole out of the oven and cool completely, then store overnight (or over two nights) in the fridge.

Depending on how long you estimate to be out of the house at the service, give the casserole a further hour's cooking at the same moderate temperature, or longer at a lower temperature, but bring the liquid to simmering point before you put the casserole into the lower oven – otherwise it will never come up to temperature and won't cook the further amount the meat will need. Scrub baking potatoes, cover them with butter papers, and leave them to bake, also at a moderate temperature, while you are out.

Root vegetable ragoût

Serves 12

---

4 tbsp oil (I use sunflower)

3 medium onions, skinned and sliced finely

4 leeks, trimmed, washed, and sliced about 1 in/ 2.5 cm thick

6 carrots, trimmed, peeled, and cut in 1 in/2.5 cm chunks

1 small turnip, skinned and cut in 2 in/5 cm long and ½ in/1 cm thick strips

4 parsnips, peeled and cut in thick strips

salt and pepper

Heat the oil in a heavy casserole-type of flameproof dish. Add the onions, and cook them for about 5 minutes, then add the rest of the vegetables. Season with salt and pepper, and cook on top of the stove for about 15 minutes, stirring from time to time to prevent any sticking and burning. Then cover the casserole with a lid and cook in a low-to-moderate oven – 325°F/160°C/Gas 3/bottom of the bottom right oven in a 4-door Aga – for the time you are at the service.

Cold chicken in a curried mayonnaise

Serves 12

This is delicious, very simple, and greatly complemented by the accompanying rice salad with its toasted flaked almonds and grapes. The curried mayonnaise can be made up a day ahead. The chicken can be cooked two days ahead, stripped off the carcasses and kept in the fridge. The rice salad can be made the day before it is needed too. You can wash the lettuce and chop the chives and mint for an accompanying green salad, and mix the French dressing for this and the rice salad and keep it in a screw-topped jar in the fridge. All you need do on the morning of the funeral is to arrange the chicken in its mayonnaise on a serving dish, do the same with the salads, and on return from the service just pour dressing on the salads.

3 chickens weighing about
    3–3½ lb/1.5 kg each
(free-range if possible, fresh
    rather than frozen
    anyway)
3 onions, skinned and cut in
    half
2–3 carrots, cut in half

3 sticks of celery
a handful of parsley
a few peppercorns
1 tbsp rock salt

FOR THE CURRIED MAYONNAISE

¾ pt/450 ml double cream,
    whipped
3 tbsp wine vinegar, white
    or red
2 tbsp runny honey
1 rounded tbsp medium curry
    powder

8 tbsp mayonnaise (I think
    it's quite all right to use
    Hellmann's or similar on
    such an occasion!)
chopped parsley for
    garnishing (optional)

Put the chickens into a big saucepan with all the other ingredients. Cover with cold water, and over a moderate heat bring the water to simmering point. Simmer for 1–1½ hours; they are ready if, when you stick the point of a knife into the flesh between the leg and body of the chicken, the juices run clear – if the juices are at all tinged with pink, let them cook a bit longer. When they are cooked, let them cool in the liquid, then take them out of the saucepan and strip the cooked chicken off the bones, cutting it into pieces as evenly sized as possible. Boil up the bones in the stock for 2–3 hours, strain, cool and keep, or freeze for use in soups.

Make the curried mayonnaise. Whip the wine vinegar, honey and curry powder into the cream. Fold together the cream and mayonnaise. Store in a covered bowl till you are ready to mix together with the cooked chicken. Scatter chopped parsley over the surface if you wish.

Rice, grape and almond salad

Serves 12

Toasting the flaked almonds makes a world of difference
to the flavour of this salad. I toast them by putting them
into a saucepan dry over a moderate heat, and shaking
them till they are golden brown. Cool before using.

---

*1 lb/500 g rice (I think
    basmati is nicest for this)*
*4 oz/100 g flaked almonds,
    toasted (see above)*
*8 oz/250 g grapes, green or
    black, cut in half and
    deseeded*

1 tbsp finely chopped parsley
*1 tbsp snipped chives – not
    essential, but good if you
    have them*
*2 tbsp vinaigrette dressing
    (see page 83)*

Cook the rice in boiling salted water till there is just a
slight bite to a grain of rice when you test it. Rinse in a
large sieve (in two or three lots) under cold running
water. Drain well, and put into a large mixing bowl. Mix
together with the flaked almonds and halved grapes, the
chopped parsley and chives. Incorporate the dressing,
mixing it through thoroughly. Arrange in a serving dish,
or around the chicken to serve, whichever is easiest.

Lemon and blackcurrant pudding

Serves 12

This is one of my favourite puddings at any time of year,

and frozen blackcurrants are always available when the fresh fruit are out of season. If any of this pudding is left over it can be frozen – I once froze a whole leftover pudding and it did so beautifully. It can be made a day in advance and warmed up before serving – worth doing as I think it is nicest served warm.

---

2 lb/1 kg blackcurrants
10 oz/275 g caster sugar
4 oz/100 g softened butter
grated rind and juice of
*   3 lemons*
8 large eggs, separated

3 oz/75 g plain flour, sieved
12 fl oz/350 ml milk
sieved icing sugar for
*   dusting*
whipped cream for serving

Divide the blackcurrants between 2 ovenproof dishes. Sprinkle 1 oz/25 g sugar over each. Put the butter in a bowl and beat it, gradually adding the rest of the sugar and beating till the mixture is pale and fluffy. Beat in the grated lemon rinds, and gradually beat in the lemon juice. Beat in the egg yolks, one at a time. The mixture will almost certainly have curdled by now – but don't worry, it will all come right in the end! Beat in the sieved flour, and lastly stir in the milk. Whisk the egg whites till they are very stiff and, with a large metal spoon, fold them quickly and thoroughly through the lemon mixture. Divide between the two dishes, and put the dishes into a roasting tin with hot water coming halfway up their sides. Bake in a moderate oven – 350°F/180°C/Gas 4/ bottom right oven in a 4-door Aga – for 40–45 minutes, until quite firm on top.

In this pudding, the mixture separates to form a light sponge on top and a thick lemony sauce with the blackcurrants underneath. Dust the tops of each pudding with sieved icing sugar to serve, and hand round whipped cream.

113

Easter

This is one of my favourite times of the year, hectic as it is for us here at Kinloch because the hotel is open, and as well we have some extra family and/or friends staying with us in our part of the house. Easter is such an important time of the year – you could say *the* most important time of the year for Christians – but how I do wish those that decide these things would peg the date of Easter! Life would be so much easier from every point of view. This year – 1989 – Easter fell as early as it was possible for it to do, but still here in Skye we were lucky and had plenty of primroses out (one of my most favourite flowers) and the small early daffodils known as Lent lilies.

I like to set the Easter scene with as many flowers as possible dotted through the house, and with a simple table centrepiece consisting of a shallow basket lined with foil or polythene, covered with moss, and within the moss tiny containers of primroses (egg-cups make good receptacles) and clusters of tiny brightly coloured foil-wrapped eggs dotted about. It is simple, very pretty, and lasts well (providing you remember to top up the water in the primroses!). I have to say that the idea is not my invention, but that of a great friend of ours, Jenny Aldridge, who several years ago made one such basket for us for Easter, and ever since I have repeated her idea.

From a food point of view, Easter holidays usually start on Maundy Thursday, so I have planned meals from dinner on that day, ending with lunch on Easter Sunday. I thought that you may well have a dinner party on Easter Saturday, but even if you don't plan to entertain other than your family or friends staying with you, it is a good and delicious menu anyway! I advise you to cook more smoked pork loin for dinner on

Thursday evening than you will need, because you will notice that it features again, thinly sliced, for brunch on Easter Saturday, served with scrambled eggs into which some goats' cheese is crumbled.

There is much in the menus planned for this weekend which can be made ahead, and some of which can be made and frozen, like the *Hot cross buns*, the *Fish pie*, the *Tapénade*, and the apple and horseradish glaze for Easter Sunday lunch's roast pork. Hopefully, you should have everything well in hand on the food front by the time your guests arrive on Thursday. I advise you to make a cake – possibly the *Orange and ginger cake* (see page 59) in the little chapter on teatime goodies because children may very well be among the guests staying – besides, not only children love cake and biscuits!

The batter for the *Deep-fried mushrooms* can be made the day before, and just needs the egg whites whisked and folded into it a couple of hours before the frying. The *Tartare Sauce* is such a delicious sauce, and simple to make, and can be made up to a week ahead and kept, covered, in the fridge. The sauce to go with the *Roast smoked pork loin* can be made in the morning, and the potato and onion dish can be made and cooked in the morning, ready to have a further hour in a slow oven before dinner. The broccoli can be prepared and trimmed and the lime quartered in the morning, all ready just to be steamed for 7–10 minutes before serving – how long you steam it depends on how crunchy you like your vegetables; test the broccoli stalks by sticking a knife into them till they feel right for your liking. The soufflé can be made in the morning up to the stage of adding the whisked egg whites, which can be done two or three hours before dinner, and the soufflé dish left till cooking time covered with clingfilm. The coffee sauce can be made the previous day and kept in a cool place till dinner time.

115

MAUNDY THURSDAY
DINNER FOR EIGHT

❧⟡⟡⟡❧

Deep-fried mushrooms with tartare sauce
Roast smoked pork loin with vermouth and tomato sauce
Baked sliced potatoes and onions
Steamed broccoli with lime
Baked chocolate and coffee soufflé with coffee sauce

Deep-fried mushrooms
with tartare sauce

Serves 8

How many mushrooms you serve per person depends on how big the mushrooms are – if they are huge flat ones like those from Marks and Spencer, which are the nicest, I allow two or three per person. If they are the more usual smaller variety, then five or six per person. Simply wipe each mushroom and remove the stalk – there is no need to skin them.

---

mushrooms (see above)   oil for deep-frying

FOR THE BATTER

6 oz/175 g plain flour   2 tbsp oil (I use sunflower)
3 large egg yolks, plus   salt and freshly ground
   2 whites   black pepper
8 fl oz/250 ml milk

Whiz together in a liquidizer or food processor everything except the egg whites. A couple of hours before cooking, whisk the whites till stiff and, with a large metal spoon, fold them quickly and thoroughly through the batter. Cover the bowl with clingfilm.

    If you haven't got a deep fryer, heat oil (again, I use sunflower) in a deep saucepan, to a depth of 3 in/7.5 cm. Dip each mushroom in the batter, and lift out using two forks. Cook them, no more than 3 or 4 at one time, in the hot oil, till they are golden brown and puffed up. Keep them warm, on several thicknesses of kitchen paper, in a low oven till you are ready to dish up. They keep warm quite well for about 20 minutes. Serve on individual serving plates, accompanied by shredded lettuce if you like, and with a good spoonful of *Tartare sauce* (see below) at the side of the mushrooms.

Tartare sauce

Serves 8

---

1 large whole egg plus one
    egg yolk
1 tsp sugar
½ tsp salt
several good grindings of
    black pepper
1 tsp French mustard
1 garlic clove, skinned and
    chopped
½ pt/300 ml oil (sunflower
    or olive, or a mixture of
    both)
2–3 tbsp white wine vinegar

1 tbsp chopped parsley
1 tsp chopped capers
2 hardboiled eggs, chopped
    finely
6–8 black olives, stoned and
    chopped
about 6 in/15 cm piece
    cucumber, skinned,
    deseeded and diced finely

Whiz the first six ingredients – the egg, egg yolk and flavourings – together, in a liquidizer or food processor, then slowly add, drop by drop at first then in a steady trickle, the sunflower or olive oil or mixture of both. When all is incorporated, whiz in the white wine vinegar – taste, and add more if you like, but remember that the capers and black olives you are going to add to this sauce

118

will themselves add a certain amount of sharpness. Stir in the rest of the ingredients.

Keep the sauce in a covered bowl in the fridge till required.

Roast smoked pork loin with vermouth and tomato sauce

Serves 8

You will need 3 smoked pork loins, each weighing about 2 lb/1 kg. Put the smoked pork loins into a roasting tin and roast them in a hot oven – 400°F/200°C/Gas 6/top right oven in a 4-door Aga – for half an hour, then continue cooking in a moderate oven – 350°F/180°C/Gas 4/ bottom right oven in a 4-door Aga – for a further 45 minutes. Let them stand, covered with foil, for 10 minutes, before you slice them. I like them sliced thick for serving hot – about ¼ in/½ cm thick.

FOR THE VERMOUTH AND TOMATO SAUCE

½ pt/300 ml red vermouth (Martini Rosso)
2 medium-sized onions, skinned and chopped very finely
2 oz/50 g butter
2 oz/50 g flour
1 pt/600 ml milk

freshly ground black pepper to taste
a grating of nutmeg
3 tomatoes, skinned, deseeded, and chopped
1 tbsp chopped parsley

Put the vermouth and finely chopped onions into a saucepan and simmer gently till the onions are very soft

119

and the vermouth is reduced almost to nothing. Melt the butter in another saucepan, and stir in the flour, let it cook for a minute or two, then stir in the milk, stirring all the time till the sauce boils. Simmer for a minute, then take the pan off the heat, and season to taste with pepper and nutmeg. You can prepare the sauce this far in the morning for dinner that evening, but cover the surface of the sauce with a piece of greaseproof paper wrung out in water to prevent a skin forming.

Prepare the tomatoes, and chop the parsley, and stir these into the sauce when you have reheated it ready to serve. Also, stir in some of the juices from the smoked pork in the roasting tin – that is why I don't include salt in the recipe, because this generally adds enough saltiness for most people's tastes. Serve in a sauce tureen accompanying the sliced smoked pork.

Reserve one of the smoked pork loins, and when it is quite cold, wrap it in foil and keep it in the fridge ready for Saturday's brunch (see page 140).

Baked sliced potatoes and onions

Serves 8

3 oz/75 g chilled butter, plus a little extra for greasing	*2 medium onions, skinned and sliced very thinly*
1 medium-to-large potato per person – this isn't being as mean as it sounds, somehow potatoes go further cooked like this!	*milk to cover the potatoes in the dish* *salt and freshly ground black pepper* *freshly grated nutmeg*

Butter well a shallow ovenproof dish. Slice the potatoes very thinly, either by hand, or in a mandolin. Arrange a layer of potatoes in the buttered dish, cover with some of the finely sliced onion, dot with small bits of butter, and season with a little salt, freshly ground black pepper and freshly grated nutmeg. Continue to fill the dish with layers of potato and onion, and seasoning each one, till the potatoes are all used up. Dot the surface with more butter. Pour in enough milk to come up to the surface of the potato, and put into a moderate oven – 350°F/180°C/Gas 4/bottom right oven in a 4-door Aga – for an hour. If you do this in the morning, which you can, then lower the heat to 200°F/110°C/Gas ½/bottom left oven in a 4-door Aga and leave in the oven till dinner time – check it occasionally and pour on a little more milk if it looks dry to you, but it will become a rich brown colour, with the potatoes and onions almost melting together. If you don't cook it from the morning on, it will need 3 hours in a moderate oven, before dinner.

Baked chocolate and coffee soufflé with coffee sauce

Serves 8

---

8 oz/250 g good dark
    chocolate
½ pt/300 ml milk, plus a
    little extra
2 tsp instant coffee granules
2 tsp cornflour

8 large eggs, separated
4 oz/100 g caster sugar
icing sugar for dusting

121

Butter a large soufflé or other ovenproof dish. Dust it with caster sugar.

Break the chocolate into a Pyrex bowl and put the bowl over a saucepan of hot water (take care not to let the bottom of the bowl touch the water, and not to let the water even simmer), melt the chocolate, and as soon as it is soft take the bowl off the saucepan. In another small saucepan heat together the milk and the coffee. Slake the cornflour with a little cold milk, then with some of the hot coffee-milk, then pour this into the saucepan with the rest of the coffee-milk and stir over a gentle heat till it thickens and boils. Take this custard off the heat and cool it for 10 minutes, stirring occasionally to prevent a skin from forming. Whisk the egg yolks, gradually adding the caster sugar, and continue whisking till the mixture is thick and pale. Whisk in the melted chocolate and the cooled coffee custard. You can complete the recipe up to this stage in the morning ready for dinner that evening.

A couple of hours before dinner, whisk the egg whites till they are very stiff and, with a large metal spoon, fold them quickly and thoroughly through the chocolate and coffee mixture. Pour into the prepared soufflé dish, and cover with clingfilm. As you clear away the first course, put the soufflé (having first removed the clingfilm) into a hot oven – 425°F/220°C/Gas 7/top right oven in a 4-door Aga – and bake for 40–45 minutes – and don't be tempted to take it out in less. A few minutes more than 45 won't hurt the soufflé, but it must be served immediately. Have ready beside the oven a sieve and a spoonful of icing sugar ready to sieve over the surface of the soufflé as it comes out of the oven.

I like to serve my *Coffee sauce* (see below) with the soufflé, but you can serve it just as well with vanilla-flavoured whipped cream.

Coffee sauce

3/4 pt/450 ml single cream   4 large egg yolks
2 tsp coffee granules   3 oz/75 g caster sugar
3 tbsp boiling water

Put the single cream into a saucepan over a low heat.
Dissolve the coffee in the boiling water and add to the
cream. Beat the egg yolks, gradually adding the sugar,
till they are thick and pale. Pour a little of the hot cream
onto the yolk mixture, mix well, then pour this into the
saucepan and stir, over a gentle heat, till the sauce
thickens enough to cover the back of the wooden spoon,
and to leave a clear path when you trace your finger
through the sauce on the back of the spoon. Take it off
the heat. Don't be tempted to hurry up the thickening
process by turning up the heat, because then you will be
in danger of curdling the sauce! If by any stroke of bad
luck your sauce should look as if it is on the point of
curdling, take it off the heat, sieve it into a clean bowl,
and beat it hard, which should do the trick. Stir the
cooling sauce from time to time, to prevent a skin from
forming. Serve cold, with the hot soufflé – delicious.

Good Friday

A solemn day, and one on which we traditionally, along
with a great many other families, don't eat meat. I
always feel rather guilty, though, about having delicious
hot cross buns for breakfast on Good Friday – I love

them so much! They are so easy to make, and they freeze very well. If you can get good whole pieces of crystallized peel, do, and cut it up yourself; it is a world apart from the little tubs of chopped mixed peel. You can also make it quite easily for yourself: dissolve together two parts of sugar to one part of water, then boil the syrup till clear, add thinly sliced citrus peel and simmer it very gently in the hot syrup for about 2 hours. Keep it wrapped in siliconized greaseproof paper, and cut up into small pieces as required.

Good Friday Breakfast

For the best possible Good Friday breakfast, I suggest just freshly squeezed orange juice, coffee or tea, with warm hot cross buns. (Remember to take them out of the freezer the night before.)

Hot cross buns

Makes 24 buns

---

2 oz/50 g dried yeast
½ pt/300 ml hand-hot
water, with 2 tsp sugar
in it
1 lb/500 g each strong white
flour and wholewheat
flour, mixed
2 tsp salt
3 oz/75 g caster sugar
4 oz/100 g raisins
2 oz/50 g sultanas (you can
substitute currants if you
like, but I much prefer
a sultana/raisin mixture)

3 oz/75 g chopped mixed
peel (see above)
2 tsp powdered cinnamon
2 tsp mixed spice
¾ pt/450 ml warm milk
3 oz/75 g butter, melted
1 large egg, beaten
sugar glaze (see below)

Mix the dried yeast into the hand-hot water and sugar, and leave in a warm place till it has trebled in size.

Add the salt, sugar, dried fruits and spices to the flour in the bowl and when the yeast is all frothed up, stir it into the flour along with the warm milk, melted butter and beaten egg. Knead well, on a floured table or work surface, till the dough feels pliable and not sticky – anyone who is a bread-maker will know just the feel! As a rough guide, I count to 200 for this kneading. Divide the dough in half, then each half in half again, and continue till you have 24 pieces of dough. Roll each one into a bun shape, and put them, not too closely together, on a baking tray. Make pastry crosses and stick one on top of each bun. Put the baking trays in a warm place, and cover each with a teatowel.

When the buns have doubled in size – about 15–20 minutes – put them straight into a hot oven – 425°F/ 220°C/Gas 7/top right in a 4-door Aga – and bake for 10–15 minutes – check them after 10, they should sound hollow when you tap the base of a bun. Cool in a warm place on a wire cooling rack – this may sound odd, but I find that bread, buns, cake etc cooled in a cold place seem to toughen up.

Brush the hot cross buns with a glaze made of 3 tablespoons of granulated sugar and 1 tablespoon of water dissolved together then boiled for 1 minute.

Good Friday Lunch

Root vegetable soup

Serves 8

This soup is actually even nicer if made a day ahead and reheated.

---

4 medium-sized beetroot (3 if one's a whopper)	2 medium onions, skinned and sliced thinly
2 carrots	2 pt/1.2 L good chicken or vegetable stock
2 parsnips	salt and freshly ground black pepper
2 medium-sized potatoes	chopped parsley for garnish (optional)
4 tbsp oil (I use sunflower)	

Peel the beetroot, and slice them into thick short strips – about 1 in/2.5 cm in size. Peel the carrots, parsnips and potatoes, and cut them in roughly the same size pieces as the beetroot. Heat the oil in a large saucepan and add the onions, cook for about 5 minutes, stirring occasionally to prevent them from burning, then add the rest of the vegetables to the saucepan. Cook for a further 5 minutes, then pour in the stock – and remember, any soup will only be as good as the stock it is made from. (I have a personal crusade against the stock cube!) Season to taste with salt and freshly ground black pepper. Simmer gently, with the pan half-covered with a lid, for 40–45 minutes, till the vegetables are tender when you stick a knife into one – try the carrot, it will need more cooking than any of the others. Take the pan off the heat, cool the soup completely and pour it into a bowl and keep in a cool place till the next day. Reheat to serve, and, if you like, sprinkle some chopped parsley over the surface of each serving.

Serve this hearty soup with warm brown rolls or bread, and cheese and fruit to follow, for a simple lunch.

Good Friday Dinner

This needn't be an elaborate dinner. In fact I advise a first course which can be eaten in the fingers before dinner, shelled *Quails' eggs with tapénade* – that is, black olive pâté which made my way includes an egg yolk, to render it of dippable consistency.

For the main course I suggest *Fish pie*, which properly made is very good, and can be made ahead and frozen, ready-covered with its creamy parsley-flecked mashed potatoes. To accompany the fish pie, *Parsnip chips* – just fat fingers of parsnip, deep-fried – are delicious, and grilled tomato halves, with a pinch of dried ginger on each half.

For pudding there is *Rhubarb meringue tart*. The pastry base can be made two or three days in advance, and the rhubarb baked and thickened with a little arrowroot, all ready to be assembled before dinner. It doesn't take a minute, and will bake happily in a moderate oven while you and your guests eat the main course.

GOOD FRIDAY DINNER
FOR EIGHT

Quails' eggs with tapénade
Fish pie
Parsnip chips
Grilled tomatoes with ginger
Rhubarb meringue tart

Quails' eggs with tapénade

allow 3–4 quails' eggs per
person

FOR THE TAPÉNADE

6 oz/175 g black olives
  weighed when stoned
1 egg yolk
1 garlic clove, skinned and
  chopped

a squeeze of anchovy paste
juice of ½ juicy lemon
¼ pt/150 ml olive oil
freshly ground black pepper

Put the stoned black olives into a food processor and whiz, add the egg yolk and the garlic, and the anchovy paste, and whiz. Still whizzing, add the oil, a drip at a time to begin with, then in a steady trickle, till it is all incorporated. Whiz in the lemon juice, and season to taste with black pepper.

Tapénade will keep in a covered bowl in the fridge for up to 5 days.

Fish pie

Serves 8

---

2 lb/1 kg smoked haddock
  (finnan haddock on the
  bone if at all possible)
2 lb/1 kg firm-fleshed white
  fish, such as cod or hake

3 pt/1.75 L milk and water
  mixed, half and half
1 onion, skinned and halved
blade of mace

FOR THE SAUCE

3 oz/75 g butter
1 onion, skinned and finely
  chopped
3 oz/75 g flour
1½–2 pt/1–1.2 L reserved
  fish liquid (see below)

freshly ground black pepper
a few gratings of nutmeg

FOR THE TOP

10 medium potatoes, peeled
  and cut in half
2 oz/50 g butter cut in pieces

½ pt/300 ml hot milk
salt and freshly ground
  black pepper
2 tbsp finely chopped parsley

Put the fish all together in a large saucepan, with the milk and water, the onion and the mace and, over a moderate heat, bring the liquid to simmering point. Simmer very gently for 2–3 minutes – no longer – then take the pan off the heat and cool the fish in the liquid for 15–20 minutes. Strain the liquid off the fish and keep it in a jug to use for the sauce. Skin the fish and flake it, and try really hard to remove all the bones. Set the flaked fish to one side.

To make the sauce, first melt the butter in a saucepan, and add the finely chopped onion. Cook for about 5 minutes, stirring occasionally and cooking till the onion is soft and transparent-looking, then stir in the flour. Cook for a further couple of minutes, before pouring in the fish liquid, a little at a time, stirring continuously, till the sauce boils. (I use rather less than 2 pt/1.2 L, but I prefer a fairly stiff sauce.) When the sauce has boiled, take the pan off the heat, and season to your taste with pepper and nutmeg. Stir in the flaked fish, taking care not to over-stir and so break up the fish into mush. Pour into an ovenproof dish big enough to take the fish in the sauce and its potato top (see below). Let the fish cool.

To make the top for the pie, boil the potatoes until they are tender, drain them well and steam dry. With a handheld electric beater, whisk in the butter and slowly add the hot milk. Whisk well, and the potatoes will become fluffy. Season with salt and pepper, and whisk in the chopped parsley. Cool, then arrange over the surface of the fish sauce, finishing by making a pattern across the surface with a fork, if you like. Cover with clingfilm, and freeze. Take out of the freezer and thaw in the fridge overnight. Reheat the pie in a moderate oven – 350°F/180°C/Gas 4/bottom right oven in a 4-door Aga – till the surface of the potato starts to become crisp, and the sauce underneath bubbles – 30–40 minutes.

Parsnip chips

Allow 2 average-sized parsnips per person, peel them and cut them into finger-thick pieces. Heat oil (I use sunflower) in a saucepan to a depth of about 3 in/7.5 cm and deep-fry the parsnip chips in small amounts, till they are golden brown. Keep them warm on several thick-nesses of kitchen paper on an ovenproof dish in a low oven.

Grilled tomatoes with ginger

When you have finished frying the parsnips, grill the tomato halves. Allow 3 halves per person, and put the halved tomatoes in a heatproof dish. Sprinkle a small amount of salt over each half, grind some black pepper over, and put a pinch of dried ginger on top. Place a small dot of butter on each half, and grill till the tomatoes are soft – 4–5 minutes.

Both the parsnip chips and the grilled tomatoes will keep warm for about 20 minutes – not much more, as the parsnips tend to lose their crispness.

Rhubarb meringue tart

Serves 8

FOR THE PASTRY

4 oz/100 g chilled butter, cut
    into small pieces

6 oz/175 g plain flour
1 oz/25 g icing sugar

FOR THE RHUBARB FILLING

2 lb/1 kg rhubarb (trimmed
    weight), cut into 1 in/
    2.5 cm pieces
4–6 oz/100–175 g soft
    brown sugar

1 tsp powdered cinnamon
1 tbsp arrowroot*

FOR THE MERINGUE

4 large egg whites

8 oz/250 g caster sugar

To make the pastry, simply whiz all the ingredients
together in a food processor till they resemble fine
crumbs. Pat around the sides and base of a 9 in/23 cm
flan dish, then put the dish into the fridge for at least half
an hour, before baking in a moderate oven – 350°F/
180°C/Gas 4/bottom right oven in a 4-door Aga – for 20–
25 minutes, till golden brown. Cool.

Put the rhubarb for the filling into a saucepan together
with the sugar and cinnamon. Cover the pan with a lid,
and cook over a moderate heat till the juices run and the
rhubarb is tender. Take the pan off the heat, and strain
the juices off the rhubarb, into a small saucepan. Slake

the tablespoon of arrowroot with 2 tablespoons water, and stir some of the hot rhubarb juice into it. Then mix this into the hot juice in the saucepan. Over a gentle heat stir till it boils – as it boils, the sauce will become clear. After it has boiled, take the pan off the heat, and stir the thickened juices into the cooked rhubarb. Keep in a bowl till shortly before assembling the tart because, if it is poured into the cooked pastry case too soon, it tends to make the pastry soft.

Finally, make the meringue. Whisk the egg whites till very stiff, then, still whisking, add the sugar a spoonful at a time, whisking till it is all incorporated and the meringue very stiff.

To assemble the tart, pour the cooled and thickened rhubarb mixture into the pastry case. Cover completely with the meringue, making sure that it comes right to the edge of the dish and that all the pastry is covered. (You can do this as you are about to dish up the main course.) Then put the tart immediately into a moderately cool oven – 325°F/170°C/Gas 3/bottom of the bottom-right oven in a 4-door Aga – for about 30 minutes. Serve, with cream if you like – which I personally don't, but Godfrey, my husband, certainly does.

* Arrowroot is marvellous as a thickener for stewed fruit, as it leaves a clear, not cloudy mixture. If you have difficulty finding it in the grocer's, or even health-food shops, you will be able to buy it from a chemist.

EASTER SATURDAY BRUNCH FOR EIGHT

───────◦⦓⦔◦───────

Fresh orange juice
Baked rhubarb and orange compôte
Smoked pork loin with scrambled eggs and goat's cheese
Cinnamon coffee bread

Easter Saturday Brunch

I thought how ideal it would be to serve brunch on Easter Saturday, so that the household could have a lazy start to the day, a leisurely breakfast-cum-lunch, and then have the rest of the day free to potter about, go for a walk, whatever. For the hostess, it leaves her free to set the table for dinner that evening and then enjoy the rest of the day with her family and friends.

Baked rhubarb and orange compôte

Serves 8

This can be made on the previous Thursday before your guests arrive, and can be kept in a cool larder or the fridge, covered.

---

2 lb/1 kg rhubarb (trimmed weight), cut into 1 in/ 2.5 cm pieces
4–6 oz/100–175 g soft brown sugar, depending on how sweet your tooth is
grated rind of 1 orange

3 oranges, peel and pith cut off with a serrated knife, and the oranges cut into segments between the pith
Greek yoghurt for serving

Put the trimmed and washed rhubarb into a saucepan with 4 oz/100 g of the sugar and the grated orange rind. Cover the pan with a lid and cook over a moderate heat till the juices run and the pieces of rhubarb are tender –

but not until the rhubarb starts collapsing, it's nicer if it retains its shape. Take the pan off the heat, taste for sweetness and add more sugar if required, and cool the compôte. Then pour it into a glass or china bowl, cover, and put the bowl in the fridge. On Saturday morning, segment the oranges and stir them through the rhubarb. Serve with Greek yoghurt, for those who like it, and a bowl of demerara sugar handed for those with a very sweet tooth!

Smoked pork loin with scrambled eggs and goat's cheese

Serves 8

You can prepare the tomatoes and cheese for this dish on the Friday and keep them in the fridge overnight.

1½–1¾ lb/750–875 kg
  smoked boned pork loin,
  sliced thinly

FOR THE SCRAMBLED EGGS

16 eggs
¼ pt/150 ml milk
salt and plenty of freshly
    ground black pepper
a dash of Tabasco

6 oz/175 g goat's cheese,
    chopped and crumbled
    into small bits
4 tomatoes, skinned,
    deseeded and cut into thin
    segments
4 oz/100 g butter

Start by slicing the smoked pork loin as thinly as possible, and arrange it on a large plate or ashet.

Next make the scrambled eggs. In a large bowl, beat the eggs with the milk. Melt the butter in a large saucepan, and pour in the egg-and-milk mixture. Over a gentle-to-moderate heat let the eggs cook, occasionally scraping round the bottom and in particular the edges of the saucepan with a wooden spoon. This amount of eggs will take about 10 minutes to reach scrambling point, but they are so much nicer scrambled slowly rather than trying to hurry the job over a higher heat. As they start to scramble, stir continuously. Season with salt, pepper and Tabasco.

Just before serving, stir through the eggs the crumbled goat's cheese and the tomato segments. Then heap this egg mixture onto a serving dish, and serve with toasted granary bread and the sliced smoked pork.

Cinnamon coffee bread

I do love the American sweet cakey breads they eat at breakfast time, and this recipe is an adaptation of my own from a couple of recipes given to me by friends from the United States. This can be made and frozen, but warm it up to serve.

FOR THE BREAD

6 oz/175 g butter
6 oz/175 g soft brown sugar
10 oz/275 g plain flour
1 tsp bicarbonate of soda

1 tsp baking powder
3 large eggs, beaten
½ tsp vanilla essence

FOR THE COVERING

4 oz/100 g demerara sugar
2 tsp powdered cinnamon

3 oz/75 g chopped pecan nuts
(you can substitute
walnuts, but pecans are
widely available now and
much nicer)
2 oz/50 g butter, melted

For the bread dough, beat together the butter and soft brown sugar really well till the mixture is light and fluffy. Sieve in the flour, bicarbonate of soda and baking powder alternately with the beaten eggs, mixing all well into the mixture. Stir in the vanilla essence. Grease a baking tin or small roasting tin measuring about 8–10 × 12 in/20–25 × 30 cm and line it with bakewell paper (siliconized baking parchment). Pour the mixture into the lined tin. Mix together the ingredients to cover the bread dough, and sprinkle this as evenly as you can over the surface. Bake the bread at 375°F/190°C/Gas 4–5/ bottom right oven in a 4-door Aga – for 30 minutes. Take it out of the oven and let it cool in the tin. Mark it into squares, and serve it warm.

EASTER SATURDAY DINNER FOR EIGHT

Spicy tomato soup with avocado cream
Roast duck with lime and gin sauce
Purée of turnip with cashew nuts
Leek and carrot ragoût
Vanilla terrine with caramel sauce

Easter Saturday Dinner

The first course of this dinner, *Spicy tomato soup with avocado cream,* has chillies in it but isn't too spicy (you can add more chillies if you like a more fiery effect, but remember your poor guests!) and it can be made ahead and frozen, or made on Thursday before everyone arrives and kept in a covered bowl in the fridge. The avocado cream does, I'm afraid, have to be made not much more than a couple of hours before dinner, but as it only takes seconds to put together this is no great hassle.

For the main course, I have chosen *Roast duck with lime and gin sauce.* This sauce is one of the best recipes I've been given *ever.* I can claim no credit for it, it was given to me by my sister Liv Milburn (who is a brilliant cook) and it was given to *her* by a great friend of hers called Zelie Mason. It's a winner. It is actually meant to be eaten with calves' liver, but I far prefer it with rich roast food, like domestic duck. The sauce is dead easy to make, can be made before your guests arrive and kept in the fridge, and only needs reheating to serve. Roast duck speaks for itself, and most people love it. I think, though, that a lot of us are put off cooking it by the thought of the carving, but we never carve duck, just cut them in quarters and trim them. I loathe the vogue for rare duck breasts, nothing can be less appealing than underdone duck with flabby fat and skin, whereas it takes a lot to beat crispy roast duck skin, and the soft rich duck flesh. You do, on the other hand, have to be careful not to overcook the duck, thereby rendering the flesh stringy.

With the duck I recommend a purée of turnip – the sweetness of turnip complements the duck very well and the purée can be made a day ahead and reheated. As a crunchy garnish and a contrast to the purée, cashew nuts fried in butter with salt are delicious. I also suggest a *Leek and carrot ragoût* which can be made and left in a low oven to cook gently until dinner is ready to be served, cutting out any last-minute vegetable cooking. I haven't included potatoes, as I don't think they are always necessary.

For pudding, we have *Vanilla terrine with caramel sauce*. Flavour-wise, this is a variation on crême brulée, caramel custard, floating islands – all those heavenly puddings which combine eggs and cream, vanilla and caramel. This pudding has the benefit of being able to be made the day before. The sauce too can be made before your guests arrive – on the Tuesday or Wednesday of Easter week, if you wish – and kept in a covered container in a cool place. This terrine is easy to slice and to serve.

Spicy tomato soup with avocado cream

Serves 8

---

2 oz/50 g butter or 3 tbsp oil
  (I use sunflower)
2 medium onions, skinned
  and chopped
1 carrot, peeled and chopped
2 leeks, trimmed and
  chopped
1 stick of celery, chopped

2 × 15 oz/450 g tins of
  tomatoes
1 tsp sugar
salt and freshly ground
  black pepper
2 dried chillies
2 pt/1.2 L good chicken
  stock

FOR THE AVOCADO CREAM

2 avocados, stoned, flesh
  scooped out
1 whole small garlic clove,
  or ½ larger clove, skinned
  and chopped

lemon juice to taste – about
  2 tsp
pinch of salt, a grinding of
  black pepper

Melt the butter or heat the oil in a large saucepan, add the chopped onions and cook for about 5 minutes, stirring occasionally. Then add the other chopped vegetables to the pan and continue to cook for a further 5–10 minutes. Add the tinned tomatoes, the seasonings, the chillies and the chicken stock. Half-cover the saucepan with a lid, and let the soup simmer gently for about 45 minutes. Cool, liquidize, and sieve into a bowl if you are going to keep or freeze it.

In the evening, make the avocado cream by simply whizzing all the ingredients together until smooth. Keep covered till required. Reheat the soup to serve, with 2 teaspoons of avocado cream in the middle of each plateful.

Roast duck with lime and gin sauce

Serves 8

---

2 × 5 lb/2.25 kg duck salt and pepper

FOR THE LIME AND GIN SAUCE

1 oz/25 g butter
2 medium onions, skinned
and chopped
grated rind and juice of
3 limes
½ tsp moutarde de Meaux
2 tbsp apricot jam
¾ tsp tomato purée

2 tsp white wine vinegar
1 rounded tbsp arrowroot
slaked with a little stock
or water
a dash of Worcester sauce
3 tbsp gin

Remove the ducks' innards, which are usually in a plastic bag inside them. Pat around inside the ducks with a wad of absorbent kitchen paper. Put them in a roasting tin, and sprinkle the skin of each with salt and freshly ground black pepper. Roast in a hot oven – 400°F/200°C/ Gas 6/top right oven in a 4-door Aga – for 2 hours. If you have just one oven and the ducks have to share it with the reheating turnip purée and the leek and carrot ragoût too, give the ducks longer than 2 hours to cook. To serve, cut them in quarters, trimming off the ends of their legs to tidy them up.

For the sauce, melt the butter and add the chopped onions. Cook till they are soft – 5–7 minutes – then stir in all the other ingredients except the gin. Simmer the sauce gently, then cool and liquidize. Reheat to serve, not forgetting to stir in the gin!

Purée of turnip with cashew nuts

Serves 8

I add a couple of potatoes to the turnip as it cooks, as otherwise the resulting purée can be rather wet.

---

1 medium-sized turnip, peeled and cut into 2 in/ 5 cm chunks
2 medium potatoes, peeled and cut in half
2 egg yolks
2 oz/50 g butter
salt and freshly ground black pepper
about 5 gratings of nutmeg
1 oz/25 g butter
salt
3 oz/75 g cashew nuts

Put the cut-up turnip and the potato halves into a saucepan and cover with cold, lightly salted water. Bring to the boil, simmer till the vegetables are tender, then drain well and steam over heat for several seconds to get rid of any excess moisture. Mash really well, or put the turnip and potato into a food processor. Whiz or mash in the egg yolks, the butter cut in bits, and the seasonings. Butter an ovenproof dish, and put the purée into it. Cool, cover, and either freeze or store in the fridge.

Melt the butter, add a couple of pinches of salt, and fry the cashew nuts in it till they are golden brown. Drain on kitchen paper, and store in a jar or bowl, covered with clingfilm.

To serve, reheat the turnip purée in a moderate oven – 350°F/180°C/Gas 4/bottom right oven in a 4-door Aga – for 30 minutes (or tip it into a saucepan and stir it over gentle heat). Scatter the cashew nuts over the surface before bringing the purée to the table.

Leek and carrot ragoût

Serves 8

---

2 oz/50 g butter or 3 tbsp oil
  (I use sunflower)
6 medium-sized carrots,
  peeled and sliced
  diagonally in 2-in/5-cm
  lengths

6 leeks, washed, trimmed,
  and cut diagonally into
  2 in/5 cm lengths
½ tsp sugar
salt and freshly ground
  black pepper

Melt the butter or heat the oil in a cast-iron casserole or similar pan, add the prepared carrots and let them cook for several minutes, stirring occasionally. Put the lid on the casserole and cook over gentle heat for 10 minutes. Then add the sliced leeks to the casserole, mix well into the carrots, season with sugar, salt and pepper, cover, and continue to cook either over gentle heat, in which case stir from time to time, or in a moderate oven – 350°F/180°C/Gas 4/bottom right oven in a 4-door Aga – for 30–40 minutes. This ragoût will keep warm for an hour in a low oven.

Vanilla terrine with caramel sauce

Serves 8, generously

Line the base and short ends of a long loaf or terrine tin measuring about 10 in/25 cm in length, and of 2½ pt/ 1.4 L capacity.

FOR THE VANILLA TERRINE

1¾ pt/1 L single cream
10 egg yolks (I know that sounds a lot, remember that (a) you are entertaining and therefore entitled to push the boat out both expense and cholesterol wise, and (b) the dinner thus far has not been rich – no cream till the pud!)

4 oz/100 g caster sugar
1 tsp vanilla essence
2 sachets gelatine (approximately 1 oz/25 g)
4 tbsp cold water

FOR THE CARAMEL SAUCE

8 oz/250 g granulated sugar
7 fl oz/200 ml water
½ tsp vanilla essence
1 oz/25 g butter

Put the cream into a saucepan over a gentle heat and heat to scalding point. Meanwhile, in a bowl, beat together the egg yolks, gradually adding the caster sugar; add the vanilla essence. Beat well, till the mixture is thick and pale in colour. Then pour on some of the hot cream, mix well, and stir the contents of the bowl into the hot cream in the saucepan. Over gentle heat (you really can't hurry this, so don't be tempted to increase the heat just to speed things up!), stir until the custard mixture thickens – it should thicken to the consistency of pouring double cream. Then take the pan off the heat.

Sprinkle the gelatine over the 4 tablespoons of cold water in a small saucepan, leave for a few minutes to sponge up, then dissolve over gentle heat. Stir this into the vanilla custard and sieve the custard into the prepared terrine or loaf tin. Let it cool, then cover and keep in the fridge.

To turn out, dip the terrine in a bowl of warm – not hot – water. (I say 'not hot' water, because then the custard melts, whereas warm water is quite enough to loosen the terrine within the metal tin.) Count to 10, then invert it over a serving plate. It should come out easily. Peel the strip of paper off, and cut in slices about ½ in/ 1 cm thick – or thicker, if you like. Serve the caramel sauce separately.

Put the granulated sugar for the caramel sauce into a heavy saucepan over a moderate heat and dissolve the sugar – nothing will appear to happen for several minutes, but don't be tempted to go away and leave it, because once it starts to melt it goes quite quickly and can burn easily. Burnt sugar tastes bitter and vile, so stand by, and shake the pan as the sugar starts to dissolve. When all is a rich golden-brown molten mixture, add the water – it will hiss, and there will be steamy clouds, so stand back, and protect your hand and forearm with a teatowel. Add the vanilla essence and butter, and let the sticky toffee stuff in the saucepan melt again in the water. When it is all melted, simmer it, with the pan uncovered, for 20–25 minutes, then take the pan off the heat and pour the caramel sauce into a jug. Cool, cover and keep in the fridge. It thickens as it cools. If there doesn't appear to be very much, remember that it is very rich and each person needs only a little.

Easter Sunday

Breakfast on Easter Day can consist simply of fresh orange juice, hot cross buns, coffee or tea.

For lunch, I thought that a *Roast loin of pork* would be good, with an *Apple and horseradish glaze*, and a *Prune and red wine sauce*. To go with the pork, I suggest *Mousseline potatoes*, which can be made ahead and frozen, and *Cauliflower with parsley sauce*. To follow, there is *Pear and ginger tart*.

If your guests are staying on till Monday morning, you could choose an item from the chapter on Sunday night suppers (see pages 357–70) for Easter Sunday evening.

EASTER SUNDAY LUNCH FOR EIGHT

*Roast loin of pork with apple and horseradish glaze
and prune and red wine sauce
Mousseline potatoes
Cauliflower with parsley sauce
Pear and ginger tart*

Roast loin of pork with apple and horseradish glaze

Serves 8

A piece of pork loin
weighing about 4 lb/2 kg
or larger, if you like. You
can then have it cold for
Monday's supper

salt and freshly ground
black pepper

FOR THE APPLE AND HORSERADISH GLAZE

3 tbsp sunflower oil
2 medium-sized onions,
skinned and chopped quite
finely
4 cooking apples, peeled,
cored and chopped

2 tsp demerara sugar
salt and pepper
1 tbsp horseradish root
(you can buy this in jars
from delicatessens)

FOR THE PRUNE AND RED WINE SAUCE

about 2 tbsp fat from the tin
the pork is roasting in
1 medium onion, skinned
and chopped
1 rounded tbsp flour

1 pt/600 ml water and red
wine mixed – about two-
thirds water, one-third
wine
about 8 prunes, stoned and
chopped

Put the meat into a roasting tin, rub the fat with some
salt, and grind some black pepper over it. Roast in a hot
oven – 400°F/200°C/Gas 6/top right oven in a 4-door
Aga – for 25 minutes per pound with 30 minutes over.

About half an hour before the cooking time is up, spread the apple and horseradish glaze (see below) over the pork. For easy carving, remove the bones first.

To make the horseradish glaze, first heat the oil in a saucepan and add the chopped onions. Cook for about 5 minutes, stirring occasionally, then add the chopped apples, the sugar, salt, pepper and horseradish. Mix well, and cook over a low-to-moderate heat till the apples are mushy. Take off the heat, and cool. You can prepare this apple sauce the previous Wednesday, providing you store it in a cool place, ideally the fridge.

A good time to make the prune and red wine sauce is when you take the pork out of the oven to smear the apple and horseradish glaze over it. Scrape some of the gooey bits from the roasting tin along with the fat, and put it into a saucepan. Heat the fat in the saucepan and add the chopped onion. Cook for about 5 minutes, stirring occasionally, then stir in the flour. Cook for a further minute, then stir in the water and red wine mixture, stirring till it boils. Stir in the chopped prunes, and reheat to serve with the sliced roast pork.

Mousseline potatoes

Serves 8

I generally allow about 4 good-sized peeled potato halves.

2½ lb/1.25 kg baking
   potatoes
½ pt/300 ml milk, warmed
3 oz/75 g butter
salt and freshly ground
   black pepper

pinch of freshly grated
   nutmeg
2 egg yolks
2 tbsp finely chopped parsley

Peel and halve the potatoes and cook them in boiling salted water till tender. Drain well, and steam for a few seconds to remove any excess moisture. Mash very well, then, with a handheld electric beater, whisk in the warm milk and the butter. Season with salt, pepper and nutmeg. Beat in the egg yolks and the chopped parsley. Butter an ovenproof dish. Put the creamily mashed potatoes into the dish, cool completely, cover, and freeze. Take out of the freezer and allow to defrost overnight, and reheat in a moderate oven till the top becomes slightly crisp.

Pear and ginger tart

Serves 8

This is a rich tart with a vanilla-flavoured pastry base and a filling of sliced pears set in a cream and egg yolk custard containing slivers of ginger. For those of you who don't like ginger you can skip the ginger and use cinnamon instead.

FOR THE PASTRY

4 oz/100 g chilled butter cut
  in pieces
6 oz/175 g plain flour

1 oz/25 g icing sugar
a few drops of vanilla
  essence

FOR THE FILLING

4 pears, if they are Comice,
  6 if they are Conference
juice of 1 lemon
½ pt/300 ml single cream
  (or double mixed half-
  and-half with milk)

4 egg yolks
3 oz/75 g caster sugar
4 pieces stem ginger, drained
  from their syrup and
  chopped

Put all the pastry ingredients together into a food processor and whiz till the mixture resembles crumbs. Pat round the sides and base of an 8–9 in/20–23 cm flan dish, and put the dish in the fridge for at least half an hour, before baking in a moderate oven – 350°F/180°C/ Gas 4/bottom right oven in a 4-door Aga – for 20–25 minutes, till the pastry is pale golden. Cool.

Meanwhile, make the filling. Peel and core the pears, and cut into quarters, then cut each quarter in half lengthwise. Put the sliced pears in a bowl, and mix the lemon juice thoroughly into them. This prevents them turning brown.

Beat together the cream, egg yolks and sugar really well. Drain the pears of the lemon juice, arrange them in the baked pastry shell, and pour the cream and egg mixture over. Scatter the chopped ginger over the surface (it will sink, it's meant to!) and bake the pie in a moderate oven – 350°F/180°C/Gas 4/bottom right oven in a 4-door Aga – till the custard is just set, about 20–25 minutes. Take the tart out of the oven, and serve warm or cold.

FESTIVAL FOOD

Pea, pear and mint soup
Courgette and fennel soup
Carrot, leek and lentil soup
Coarse pork terrine
Sardine and mushroom pâté
Granary bread
Brioche
Rich tomato sauce
Chicken, tomato and pepper casserole
Sliced nectarines with raspberries
Vanilla meringues with cream, and raspberry
and blackcurrant sauce
Chocolate fudge squares

Festival Food

Throughout Great Britain cities and towns are hosts to annual festivals of all kinds – musical, artistic, dramatic, or a mixture of the lot. Probably the best-known and longest established all-round festival is the Edinburgh Festival, which lasts for three weeks in August, but the Aldeburgh Festival in Suffolk and the Bath Music Festival are both long-established and well known too. Keen festival-goers need to plan ahead, for the physical side of life needs to be catered for just as much as does the aesthetic, which will in any case need to be fortified against a possible culture overdose. If you live in a festival city or town you will most probably have friends to stay for some or all of its duration, and you will almost certainly find yourself wondering what on earth to feed yourself and your guests because festival-goers, of necessity, eat at strange times. The most important thing to bear in mind when planning food for eating during a festival is that it may very well be 11 o'clock in the evening or later before you sit down to eat, and no-one feels like eating the sort of three-course dinner one would consume with such relish two or more hours earlier on. The other great thing to bear in mind is that on return from the theatre, cinema or concert you and your guests will want to eat almost immediately; you most certainly will not want to finish off something which needs much further cooking on your return. So, you need food which can be ready to eat as soon as you and your guests have a glass of wine in hand – food which, at most, needs

5 minutes' reheating, or pasta, which takes scarcely 10 minutes' cooking, with a ready-made sauce.

You can leave the table set before you go out, a salad made with its dressing in a screw-topped jar ready to be shaken and poured over the salad. Good festival-food planning could include a quantity of good tomato sauce, which can be served one evening with fried diced aubergines and cubes of mozzarella cheese stirred through with pasta and a salad; and the next evening as part of a sauce, together with sliced sautéed red and yellow peppers and chicken, for a casserole which can be left gently cooking in a low oven ready to eat on your return; or, such a casserole could be already cooked, merely needing 20 minutes to bring to simmering point.

You will also find in this chapter three good soup recipes, all of which can be served with granary bread or rolls, or with warm brioche and a coarse meaty terrine; I have included too a fishy pâté made of sardines and mushrooms, which is a great favourite of my husband Godfrey.

Puddings for post-festival eating should be simple. Try sliced nectarines and raspberries, meringues filled with whipped cream and served with thick raspberry and blackcurrant purée – or just serve coffee, with rich chocolatey squares for eating in the fingers.

Pea, pear and mint soup

Serves 8

As with all soups, this one is only as good as the stock used in its making.

2 oz/50 g butter, or 3 tbsp oil (I use sunflower)	2 pt/1.2 L good chicken stock
2 medium onions, skinned and chopped	salt and freshly ground black pepper
1 lb/500 g peas, weighed when shelled	juice of ½ lemon
3 pears, cored (no need to peel them) and chopped	a handful of applemint, leaves stripped from the stalks

Melt the butter in a saucepan and add the chopped onions. Cook for about 5 minutes, stirring occasionally, till the onions are soft and transparent. Then add the peas, the chopped pears, and the chicken stock. Half-cover the pan with a lid, and simmer the soup for 20 minutes. Liquidize and sieve the soup, and season to taste with salt, pepper and lemon juice. To finish, finely chop the mint leaves, and stir them through the soup.

This soup is equally delicious served chilled, with a spoonful of Greek yoghurt in the middle of each plateful.

Courgette and fennel soup

Serves 8

This is another soup which is equally good served hot or chilled.

2 oz/50 g butter	2 pt/1.2 L good chicken
2 medium onions, skinned	stock (do try and use the
and chopped	Real Thing, water and a
1 lb/500 g courgettes,	stock cube just doesn't
trimmed and cut in 1 in/	give the same result
2.5 cm chunks	at all)
2 heads of fennel, chopped	salt and pepper
	lemon juice

Melt the butter and add the chopped onions. Cook for about 5 minutes, till the onions are soft and transparent-looking. Add the chopped courgettes and the fennel, and pour on the stock. Half-cover the pan with a lid, and simmer for about 30 minutes. Then liquidize and sieve the soup. Season with salt and pepper, and lemon juice to your taste, and either reheat to serve, or serve chilled.

Carrot, leek and lentil soup

Serves 8

This is one of my favourite soups. More substantial than the previous two, it is ideal for a chilly evening. Again, it is only as good as the stock it is made with.

2 oz/50 g butter or 3 tbsp oil
(I use sunflower)
2 medium onions, skinned
and chopped
2 carrots, peeled and
chopped
3 leeks, washed, trimmed
and sliced

4 oz/100 g orange lentils
2 pt/1.2 L good chicken
stock
salt and freshly ground
black pepper
2 tbsp finely chopped parsley

Melt the butter and add the chopped onions to the butter in a saucepan. Over a moderate heat, cook the onions for about 5 minutes, stirring occasionally, then add the chopped carrots and sliced leeks. Cook for a further 5 minutes or so, then stir in the lentils and the chicken stock. Half-cover the pan with a lid, season, then simmer the soup for 35–40 minutes. Liquidize, and sieve into a clean saucepan. When ready to eat reheat the soup, stirring the chopped parsley through just before serving, to prevent the parsley losing its bright fresh green colour by sitting for too long in the hot liquid.

Coarse pork terrine

Makes 2 terrines, each serving 10–12

This terrine can be made several days in advance and stored, tightly wrapped in clingfilm or in foil, in the fridge. It also freezes well, but not for too long.

FOR LINING THE TERRINE

6 bay leaves   about 16 rashers of streaky
                                bacon

FOR THE TERRINE

4 oz/100 g butter

4 medium onions, skinned
and chopped finely

6 spring onions, sliced thinly
– green stalks as well as
bulbs

3 lb/1.5 kg good pork
sausagemeat (I use
Lincoln sausages from
Marks and Spencer slit
down their lengths with
the point of a sharp knife,
and their skins removed)

1 lb/500 g lambs' liver,
trimmed, and chopped
finely (slithery but
possible)

2 lb/1 kg lean pork meat,
minced

1 tsp thyme

a good pinch of salt, and
plenty of black pepper

4 tbsp chopped parsley

4 large eggs, beaten

Carefully (because foil seems so thin these days, and it is easy to stick your finger through it) line two loaf or terrine tins about 9–10 in/20–23 cm long and 3 in/7.5 cm wide with foil. On the base of each place 3 bay leaves. Then stretch the streaky bacon rashers with the blunt edge of a knife, and line the tins widthwise with them. You will need about 8 rashers per tin.

In a large bowl mix together all the terrine ingredients really well. The *only* way to do this job thoroughly is the messy way, by using your hands! Divide the mixture between the two prepared tins. Fold the ends of the bacon rashers over the top of the meat. Cover tightly with foil, and put the tins into a roasting tin, with enough hot water to come halfway up the sides of the terrines.

Cook in a moderate oven – 350°F/180°C/Gas 4/bottom right oven in a 4-door Aga – for 2 hours. Take out of the oven, and leave overnight in a cool place, with weights on top of each terrine.

These terrines keep well for up to a week, wrapped, in the fridge.

Sardine and mushroom pâté

Serves 6–8

I make no apology for including this recipe from my first book, *Seasonal Cooking from the Isle of Skye*. It is just such a good recipe, and very quick to make, at its best when served with granary bread either as it is or toasted; even confirmed sardine loathers like my husband Godfrey love this pâté. It doesn't freeze well – it goes watery on thawing – but it can be made three or four days in advance, and is ideal for a festival supper, served with granary bread and a green salad after one of the soups.

---

3 oz/75 g butter
1 lb/500 g mushrooms, wiped and chopped
8 oz/250 g cream cheese
2 × 5 oz/150 g tins of sardines, well drained of their oil

lots of freshly ground black pepper
juice of ½ lemon – more if you like a sharper taste
dash of Tabasco

Melt the butter and cook the chopped mushrooms for 2–3 minutes, then take the pan off the heat, and cool the cooked mushrooms completely. In a food processor, whiz the cooled mushrooms, the cream cheese and the drained sardines till well mixed. Season to taste with lots of black pepper, lemon juice and Tabasco. Store in a covered container in the fridge.

Granary bread

Makes 3 1 lb loaves

---

2 oz/50 g dried yeast, such
    as Allinsons or DCL
½ pt/300 ml hand-hot water
2 tsp sugar
1 tbsp salt

2 tbsp demerara sugar
1¼ pt/750 ml hot water
3 lb/1.5 kg granary flour
4 tbsp oil (I use sunflower)

Stir the dried yeast into the ½ pt/300 ml of hand-hot water and 2 tsp sugar and leave in a warm place until it trebles in volume.

Stir the salt and demerara sugar into the generous pint/600 ml of *hot* water.

Leave the flour in a large mixing bowl in a warm place while the yeast trebles in volume – the secret of good breadmaking lies in keeping everything warm. Mix the yeast-and-water into the flour, pour in the sugar-and-salt water, and measure in the oil. Mix all together, then turn the dough onto a well-floured surface and knead well (I knead and count to 200), then divide the dough into three pieces, and knead each to a further count of 50. Put each piece of dough into an oiled loaf tin, and leave all three tins in a warm place, covered with a teatowel, to double in size – about 20–25 minutes. Bake in a hot oven – 425°F/220°C/Gas 7/top right oven in a 4-door Aga – for 20–25 minutes – try not to overcook them as this toughens the dough. The loaves are cooked when they sound hollow when tapped on their base. Cool on a wire rack in a warm place – if they cool in a draught or a cold place that toughens the dough, too. Slice thickly, and toast if you like.

Brioche

Makes 1 1 lb/500 g loaf

I love thickly sliced and toasted brioche with any meaty pâté – this loaf is very good with the coarse pork terrine.

---

8 oz/250 g strong plain flour	*2 tsp dried yeast*
½ tsp salt	*2 large eggs, beaten*
1 tbsp caster sugar	*2 oz/50 g butter, melted*
½ tsp sugar	*1 egg, beaten with 1 tbsp*
2 tbsp warm water	*water, to glaze*

Mix the flour, salt and tablespoonful of caster sugar in a bowl and put in a warm place. Mix together the ½ teaspoon of sugar with the warm water and the dried yeast, and leave this mixture in a warm place till it is well risen and frothy. Then mix it into the flour, together with the beaten eggs and melted butter, mixing all together to form a dough. Turn on to a lightly floured surface, and knead well with floured hands – I count to 200 as I knead, which gives about the right kneading time. Put the dough into an oiled loaf tin, cover with a teatowel, and leave in a warm place till the dough is well risen. Brush the loaf with the beaten egg and water glaze, and bake for 15 minutes in a hot oven – 425°F/220°C/Gas 7/ top right oven in a 4-door Aga.

Rich tomato sauce

Serves 8

This sauce has sautéed cubed aubergine and cubed mozzarella cheese mixed through, and is here used for pasta.

Keep a half-pint of sauce aside for a chicken casserole.

---

4 tbsp good olive oil
3 medium onions, skinned
    and chopped finely
1 stick of celery, washed and
    chopped
1–2 garlic cloves, skinned
    and chopped finely
2 carrots, scraped and diced
4 × 15 oz/450 g tins of
    tomatoes

1 tbsp pesto
1 tsp salt and freshly ground
    black pepper
½ tsp sugar
2 aubergines, cut into ½ in/
    1 cm dice
oil for frying (I use
    sunflower)
8 oz/250 g real mozzarella
    cheese, cut into ½ in/1 cm
    dice

Heat the olive oil in a saucepan, and put in the chopped onions. Cook over a moderate heat for about 5 minutes, stirring occasionally, then add the chopped celery, one or two cloves of chopped garlic depending on your taste for it, and the diced carrots. Cook for a further 5 minutes, then add the tomatoes, but include the juice of only one of the tins. Stir in the pesto, salt and pepper and sugar, and simmer the sauce gently for 40–45 minutes. Liquidize the sauce, and reserve ½ pt/300 ml.

Sauté the diced aubergines in oil till soft, then stir them into the tomato sauce along with the diced mozzarella cheese. Reheat this sauce to serve with pasta of your choice. Personally, I like green fettucine.

Chicken, tomato and pepper casserole

Serves 8

This superb, rich casserole can be left cooking in a slow oven while you are out festivalizing. It can be eaten with boiled brown rice – boiled before you go out and kept in a cool oven with a couple of layers of buttered greaseproof paper on top and foil over that – and a green salad.

---

8 chicken joints – on the bone, don't be tempted to substitute chicken breasts for this, because they would overcook

6 tbsp olive oil

FOR THE SAUCE

2 medium onions, skinned and sliced thinly

2 red and 2 yellow peppers, halved, deseeded and sliced into thin strips

1 garlic clove, skinned and chopped

1 rounded tbsp flour

1 pt/600 ml chicken stock

½ pt/300 ml red wine

salt and pepper

½ pt/300 ml Rich tomato sauce (see page 172)

Heat the oil and brown the chicken joints in it. Remove them to a dish to keep warm while you make the sauce. Add the sliced onions to the casserole, and cook for about 5 minutes, stirring occasionally. Add the sliced peppers, and continue cooking for a further 10 minutes, stirring from time to time to prevent them sticking. Stir in the chopped garlic, and the flour. Cook for a further couple of minutes, then stir in the stock and red wine and stir continuously till the sauce boils. Season to your taste with salt and pepper, and stir in the tomato sauce. Replace the chicken joints, and put into a low-to-moderate oven – 300–325°F/150–160°C/Gas 2–3/top left oven in a 4-door Aga – (if the sauce is actually bubbling when you put it in) and leave for 2½ hours. The chicken will be falling off the bone, but it will be quite delicious! Alternatively, you can cook the casserole in a moderate oven – 350°F/180°C/Gas 4/bottom right oven in a 4-door Aga – for 1 hour. Leave it at room temperature while you are out, and reheat it on the surface of your cooker, letting the sauce bubble round the joints, for a good 10 minutes – the whole heating-up process will take you about 25 minutes.

Sliced nectarines with raspberries

Serves 8

This makes a perfect, simple end to a meal following a festival outing. I like to serve it with Greek yoghurt and demerara sugar, but you could serve it with whipped cream just as well. Any fruit left over would be delicious for breakfast.

---

8 nectarines (I like to leave the skins on)   *2 lb/1 kg raspberries*
3 oz/75 g caster sugar

Slice the nectarines in slanted cuts towards each stone. Mix them in a serving bowl with the raspberries, and sprinkle the sugar over them. Cover the dish with clingfilm.

Vanilla meringues with cream, and raspberry and blackcurrant sauce

Serves 8

You can sandwich together the meringues with whipped cream and leave them ready for your return. The raspberry and blackcurrant sauce can be served in either a jug or a bowl, to accompany the meringues.

6 large egg whites
12 oz/350 g vanilla sugar
(caster sugar kept in a
sealed container with a
vanilla pod or two)

½ pt/300 ml double cream,
whipped

FOR THE SAUCE

1 lb/500 g each raspberries
and blackcurrants – there
is no need to strip the
currants from their stems,
as the sauce will be
liquidized and sieved

4 oz/100 g granulated sugar
icing sugar (optional)

To make the meringues, whisk the egg whites till they are very stiff then, still whisking, gradually add the vanilla sugar a spoonful at a time. Whisk till all the sugar is incorporated and then pipe the meringue into even-sized rounds about 2½ in/6 cm in diameter onto bakewell paper-lined baking trays. Bake in a cool oven – 225°F/110°C/Gas ¼–½/top left oven in a 4-door Aga – for about 2 hours or till they lift easily off the bakewell paper. Store the meringues in an airtight tin till you are ready to stick them together with the whipped cream

To make the sauce, put the raspberries and blackcurrants together in a saucepan with the sugar. Over gentle heat, cook till the juices run and the currants are soft. Take them off the heat, cool, liquidize and sieve. If you would like a sweeter sauce, add sieved icing sugar to sweeten.

Chocolate fudge squares

Makes about 18 squares

These delicious squares of dark chocolate-covered fudgey biscuit mixture make a perfect end to a meal, served with cups of coffee, when you haven't time to make a pudding. They aren't my invention – we had a wonderful nanny cum mother's help called Wendy Stephen (Middleton now, that's why she left us) and she first made these for us. We are now lucky enough to have Wendy's sister Annette, who although she is the prop and mainstay of our lives and a dear friend as well, is nonetheless responsible for several unnecessary inches round my middle, by baking such irresistible things!

---

8 oz/250 g dark chocolate
12 oz/350 g caster sugar
8 oz/250 g butter
4 tbsp golden syrup
large (7 oz/200 g) tin of
    condensed milk

1 × 15 oz/450 g packet of
    digestive biscuits,
    pulverized to crumbs in a
    food processor
a few drops of vanilla
    essence

Break the chocolate into a bowl and put it over a

Buy Sugar (gran.)
2 oz. Butter
1 Large Spoon Syrup
10 Fluid Oz. Full Cream
                    milk

Stir until all sugar
dissolved

add small teaspoonsfuls
            condensed milk

Boil for 20/30 mins.

Pan off
Stir until
converts to sugar

POUR!! into
buttered dish

saucepan of barely simmering water till the chocolate is just melted.

Put the sugar, butter, syrup and condensed milk into a saucepan over a low heat, and melt and dissolve all together. When the sugar has dissolved completely, boil the mixture for 5–8 minutes. Stir the crushed digestive crumbs and vanilla essence into the fudge mixture. Grease a baking tray – or line it with a piece of bakewell paper (siliconized greaseproof paper) – measuring about 12 × 14 in/30 × 35 cm and pour the biscuit fudge into it. Cool a bit, then pour the melted dark chocolate over. When it is cold, cut into squares, and store in an airtight tin. These fudgey squares freeze very well.

BARBECUES FOR EIGHT

Stilton and celery dip for quails' eggs
Curried egg mousse
Marinated pork fillets with orange sauce
Barbecued fillet of beef with horseradish mousse
Barbecued salmon with tomato and dill mayonnaise

The best potato salad
Marinated mushrooms
Avocado salad
Strawberry and orange terrine with strawberry sauce
Cinnamon pavlova with blackcurrant cream

Barbecues and Picnics

I love the two forms of entertaining out of doors that summertime makes possible (weather permitting), barbecues and picnics. There are varying standards of elegance which apply to both – from the spur-of-the-moment family occasion involving buns, sausages, chicken drumsticks, tomato ketchup and yards of kitchen paper to mop up the younger or messier of the group, via the semi-sophisticated picnic or barbecue food, to the positively elegant occasions exemplified by events such as Henley Royal Regatta or the opera at Glyndebourne. For me, though, I like best an informal barbecue or picnic, both, of course, with good food.

BARBECUES

I love barbecues for two reasons, one is that I love charcoal-grilled food, be it meat or fish, and the other reason is that however smart the food a barbecue has an inescapable informality dear to my heart! As with picnics, barbecue food can be very mundane, just grilled sausages, chops or chicken drumsticks, or it can be more elaborate, like some of the suggestions here. For instance, *Barbecued salmon with tomato and dill mayonnaise, Marinated pork fillets with orange sauce*, or the *Barbecued fillet of beef with horseradish mousse*. There are several salad accompaniments, to complement these barbecue suggestions, such as *Marinated mushrooms*; or *Avocado salad*; or my favourite of all, *The best potato salad*, which has hardboiled eggs, finely sliced celery and lots of chopped chives in it. There are a couple of suggestions for first courses if you plan to serve one; try *Quails' eggs with Stilton and celery dip*, or *Curried egg mousse*, which is a great favourite of ours.

For pudding, I suggest *Strawberry and orange terrine with strawberry sauce* coulis or a *Cinnamon pavlova with blackcurrant cream* – or you could make the *Raspberry and almond tart* from the picnics section (see pages 210–12).

Whatever you provide for your guests, barbecues are my ideal form of summer entertaining, our only problem living here in Skye is the weather, its unpredictability; and the midges which can come down like dark clouds and never mind their terrible biting of people, they manage to provide a midge covering for any creamy surface, which can be explained away in savoury dishes as an over-enthusiasm with the pepper grinder but which it's harder to find an explanation for with the sweet dishes. These obstacles do not in any way put us off barbecuing in the summer, we just tend to move our barbecue into the ping-pong shed and dash between it and the back door with teatowels draped over our heads to protect us from either driving rain or the dreaded midges!

The one thing to remember about barbecued food is to start cooking early, keeping the cooked food warm, so that all your guests can eat at once when it's ready. Many is the barbecue I've attended where the cooking has started too late and half the guests look on hungrily as the food cooks slowly in relays and guests eat in stages. This does not make for a good party. So get the fire lit early, start cooking when the coals are glowing white, and don't be tempted to cook too soon as the flames will leap and your food will be cremated rather than charcoal-grilled.

Stilton and celery dip for quails' eggs

Quails' eggs are now widely available wherever you live, and this makes an ideal first course which can be eaten in the fingers with a drink in hand. There is very finely sliced celery stirred through the smooth Stilton cream dip, providing a good contrasting crunch. I like to stir snipped chives through too, for the appearance as well as the flavour.

As well as this dip for quails' eggs you could serve the *Crudités with garlic, parsley and tomato dip* from the section on picnics (see page 201).

---

8 oz/250 g Stilton cheese   1 tbsp snipped chives
¼ pt/150 ml single cream
1 good stick of celery, sliced
    as finely as possible

Put the Stilton in a food processor and whiz, gradually pouring in the single cream. When it is all a smooth thick mixture, pour it into a serving bowl, and stir through the finely sliced celery and snipped chives. Cover with clingfilm till you are ready to serve it.

Curried egg mousse

Serves 8

This makes a good first course before a barbecued

dinner, and a convenient one too because it can be made a couple of days in advance. You can put the mousse in a glass or china serving dish, or in individual ramekins, but I like to set it in a ring mould and turn it out, with a bunch of watercress in the middle. Serve granary bread to accompany the mousse.

FOR THE EGG MOUSSE

1 pt/600 ml chicken stock
1½ sachets (approximately
*   1½ oz/40 g) powdered*
*   gelatine*
8 large eggs, hardboiled,
*   shelled and chopped*

½ pt/300 ml double cream
2 tbsp Worcestershire sauce
a bunch of watercress for
*   garnish*

FOR THE CURRY SAUCE

3 tbsp oil (I use sunflower)
1 onion, skinned and
*   chopped*
1 garlic clove, skinned and
*   chopped*
1 slightly rounded tbsp
*   medium-strength curry*
*   powder*

1 tbsp tomato purée
1 tbsp apricot jam
½ pt/300 ml chicken stock
salt and freshly ground
*   black pepper*

Start by making the curry sauce: heat the oil and add the chopped onion and chopped garlic. Cook for 5–7 minutes, stirring occasionally to prevent them sticking. Then stir in the curry powder, cook for a minute, then add the tomato purée, apricot jam, stock and seasoning. Simmer gently till the stock reduces by about a third. Liquidize or sieve, and leave to cool.

Meanwhile, make the mousse. Sprinkle the gelatine over the chicken stock, then dissolve it over a gentle heat.

Stir the chopped eggs into the stock and gelatine. Whip the double cream with the Worcestershire sauce, fold in the cool liquidized or sieved curry sauce, and fold together the cream and the egg mixtures. Pour into a ring mould and leave to set. Dip the mould in warm (not too hot) water for a few seconds, then turn out onto a serving plate. Fill the centre with a bunch of watercress.

Marinated pork fillets with orange sauce

Serves 8

As barbecuing is a rather drying form of cooking, it is as well to marinate the meat. These pork fillets are bashed thin between two pieces of bakewell paper (because it's thicker than ordinary greaseproof) with a rolling pin then marinated overnight (or over two nights) and patted dry with kitchen paper before being grilled on the barbecue. They need only 3–4 minutes' cooking each side. One average-sized pork fillet will give you two escalopes, when bashed thin, about ¾ lb/750 g meat.

4 pork escalopes

FOR THE MARINADE

½ pt/300 ml sunflower oil
¼ pt/150 ml fresh orange juice
1 onion, skinned and cut in quarters

2 garlic cloves, skinned and halved
6 tbsp soy sauce
a bunch of parsley

183

Put all the marinade ingredients into a saucepan and simmer them for 5 minutes, then cool. Strain the cold marinade over the bashed pork escalopes, and leave in a cool place for several hours – the longer the better, but at the most for 2 days. Remove from the marinade and pat dry with kitchen paper before grilling them. Serve with *Orange sauce* (see below).

Orange sauce

Serves 8

This thin orange sauce has snipped chives stirred through it, for both colour and taste.

¾ pt/450 ml orange juice, fresh if possible
2 sprigs of rosemary
½ pt/300 ml chicken or vegetable stock

1 tbsp arrowroot slaked with 2–3 tbsp water
salt and freshly ground black pepper
1 heaped tbsp snipped chives

Put the orange juice, rosemary and stock in a saucepan and bring to simmering point. Simmer for 5 minutes, then stir some of the hot liquid into the slaked arrowroot, pour this back into the saucepan, season and stir till the sauce boils. Take it off the heat, cool, take out and throw away the rosemary, and stir in the snipped chives. Serve this sauce either warm or cold, with the barbecued pork escalopes (see above).

Barbecued fillet of beef with horseradish mousse

Serves 6

Barbecued fillet of beef is, for me, the nicest, most delicious way to eat beef, and I prefer it cooked then cooled and served cold. Last May I was at a pre-confirmation lunch for Melanie Palmer whose parents John and Carol are great friends of ours. They live near Kirkmichael in a part of Perthshire which is high and remote and beautiful. We had a most delicious lunch and one of the two main courses was cold sliced barbecued fillets of beef – lucky me! Whether you serve the meat hot or cold, the horseradish mousse goes so well as an accompaniment and it can be made two days ahead and kept, covered, in the fridge. The dried grated horseradish is easily obtainable from good delicatessens.

An average-sized fillet of beef weighs about 2½ lb/1.25 kg and will serve 5 when hot from the barbecue, 6 if served cold. Trim the fillet of excess fat and gristle, and tuck the flat end under so that there is much the same thickness the length of the fillet, which prevents the thinner end from overcooking. It isn't necessary to marinate but if you like to do so, use the marinade below which I use for beef.

1 fillet of beef, weighing
about 2½ lb/1.25 kg,
trimmed of gristle and
excess fat

FOR THE OPTIONAL MARINADE

6 tbsp olive oil
1 onion, skinned and
quartered
1 garlic clove, skinned and
halved
1 stick of celery, halved

handful of parsley
1 good tsp black peppercorns
and 1 tsp rock salt
1 pt/600 ml red wine

FOR THE HORSERADISH MOUSSE

1 sachet powdered gelatine
(approximately ½ oz/
15 g)
¼ pt/150 ml cold water
2 heaped tsp grated
horseradish
juice of ½ lemon

1 rounded tbsp chopped
parsley and chives mixed
½ pt/300 ml double cream,
whipped
2 egg whites

For the marinade, heat the oil and add the onion, garlic, celery and parsley. Cook for a few minutes, then pour in the red wine, and add the peppercorns and salt. Simmer for 5 minutes then take off the heat and cool. Pour this cold marinade over the ready-trimmed fillet in a dish. Leave for several hours, turning the fillet so that it marinades on each side.

Before barbecuing take the fillet out of the marinade and pat it dry with kitchen paper. How long you grill it for depends on how rare you like to eat your beef. Turn it regularly on the barbecue so that it cooks evenly, and for a rare result give it about 10 minutes' grilling each side.

To prepare the mousse, sprinkle the gelatine over the water, in a saucepan, then dissolve over gentle heat. Mix the horseradish into the gelatine mixture and stir in the lemon juice, parsley and chives. Stir this into the whipped cream. Whisk the egg whites till stiff and, with a metal spoon, fold them into the horseradish cream. Put into a dish, and serve a small spoonful at the side of each helping of beef.

Barbecued salmon with tomato and dill mayonnaise

This is my all-time favourite barbecue main course. I get such satisfaction each time I give it to people because those for whom barbecued salmon is a first-time experience all say the same thing – that they just can't believe how perfect and delicious it is. I think that, being a rich fish, it is ideal barbecue material, and the flavour of charcoal just seems to be made for salmon more than anything else. The salmon has to be foil wrapped, with the foil slashed in several places to allow the charcoal to penetrate. I have often cooked whole fish this way, but it does take time; a much quicker way is to have the salmon filleted, place it on butter-smeared foil, grind black pepper liberally over it, lay sprigs of parsley and slices of lemon on top, dot with more butter then seal it into a foil parcel. Slash the foil a few times, put the parcel on the barbecue and cook for several minutes each side depending on the thickness of the fillets of salmon – allow 3–5 minutes – then turn it over and give it the same amount of time on the other side. Open the foil, test to see if it is cooked and give it a further couple of minutes if not. Serve with *Tomato and dill mayonnaise* (see below).

Tomato and dill mayonnaise

Makes ¾ pt/450 ml

This is, to my taste, the ideal sauce for barbecued salmon. You can leave out the garlic if you prefer. Dill is one of my favourite flavours (garlic, coffee, chocolate, lemon, vanilla and basil are the others!)

---

1 whole egg plus 1 yolk	*½ pt/300 ml sunflower oil*
1 rounded tsp caster sugar	*3–4 tbsp wine vinegar*
½ tsp salt and lots of freshly	*(depending on how sharp*
ground black pepper	*you like your mayonnaise)*
1 rounded tsp mustard	*2 tbsp chopped dill fronds*
powder	*4 tomatoes, skinned,*
1 garlic clove, skinned and	*deseeded and chopped*
chopped	

If you make this mayonnaise the day before don't worry that the chopped tomatoes will make it watery; they won't, because their seeds have been removed and it is they that make for wateriness.

Put the mayonnaise ingredients – save for the dill and tomatoes – into a food processor and whiz together. Stir the dill and chopped tomatoes into the mayonnaise to serve.

The best potato salad

Serves 8

There are potato salads and potato salads. Some of the

ones you come across are enough to put you off eating it again for life. This recipe, originally given to me by my American Aunt Janie, is the best potato salad of all. I have jiggled about a bit with the ingredients over the years, but we all eat it with glee – it is worth making just for the family to have with a tomato salad and a green salad, it is so totally delicious. You can make it the day before.

---

8 good-sized potatoes,
    scrubbed
4 hardboiled eggs, shelled
    and chopped
2 sticks of celery, sliced very
    finely
8 spring onions, bulbs and
    stalks, sliced thinly

salt and plenty of freshly
    ground black pepper
2 tbsp chopped parsley
6 tbsp good mayonnaise
shredded lettuce for garnish

Boil the potatoes until they are tender. Drain them and steam off excess water. When they are cool enough to hold without burning your hands, peel the skins off and chop into even-sized bits.

Fold all the ingredients together and put them in a serving dish with shredded lettuce round the sides – it is a pretty potato salad as well as being delicious.

Marinated mushrooms

Serves 8 as a salad, 6 as a first course

There are so many differing versions of marinated mushrooms, each introducing different flavours depending on what herbs or spices are used. In this marinade recipe there is red wine, garlic, tarragon and chives. If you can get small mushrooms of a fairly even size, just

189

slice off their stalks level with the cap. If your mushrooms are larger, flatter, and of unequal size (and
actually these have far more flavour than the small
button mushrooms) just slice them in thickish slices.

---

4 tbsp olive oil
1 garlic clove, skinned and
   chopped finely
½ pt/300 ml red wine
2 lb/1 kg mushrooms, wiped
   and sliced

2 tbsp chopped fresh
   tarragon
salt and lots of freshly
   ground black pepper
2 tbsp snipped chives

Put the oil, garlic, and red wine into a saucepan and
simmer for 5 minutes, then add the mushrooms. Cook for
3–5 minutes, then take the mushrooms out of the liquid
with a slotted spoon and put them into a serving dish.
Add the chopped tarragon to the liquid, and the salt and
pepper. Simmer for 3–5 minutes to reduce the liquid,
then pour this over the mushrooms, and stir in the
snipped chives. Leave to cool completely, or overnight.

Avocado salad

Serves 8

The trouble with most avocado salads is that there is
never enough of them, or that they are combined with
another ingredient (as in many instances in this book!)
and the ratio of avocado to the other ingredients – say,
orange – is two-to-one in favour of the orange. This salad
is purely avocado, and I serve it with my father in mind if
not in presence as he loves avocados nearly as much as
he loves chocolate.

6 large avocados – 8 if they
are the small dark
knobbly variety (which I
think have the best
flavour)

juice of 1 lemon

FOR THE FRENCH DRESSING

½ tsp salt
½ tsp sugar
lots of freshly ground black
pepper
1 tsp mustard powder
¼ pt/150 ml oil – sunflower
or olive

2 tbsp wine vinegar
2 tsp each chopped parsley,
snipped chives and
chopped mint (applemint
if possible)

Put all the ingredients for the French dressing into a
liquidizer and whiz till you have a thick green dressing.
Score each avocado in quarters and peel the skin off
each. Cut each in half, then in neat slices lengthways.
Brush lemon juice over the slices, arrange them in a dish,
with the slices all going in the same direction, and pour
over the green dressing.

Try not to prepare this salad much more than 3–4
hours before your guests arrive.

Strawberry and orange terrine
with strawberry sauce

Serves 8

This looks beautiful, tastes wonderful with the

complementing flavours of strawberry and orange, and as a bonus isn't too dire calorie-wise.

FOR THE TERRINE

1 lb/500 g strawberries
1 pt/600 ml fresh orange
   juice
½ pt/150 ml orange liqueur
   (such as Cointreau) and
   water mixed

2 sachets of powdered
   gelatine (approximately
   1 oz/25 g)

FOR THE STRAWBERRY SAUCE

8 oz/250 g strawberries,
   hulled

3 oz/75 g icing sugar

For the terrine, hull the strawberries and cut them in half. Try to keep the medium-sized ones together, the smaller ones to one side, and the larger halves in a third group. By doing this you can jigsaw-puzzle the layers much quicker than if they are all mixed together. Sprinkle the gelatine over the orange juice in a saucepan and dissolve it over a gentle heat. Stir in the orange liqueur and water.

Take a long loaf or terrine tin, approximately 10 in/ 25 cm long, pour in a layer of the gelatine, orange and water mixture and put it in the fridge to set. When it is set, arrange on top a layer of strawberry halves, cut-side uppermost. Pour over a little orange-gelatine liquid to hold them in place and return to the fridge to set. Continue doing this till the terrine is full to the top. It sounds a fiddle I know, having to leave the liquid to set between each layer, but it makes for a far neater terrine when turned out. Leave the terrine in a cool place or fridge for several hours. Meanwhile, make the strawberry sauce by liquidizing the strawberries with the icing sugar, then sieving the purée.

When ready, dip the terrine tin in warm (not hot) water for a few seconds and it will then turn out onto a serving dish or plate. Slice to serve, with the strawberry sauce spooned over each slice or in a pool around each slice.

Cinnamon pavlova with blackcurrant cream

Serves 8

This cinnamon-flavoured soft marshmallow-textured pavlova goes so well with the blackcurrants and whipped cream on top. If you really don't like blackcurrants, you could substitute raspberries, whose flavour are also well complemented by cinnamon.

FOR THE PAVLOVA

4 large egg whites
8 oz/250 g caster sugar

1 tsp wine vinegar
2 rounded tsp powdered cinnamon

FOR THE BLACKCURRANT CREAM

1 lb/500 g blackcurrants, stripped of their stalks
4 oz/100 g sugar

pared rind of 1 small lemon
½ pt/300 ml double cream, fairly stiffly whipped

Line a baking tray with bakewell paper (siliconized greaseproof paper) and mark on it a large circle, about 9 in/23 cm diameter.

Whisk the egg whites till stiff then, still whisking, gradually add the caster sugar, a spoonful at a time. When the sugar has all been whisked in, fold in the wine vinegar and powdered cinnamon. Spoon the cinnamon meringue onto the marked circle, smoothing it even. Bake in a moderate oven – 350°F/180°C/Gas 4/bottom right oven in a 4-door Aga – for 5 minutes, then in a cooler oven – 250°F/120°C/Gas ½/top left oven in a 4-door Aga – for a further 45 minutes. Take it out of the oven and cool it on its bakewell paper on a wire cooling rack. Then carefully peel off the paper and put the pavlova onto a serving plate.

For the blackcurrant cream, first cook the fruit gently with the sugar and pared lemon rind till the currants are soft. With a slotted spoon, spoon the currants from their juices, throwing out the lemon rind and draining off as much juice as you can. Fold the currants into the whipped cream and spoon this mixture onto the Pavlova. It needs no further decoration.

PICNICS FOR SIX–EIGHT

~~~~~~~~~~~~~~~~~~~~~~~~~~~

Egg mayonnaise and crispy bacon buns
Sausagemeat and thyme pastry roll
Crudités with garlic, parsley and tomato dip
Fresh salmon and dill tart
Watercress and smoked salmon roulade
Chicken terrine with pistachios and Cumberland jelly
Brown sugar meringues
Lemon and elderflower curd
Raspberry and almond tart

PICNICS

The picnics I remember best from my childhood took place by the river and consisted of tea-food – lots of sandwiches in boxes with lids which although made of plastic somehow managed to be elegant, biscuits, cake, tea and milk. We seemed to have a picnic tea by the river virtually every day and, as is the way with memory, there were endless hot days for swimming in the river. Picnics for us now rarely involve teatime food, they are more usually lunch picnics. Our big annual picnic, whatever the weather, takes place on our girls' open day at their school near Perth, and as we have to make a *very* early start in order to be there in time for the first event at the end of the morning all the food has to be packed up the night before, ready to be taken from the fridge and put into the car very early the next morning. The first open day, I provided rather an elaborate picnic which was definitely inappropriate to satisfy the needs and appetites of our children and two or three friends. What they really like are cold sausages (the Lincoln sausages from Marks and Spencer are definitely the nicest) and fat buns filled with the universal family favourite filling of egg mayonnaise with crispy bacon and lettuce and cherry tomatoes, which are ideal for picnics. Gooey fudge brownies and/or carrot cake (see page 228 for the recipe) are all they ask for pudding, with lots of fruit, cherries, strawberries and so on to pick at. This sort of picnic is *not* suitable for smart occasions, but is eminently so for all the many family outings which families enjoy each summer. The *Sausagemeat and thyme pastry roll* is ideal for such an occasion, too. In this chapter there are recipes for filled buns, a six-serving sausage roll, and also for rather more up-market picnic food. The point to bear in mind when planning picnic food is that it has to travel –

197

if you are lucky, on a hot day – so you don't want lots of food which will melt and be a sloppy mess on arrival. I remember helping a friend with the food for a School Founder's Day lunch for the governors many years ago. Because there were no cooking facilities where it was to be held, we had to make the entire lunch and transport it in the morning; the first course was to be jellied consommé with caviare stirred through it and we set off with me holding the vast bowl containing the jellied soup between my knees to keep it more or less stable. As we wended our way along the country lanes, the hot sun beating through the car windscreen reduced the jellied consommé to a sloppy mess and I arrived looking as though I had been wading through frog spawn . . . This is an example of what *not* to plan for a smart picnic!

Egg mayonnaise and crispy bacon buns

Enough to fill 8 buns

---

8 large white or brown soft
buns, cut nearly in half
with a serrated knife, and
some of the dough from
the top and bottom halves
pulled out

FOR THE FILLING

4 tbsp mayonnaise
1 rounded tsp Dijon mustard
6 eggs, hardboiled, shelled
and chopped

6 rashers streaky bacon,
grilled till crisp, cooled
on kitchen paper then
broken into bits
salt and freshly ground
black pepper
8 leaves Iceberg lettuce

Mix the mayonnaise mixture with the mustard, chopped
hardboiled eggs and broken-up bacon. Season to taste.
Butter the top and bottom of each half bun, put a leaf of
iceberg lettuce on one half, and a generous spoonful of
the egg-and-bacon mixture. The lettuce keeps the buns
moist, and you can make these up and wrap them in
clingfilm or foil and leave them in the fridge overnight.

Sausagemeat and thyme pastry roll

Serves 4–6

This delicious savoury roll makes a fat roulade shape, which I like to slice in thick slices (about 1½–2 in/4–5 cm wide) on the diagonal. I personally like to use shortcrust pastry, but you could substitute puff pastry if you prefer. The goodness of the filling depends on the quality of the sausagemeat – I like to use Lincoln sausages from Marks and Spencer, which I think the most delicious sausages one can buy. With the tip of a sharp knife you slit them lengthways and the skin peels off easily.

---

2 oz/50 g butter
1 onion, skinned and
    chopped finely
1 garlic clove, skinned and
    chopped finely
1 lb/500 g pork sausagemeat
    (see above)

a large pinch of dried thyme
a pinch of salt and lots of
    freshly ground black
    pepper
1 lb/500 g shortcrust pastry
beaten egg to glaze

Melt the butter and cook the finely chopped onion and garlic till the onion is soft – 5–7 minutes. Take it off the heat, and cool it thoroughly. Skin the sausages and put them into a bowl, with the thyme, salt and pepper and cooled cooked onion and garlic mixture. Mix all thoroughly together – the only way to do this properly is to use your hands to squelch through the sausagemeat, no wooden spoon will do the job so well! Roll out the pastry into a neat oblong about 8 in/20 cm wide and 10 in/25 cm long. Put the sausagemeat mixture down the middle. Fold the sides up to meet in the middle, and seal the two sides together by pinching the pastry. Do this to seal the ends, too. Make pastry leaves from any trimmings, and slash the pastry in several places down either side of the pinched middle and put the pastry leaves alternating with the slashes. Put the pastry roll onto a baking tray. Brush the pastry with the beaten egg, and bake in a hot oven – 425°F/220°C/Gas 7/top right oven in a 4-door Aga – for 15–20 minutes till the pastry is browned, then lower the heat, and cook for a further 30–35 minutes at a moderate temperature – 350°F/180°C/Gas 4/bottom right oven in a 4-door Aga. Cool before serving, and slice on the diagonal before packing it for the picnic.

Crudités with garlic, parsley and tomato dip

Serves 8

For a smart picnic where you would like to provide a first course of a sort, I can think of nothing more suitable than a selection of crudités – vegetables peeled and sliced in thin, even-sized sticks to dip into a good sauce. This is a very portable idea – the crudités and dip can be prepared the day before. This dip tastes wonderful, looks good with its flecks of parsley and small bits of tomato, and, most important for a picnic, transports well. Take it along in its serving dish, covered with clingfilm.

FOR THE CRUDITÉS

1 red, 1 green and 1 yellow
pepper cut in strips
3 medium-sized carrots, cut
in narrow, even sticks
1 head celery, cut in narrow,
even sticks

1 medium-sized cauliflower
cut into florets, blanched
in boiling water for 2–3
minutes, then refreshed
under cold water and
drained

FOR THE DIP

1 whole egg plus 1 yolk
½ tsp salt and plenty of
freshly ground black
pepper
1 garlic clove, peeled and
chopped
1 rounded tsp Dijon mustard
½ pt/300 ml sunflower oil
a small bunch of parsley,
heads stripped from
stalks (keep the stalks for
stock)

3–4 tbsp wine vinegar,
depending how sharp you
like the taste
3 tomatoes, skinned,
deseeded and diced quite
small

Whiz the eggs and extra yolk, salt and pepper, garlic and mustard in a food processor or liquidizer. Then, drop by drop at first, then a steady stream add the sunflower oil. Lastly, whiz in the parsley, and the wine vinegar to taste.

Fold the diced tomatoes into the dip, and don't worry that the tomatoes will make the dip watery – they won't, because the seeds are removed and it is they that cause the wateriness.

Pack the crudités in a wide polythene box or on a serving dish, with dampened kitchen paper pressed over their surface.

Fresh salmon and dill tart

Serves 6–8

I made this once for an elegant picnic competition sponsored by a champagne firm. I was among four contestants selected by the judges to take part in the finals at Henley, in the beautiful garden of some very kind people who had lent their house and garden for the occasion. I travelled down from Skye by plane for the event, with some of my picnic food made (bread, spinach terrine) and I got up early to make the tart. I thought it ideal picnic food for a smart occasion, but my three fellow contestants were Real Chefs, who arrived with stage props undreamt of by me – flower arrangements as for a wedding, hatstands laden with stripey blazers and boaters, spun sugar helmets to put over their pudding concoctions, and two of them really amazed me when I saw that they had brought portable ovens in which to cook their main courses! I was not in the same league at all, with my tablecloth on a rug, fat white pot of garden roses in the middle, and picnic food which could be cooked by anyone but which did *not* involve baking duck breasts on the spot!

FOR THE PASTRY

4 oz/100 g chilled butter, cut
  in pieces
6 oz/175 g plain flour

1 heaped tsp icing sugar
salt and pepper

FOR THE FILLING

1 lb/500 g salmon, cut in
  1 in/2.5 cm chunks
3 large egg yolks plus
  1 whole large egg
1 pt/600 ml single cream
good pinch of salt and plenty
  of freshly ground black
  pepper

a handful of dill fronds –
  less if you prefer, but dill
  and salmon are so
  delicious together that,
  for me, the more the
  better!

Put the pastry ingredients into a food processor and whiz till the mixture looks like fine crumbs. Pat them round the sides and base of an 8–9 in/20–23 cm flan dish, and put the flan into the fridge for at least half an hour before baking it in a moderate oven – 350°F/180°C/Gas 4/ bottom right oven in a 4-door Aga – for 20–25 minutes, till the pastry is golden and cooked. Take it out of the oven.

Put the chunks of salmon into the cooked pastry shell. Beat together the egg and yolks, and beat the cream into this. Season with salt and pepper and pour over the salmon. Place the dill fronds over the surface, and bake the tart in a moderate oven – 350°F/180°C/Gas 4/bottom right oven in a 4-door Aga – until the filling is just set when you touch it with your finger or when you gently shake the flan dish – 20–25 minutes. Take care not to overcook it, and remember that it will go on cooking a bit once it is taken out of the oven.

Watercress and smoked salmon roulade

Serves 8

This pale green roulade looks beautiful with its pink-flecked cream filling; it also tastes very good. We make it here at Kinloch to serve as a first course for our guests, but it makes a perfect smart picnic main course too.

FOR THE FLAVOURED MILK

1 pt/600 ml milk
1 onion, skinned and halved
a stick of celery, washed and
  halved

frond of fennel (optional)
a few black peppercorns
1 tsp rock salt
a handful of parsley

FOR THE ROULADE

2 oz/50 g butter
2 oz/50 g flour
2 handfuls of watercress or
  1 box of watercress as
  sold by Marks and
  Spencer

salt and freshly ground
  black pepper
4 large eggs, separated, plus
  1 whole egg

FOR THE FILLING

¾ pt/450 ml double cream,
  whipped
grated rind and juice of
  1 lemon

plenty of freshly ground
  black pepper
8 oz/250 g smoked salmon,
  cut into fairly fine shreds

205

Bring the milk to scalding point in a saucepan, together with the flavourings. Once the milk has reached scalding point, take the pan off the heat and leave it to stand for an hour, then strain the milk, throwing away the flavourings.

Line a baking tray with bakewell paper (siliconized greaseproof paper). Melt the butter in a saucepan, stir in the flour and let it cook for a couple of minutes to make a *roux*. Liquidize the watercress with the flavoured milk and add gradually to the *roux*, stirring continuously till the sauce boils. Season with salt and pepper, and take the pan off the heat. Beat in the whole egg and 4 egg yolks. Whisk the 4 egg whites till they are very stiff, then, with a large metal spoon fold them quickly and thoroughly into the sauce. Pour this into the bakewell paper-lined baking tray, and bake in a moderate oven – 350°F/180°C/Gas 4/bottom right oven in a 4-door Aga – for about 25 minutes, till it feels firm to the touch. Take it out of the oven, cover with a fresh piece of bakewell paper and a damp teatowel over that, and leave to cool.

To make the filling, whip the lemon juice and rind into the whipped cream, and season with black pepper. Fold the shredded smoked salmon into the cream.

To roll up the roulade, lay a piece of bakewell paper on a table or work surface, uncover the roulade and, taking the short ends of its bakewell paper in either hand, flip it over onto the work surface. Carefully peel the paper off its back, in strips parallel to the roulade which will prevent the roulade tearing with the paper. Cover the surface with the smoked salmon cream, and roll up. Slip it onto a serving plate and slice it thickly (one less thing to do on the picnic site) before loosely wrapping the roulade and its plate in foil. Take a large palette knife or fish slice to serve the roulade from the serving dish to each plate.

Chicken terrine with pistachios and Cumberland jelly

Serves 6–8

This tastes delicious, and is very portable. I would advise slicing it before packing it in with the other picnic contents.

FOR THE TERRINE

3 bay leaves
8 streaky bacon rashers
1½ lb/750 g white chicken meat, diced quite finely – this is quick to do providing you have a sharp knife

1 lb/500 g good pork sausages (I use Marks and Spencer's Lincoln sausages)
2 oz/50 g pistachio kernels

FOR THE MARINADE

4 tbsp olive oil
¼ pt/150 ml port (you can use red wine instead, but port gives a richer flavour)
1 onion, skinned and chopped finely

pared rind of 1 lemon (I use a potato peeler to avoid getting bitter white pith too)
½ tsp salt and plenty of freshly ground black pepper
pinch of dried thyme

Line a 1½–2 lb/approximately 1 kg loaf or terrine tin with foil, then lay the bayleaves down the centre. With the blunt side of a knife, flatten the rashers of streaky bacon and lay them across the tin widthways; their ends will overhang at either side.

Put the marinade ingredients into a saucepan and bring to the boil, simmer for 3–5 minutes, then take off the heat and leave to cool completely before pouring over the diced chicken in a dish. Leave for several hours or overnight, then discard the strips of lemon peel, and mix the chicken, the marinade, the pistachio kernels and sausagemeat together – the only way to do this job thoroughly is to use your hands. When thoroughly mixed, pack this into the bacon-lined tin. Fold the overhanging flaps of bacon over the meat surface, and fold over the foil to seal it, then put the loaf or terrine tin into a roasting tin with water coming halfway up the sides. Cook in a moderate oven – 350°F/180°C/Gas 4/ bottom right oven in a 4-door Aga – for 2 hours, until when you stick a skewer into the middle of the terrine the juices run clear. If you are in any doubt give it a further 20 minutes' cooking time. Take the tin out of the roasting tin, put a weight on top – I use a couple of tins of tomatoes or something similar – and leave to get quite cold. When cold, keep the terrine in the fridge. Serve with *Cumberland jelly* (see below).

Cumberland jelly

This is very good served with the chicken and pistachio terrine, or with any cold meat or game for that matter.

8 oz/250 g redcurrant jelly	2 tsp powdered gelatine
1 tbsp Dijon mustard	grated rind and juice of
¼ pt/150 ml port	1 lemon
	grated rind and juice of
	1 orange

Put all the above ingredients together into a saucepan

and heat gently till the jelly has dissolved. Pour into warmed jars, seal and store in a cool place.

Brown sugar meringues

Serves 6

This recipe has appeared in my book *Sweet Things*, but I make no apology for including it here too, because it is such a perfect pudding for a picnic when combined with lemon and elderflower curd and whipped cream, and strawberries.

---

4 oz/100 g granulated sugar   4 large egg whites
4 oz/100 g demerara sugar

Mix together the two sugars. Line a baking tray with a piece of bakewell paper (siliconized greaseproof paper). Whisk the egg whites till stiff then, whisking continuously, add the sugar a spoonful at a time. When the sugar is all incorporated, pipe, using a fluted nozzle, the meringue onto the prepared baking tray in even-sized rounds – I aim for about a 2–2½ in/5–6 cm diameter. Bake in a cool oven – 250°F/120°C/Gas ½/top left oven of a 4-door Aga – for 2–2½ hours. Cool on a wire rack, and store the meringues in an airtight tin. Transport them in the tin to the picnic, and sandwich them together with whipped cream and *Lemon and elderflower curd* (see below) to serve.

Lemon and elderflower curd

You can keep this curd for 3–4 weeks in the fridge. The flavour of lemon and elderflower is so perfectly delicious that I like to make the most of the elderflowers while they are in bloom.

---

2 large eggs plus 2 large egg yolks
3 oz/75 g butter
3 oz/75 g caster or granulated sugar

grated rind of 2 lemons and juice of 1
a handful of elderflowers, plucked from their stalks

Beat the eggs and egg yolks together, then sieve them into a Pyrex or other heatproof bowl. Cut the butter into bits and put it into the bowl of sieved egg; add the sugar, lemon rind and juice, and elderflowers. Put the bowl over a saucepan of barely simmering water, and stir occasionally as the butter melts and the sugar dissolves, and the curd gradually thickens. When it is thick, cool it in the bowl then put it into jars, seal them and store in the fridge.

Raspberry and almond tart

Serves 6–8

It really is worth the small effort involved in toasting the ground almonds for the pastry case for this tart – their flavour is wonderful with the jewel-like raspberry filling.

By the way, if you have any trouble getting arrowroot, you can always find it in a chemist's shop. It is invaluable for thickening fruit as once boiled it leaves their colour jewel-clear and unclouded.

FOR THE ALMOND PASTRY

4 oz/100 g ground almonds
4 oz/100 g chilled butter, cut in pieces

1 oz/25 g icing sugar
2 oz/50 g plain flour

FOR THE FILLING

1½ lb/750 g raspberries
4 oz/100 g granulated sugar

1 heaped tbsp arrowroot, slaked in 2 tbsp cold water

Toast the ground almonds to a golden brown; I find the easiest way of toasting them is to dry-fry them in a saucepan.

Put the cut-up butter, icing sugar, flour and cooled toasted ground almonds in a food processor, and whiz till the mixture resembles crumbs – but take care not to let it go into a ball, as you won't have enough pastry to roll out to cover the flan dish. Pat the crumb-like mixture round the sides and base of a flan dish about 9 in/23 cm in diameter, and put it into a fridge for at least an hour before baking in a moderate oven – 350°F/180°C/Gas 4/ bottom right oven in a 4-door Aga – for 25–30 minutes, till the pastry is firm to the touch. Cool.

To make the filling, put the raspberries and sugar together in a saucepan, and heat gently till the juices just begin to run from the fruit and the sugar has dissolved. Stir some of the hot juice into the slaked arrowroot, and pour this into the saucepan with the raspberries. Stir over a gentle-to-moderate heat till the raspberries have thickened and boiled. Take the pan off the heat, and cool the raspberries, then pour them into the cooled almond-pastry flan. Leave to set.

CHILDREN'S PARTY FOOD

Tiny fairy cakes
Flapjack fingers
Pink and white miniature meringues
White-iced vanilla biscuits with hundreds and thousands
Marshmallows with chocolate and Smarties
Chocolate Rice Krispies
Gingerbread men
Lemonade and orangeade

and

Egg and Marmite open sandwiches
Mashed sardine and chopped tomato open sandwiches
Tuna fish-filled tiny vol-au-vents
Sausages

Birthdays

Like it or not, birthdays are an annual occurrence and in my opinion they are best marked with a celebration! It eases the pain for those who mind about the speed with which birthdays seem to come round the older one gets. It's ironic that when young there seems an age between each birthday, and when one gets older, they just keep coming, seemingly faster and faster. But really, apart from the, to them, all-important children's birthdays, other major birthday celebrations are geared to eighteenth or twenty-first (*never* both, too greedy for words) birthdays, and thereafter each decade seems to be a milestone – thirtieth, fortieth, fiftieth, sixtieth, seventieth, and dare one go much further?! The allotted three-score years and ten and every year thereafter, never mind decade, should be considered a bonus and therefore worth celebrating annually, and with gusto.

In this chapter I give recipes for a wide range of parties: a child's birthday, a teenager's birthday party, a twenty-first, a fortieth birthday party based on my husband Godfrey's last year, and a seventieth, with food which I think appropriate for each.

Children's Birthday Parties

Little did I realize, the day our eldest was born, that I would view the anniversary of that day, and the birthdays of our subsequent three children for the next ten years with dread. I discovered that I hate giving children's birthday parties – and what an admission. I always feel envious of my friends who live in less rural areas who tell me that they are taking a group of small

215

children to a trampoline centre where a birthday tea will be laid on after they have all bounced themselves to exhaustion; or that there is a suitable stage entertainment to take the group of small friends to for a birthday treat. Others mothers employ hired entertainers who take the heat off them and organize all the games for the party. Here in Skye there is none of that, and it's up to us mothers to take the lead (I have never got over my cringing embarrassment of this role, not being a natural Joyce Grenfell character) in all the children's games such as 'Nuts in May', 'Grand Old Duke of York', 'I sent a Letter to my Love and on the way I dropped it' – all those games that are dying out in more populated areas, thanks to the aforementioned entertainers.

At our parties we have such games and 2 goes of pass the parcel, and lots of Musical Bumps and Statues, to hopefully wear them (and me) all out before sending them home. When they reach school age, there is a half hour between the arrivals of the 2 school buses during which I long to start their tea, because things loosen up no end once they are all fed, but we can never start without the full complement of party guests. I always feel guiltily disloyal about these feelings about my children's parties, but I can't help it. Thankfully, they are getting older now, and real children's parties will soon be a thing of the past – just another year or two to go!

When it comes to food, one vital ingredient for a successful birthday tea is one or two large dishes of sausages, which are universally popular. I refuse to have bowls of crisps, but make two or three savoury items, two being open sandwiches and a third tiny vol-au-vents called bouchées, with a tuna fish filling, which they all seem to love. If everything is kept small or miniature it seems to have far more appeal to their eyes and stomachs, so we make tiny cakes in sweet paper cases, and miniature biscuits. Marshmallows with a blob of chocolate and a Smartie on top are extremely popular, as are tiny pink and white meringues, unfilled, as a dislike of cream seems quite common among the young. Small fingers of flapjacks, and miniature biscuits, and, of course, The Cake. I am not in the Jane Asher cake-decorating league, in fact only yesterday Hugo, my six-year-old, was looking through Jane Asher's cake-decorating book ('Mummy, please can I have a Vampire in a Coffin for my next birthday?') when he said wistfully, 'Just think what it must be like to have Jane Asher for your Mum.' In my time I have made a passable aeroplane, and a hedgehog but I don't think anyone else knew what it was supposed to be, but otherwise I have played safe and stuck to the number of their age.

When it comes to drinks, I suggest jugs of lemonade rather than endless fizz, like Coke. And a vital tray of tea for any adults who may be present – with the promise of a good tea you can rope in a few friends to help with the Nuts in May etc!

Tiny fairy cakes

Makes about 48 cakes

These are small vanilla cakes with either pink or chocolate icing, whichever you prefer. If the birthday cake is chocolate, I would ice them pink. They are baked in sweet paper cases.

---

4 oz/100 g softened butter	*4 oz/100 g self-raising flour,*
4 oz/100 g caster sugar	*sieved*
2 large eggs	*a few drops of vanilla*
	essence

Beat the butter very well, gradually adding the sugar, and beating till the mixture is light and fluffy. Beat in 1 egg, beating well, then beat in a spoonful of the sieved flour, then the other egg, then beat in the remaining flour, sieved, and a few drops of vanilla essence. Put the sweet paper cases onto a baking tray and, with a teaspoon, spoon the cake mixture into the cases, filling each three-quarters full. Bake in a moderate oven – 350°F/180°C/Gas 4/bottom right oven in a 4-door Aga – for 10 minutes. Cool on a wire rack, and ice them the morning of the party.

Flapjack fingers

Makes about 30

This is the nicest flapjack recipe I have ever come across, given to me by Minty Dallmeyer and Margaret Taylor. Cut the baked flapjack into fingers approximately 2 in/ 5 cm long and 1 in/2.5 cm wide. Children love them – ours do, anyway.

---

4 oz/100 g butter
1 tbsp golden syrup (dip the spoon in very hot water first, the syrup will then slip easily off the spoon)
2 oz/50 g rolled oats

2 oz/50 g self-raising flour, sieved
4 oz/100 g soft brown sugar
3 oz/75 g cornflakes

Melt together the butter and golden syrup, then stir in the oats, sieved flour, sugar, and cornflakes. Butter a baking tray measuring approximately 9 × 13 in/23 × 32 cm and spread the flapjack mixture into this. Bake in a hot oven – 400°F/200°C/Gas 6/top right oven in a 4-door Aga – for 10 minutes. Cool in the tin, but cut into fingers while still warm.

Pink and white miniature meringues

Makes about 24–30 meringues

All but one of our children (Meriel) love meringues, and judging how they disappear at parties so do most of their friends.

---

3 large egg whites
6 oz/175 g caster sugar

a few drops of pink food colouring

Line a large baking tray with bakewell paper (siliconized greaseproof paper). Whisk the egg whites till stiff then, whisking continuously, add the sugar a spoonful at a time, till all the sugar is incorporated. Divide the mixture – put about half into a separate bowl and fold in a few drops of pink food colouring. Pipe first the white meringue, with a small star nozzle or fluted nozzle, into small blobs about the size of a 5-pence piece. Then pipe the pink (you will have some pink and white stripey ones, too, but it doesn't matter!) Bake in a cool oven – 250°F/120°C/Gas ½/top left oven in a 4-door Aga – for about 2 hours. Cool, then store in an airtight container. You can make these meringues a week or more in advance.

White-iced vanilla biscuits with hundreds and thousands

Makes about 24

These biscuits are cut in small rounds, a little larger than a 10-pence piece. To avoid the colour weeping from the hundreds and thousands into the icing, ice them the morning of the party. Alternatively, you could put a jelly tot or similar on the icing, instead of the hundreds and thousands. These aren't just decorative biscuits, they taste delicious too.

---

4 oz/100 g softened butter
2 oz/50 g caster sugar

5 oz/150 g self-raising flour, sieved
a few drops of vanilla essence

Cream the butter and sugar together very well, then work in the sieved flour and vanilla essence. On a lightly floured work surface, with a floured rolling pin, roll out the dough to about ¼ in/5 mm. Cut out the biscuits with a 1½–2 in/3–5 cm diameter scone cutter or glass. Put the rounds of biscuit dough onto a baking tray, and bake in a moderate oven – 350°F/180°C/Gas 4/bottom right oven in a 4-door Aga – for about 10–12 minutes, till the biscuits are pale golden and just firm to the touch. Take them out of the oven, cool for a couple of minutes on the baking tray, then with a palette knife carefully lift them onto a wire cooling rack.

When cold, ice the biscuits with a small amount of white glacé icing (see page 59), and decorate with either a pinch of hundreds and thousands, or whatever you like – a half glacé cherry, a jelly tot, are two alternatives.

Marshmallows with chocolate and Smarties

These are so simple they don't really warrant a recipe. Just break a small amount of dark chocolate into a bowl, and put the bowl over a saucepan of barely simmering water, taking care not to let the bottom of the bowl touch the water. Heat till the chocolate has just melted. Dip half of each marshmallow in the melted chocolate, and put a Smartie on top. Store in an airtight container. You can make these a day ahead.

Chocolate Rice Krispies

Makes about 30–40

Never mind the children, I find the adults go for these! I love them, providing they are made to this rather rich recipe. And whatever you do, do use proper, *good* dark chocolate – never the chocolate flavouring marketed as Cakebrand south of the border and Scotchoc north of the border.

---

3 oz/75 g butter
3 oz/75 g good dark
   chocolate
a few drops of vanilla
   essence

2 tbsp golden syrup (dip the
   spoon in very hot water
   first)
Rice Krispies (see below)

Put the butter and chocolate, vanilla essence and syrup

221

into a large saucepan and melt it over fairly gentle heat. When all is melted and mixed together, take the pan off the heat and stir in enough Rice Krispies to take up the chocolate mixture without making them too sparsely coated – about 4 cupfuls. Let it cool, stirring from time to time, otherwise the chocolate mixture sinks to the bottom of the pan. Spoon into paper cases to set.

Gingerbread men

Makes 10–12

These look attractive and taste good too. You can buy gingerbread men cutters from most cookshops. Being of a rather simple mentality, I always have a small expectation that one of them will actually jump off the baking tray and run off, as in the children's story.

---

4 oz/100 g plain flour
good pinch of bicarbonate
  of soda
4 oz/100 g caster sugar
2 tsp ground ginger

3 oz/75 g butter
2 tbsp golden syrup (dip the
  spoon in very hot water
  first)
currants for decoration

Sieve together the dry ingredients. Melt the butter and syrup, let it cool a bit, then stir them into the dry ingredients, mixing well. On a lightly floured surface and with a floured rolling pin, roll out the dough thinly – about ⅛ in/3 mm thick. Cut into gingerbread men and place them carefully on a greased baking tray. Bake in a moderate oven – 350°F/180°C/Gas 4/bottom right oven in a 4-door Aga – for 10 minutes. As soon as you take them out of the oven stick currants into them for eyes, mouth and buttons. Then carefully lift the gingerbread men onto a wire cooling rack to cool completely – if they become too brittle to lift off the baking tray, put the tray back in the oven for a few moments, and they will then lift off more easily.

Lemon and orangeade

Makes 2 pt/1.2 L

Wash 2 lemons and 2 oranges. Cut each into quite fine dice, and put them into a large bowl. Add 3 tablespoons caster sugar, and pour on 2 pints/1.2 litres of boiling water. Leave to stand for 30 minutes, but no longer as the juice tends to become bitter if left for any length of time. Strain, and serve in jugs with sliced oranges and ice cubes floating in it.

A TEENAGE BIRTHDAY PARTY FOR SIXTEEN–EIGHTEEN

Baked potatoes with:
Barbecue sauce with sliced sausages
Cream cheese, crispy bacon and garlic sauce
Tuna fish and sweetcorn dip
Salad of lettuce and spinach, avocado and chopped bacon
Carrot cake with vanilla cream cheese icing
Meringues (choose from recipe on page 209 or 353)

A teenage birthday party

There comes a time, it came to us during the summer holidays, when there is expressed a wish from a teenage member of the family to have a birthday party which she (I don't yet know about hes) can 'do myself'. Not wishing to dampen budding entrepreneurial desires, I and my great friend Caroline Fox gave in to the requests of our eldest daughters, our Alexandra and their Harriet, to give a party around the time of Alexandra's fifteenth birthday. They spent hours on the telephone discussing the menu – Harriet being in Edinburgh, and Alexandra in Skye. For geographical reasons it was held in the Foxes' house – I shall always be grateful to them and thankful it wasn't in our own, due to the number of days it took to get rid of the stale cigarette smoke clinging to the curtains . . . But that is another story.

The menu was as follows, and to the credit of both girls they not only did a large part of the preparation, but they cleared up immaculately too.

Barbecue sauce with sliced sausages

Serves 16–18 with baked potatoes and two other sauce-cum-fillings

---

2 lb/1 kg good pork sausages, grilled till browned all over, then cooled and sliced about ½ in/1 cm thick

FOR THE BARBECUE SAUCE

3 tbsp sunflower oil
2 onions, skinned and chopped finely
1 large garlic clove, skinned and chopped finely
1 rounded tbsp soft brown sugar

2 × 15 oz/450 g tins of tomatoes
4 tbsp tomato ketchup
1 tbsp wine vinegar
salt and freshly ground black pepper

To make the sauce, first heat the oil and add the chopped onions and garlic. Cook for several minutes, stirring occasionally to prevent them sticking, then add the brown sugar. Cook for a minute or so, then liquidize the tins of tomatoes, and add those to the contents of the saucepan. Stir in the ketchup, wine vinegar and salt and pepper to taste, and let this sauce simmer for 35–40 minutes, with the pan uncovered. Serve hot or cold. If you intend serving the sauce hot, let it cool before you add the sliced sausages to it, then reheat to serve.

Cream cheese, crispy bacon and garlic sauce

With two other choices, serves 16–18

If I could only choose one sauce out of the three suggestions, this would be my favourite.

---

12 rashers bacon, smoked or unsmoked (I prefer smoked myself)

1½ lb/750 g cream cheese, such as Philadelphia

2 garlic cloves, skinned and chopped

¼ pt/150 ml milk

1 heaped tbsp chopped parsley

First, cook the bacon till crisp, then drain and cool it on kitchen paper, and break it into small bits.

Put the cream cheese into a food processor with the chopped garlic and whiz till smooth, gradually adding the milk till you have a thick cream. Whiz in the broken-up bacon and chopped parsley, then put the cream cheese and bacon mixture into a serving bowl. You can make this sauce two days in advance providing you cover the bowl and keep it in the fridge.

Tuna fish and sweetcorn dip

Serves 16–18, when served with two alternatives

This is simply a combination of tuna and sweetcorn, bound together with mayonnaise, and with a tablespoon of snipped chives to add colour and flavour.

3 large tins tuna fish, well
drained of their oil
3 × 15 oz/450 g tins of
sweetcorn, well drained
of their brine

4 rounded tbsp mayonnaise
2 tbsp snipped chives

In a large bowl, mash the drained tuna fish with a fork. Add the drained sweetcorn, the mayonnaise and the chives, and mix all well together. Heap into a serving dish.

Carrot cake with vanilla cream cheese icing

Serves 14–16

We make this carrot cake in an oblong baking tin (12–14 in/30–35 cm) lined with bakewell paper (siliconized greaseproof paper) and then, when cool, cover it with its yummy vanilla-flavoured cream cheese buttercream. You can make this cake two or three days in advance, but I suggest you cover the baking tin with foil or cling-film, rather than try to take out the cut squares of cake to keep them in a storage tin.

a scant ½ pt/275 ml
   sunflower oil
8 oz/250 g caster sugar
3 large eggs
6 oz/175 g plain flour, sieved

¾ tsp baking powder
¾ tsp bicarbonate of soda
¾ tsp powdered cinnamon
8 oz/250 g grated raw carrot

FOR THE CREAM CHEESE ICING

6 oz/175 g cream cheese
   (such as Philadelphia)
6 oz/175 g softened butter

8 oz/250 g icing sugar,
   sieved
½ tsp vanilla essence

Beat together the oil and sugar in a mixing bowl, then beat in the eggs, one by one, beating really well. Sieve the dry ingredients into the same bowl, stir in, add the grated carrots and mix all together well. Pour the mixture into the lined baking tin, and bake in a moderate oven – 350°F/180°C/Gas 4/bottom right oven in a 4-door Aga – for about 40 minutes, or till when you stick a knife in the centre it comes out clean. Cool the cake in the tin, and when it is quite cold cover it with the cream cheese icing. Cut into squares to serve.

To make the icing, in a food processor or in a bowl beat together the cream cheese, butter, icing sugar and vanilla essence until smooth. Spread on the cake and make a pattern with a fork.

EIGHTEENTH OR TWENTY-FIRST BIRTHDAY PARTY FOR THIRTY

Garlic cheese-stuffed cherry tomatoes
Small squares of pizza
Mushroom and rice filo parcels
Crab-stuffed profiteroles
Smoked salmon and dill cream cheese spread
Crudités with avocado dip
Pieces of melon wrapped in parma ham
Sesame toast fingers with a curried dip

Eighteenth or Twenty-first Birthday Party

Since the vote was given to young people at the age of eighteen, there has been a vogue for celebrating the coming of age at eighteen instead of twenty-one, although most people do still favour a twenty-first birthday party to mark their official majority. So here are some ideas for good food to serve with champagne at the celebration.

The aim with these cocktail eats is to provide really tasty food which is not too messy to eat and which looks attractive as well. Have stacks of small decorative paper table napkins at strategic points for your guests to use.

Garlic cheese-stuffed cherry tomatoes

For 60 tomatoes

Cherry tomatoes are perfect cocktail food – they can be popped in the mouth in one! This is an easy, tasty stuffing, and the simplest way to stuff these tomatoes is by using a piping bag with a small fluted nozzle.

2½ lb/1.25 kg cream cheese, such as Philadelphia	salt and lots of freshly ground black pepper
2 garlic cloves	parsley
2 tbsp chopped parsley	a few black olives

Put the cream cheese and the garlic into a food processor and whiz till the mixture is very smooth, then add the chopped parsley, salt and pepper, and whiz again.

With a very sharp knife, cut a tiny slice off the bottom of each tomato at the opposite end to the stalk – this makes them sit straight. Slice off the top of each tomato and, using a salt spoon or a similar small spoon, scoop out the insides of each tomato. As you finish each, put them face down on a tray lined with several thicknesses of kitchen paper, to drain any excess juice. Fill a piping bag half-full of the cream cheese mixture, and fill each tomato, putting them onto a serving plate or dish as you finish each one. Put a tiny piece of parsley on top of each, or a piece of black olive.

Small squares of pizza

Serves 10

These taste delicious. I wouldn't be tempted to serve them on a dish with anything else. If you have a wide shallow basket you could line the base with foil, and put the pizza squares on it – I think quite a large area of pizza is very appealing.

This recipe fills one tin about 10 × 12 in/25 × 30 cm so I would make it three times over for thirty people, but make the dough for all three tins in one go. Bake the pizza not long before it is to be handed round – pizza is nicest eaten as freshly baked as possible.

FOR THE PIZZA DOUGH

½ pt/300 ml hand-hot water
2 tsp sugar
1 rounded tbsp dried yeast
2 lb/1 kg plain flour

1 tsp salt
2 large eggs, beaten
¼ pt/150 ml warm water
3 tbsp sunflower or olive oil

FOR THE PIZZA FILLING

3 tbsp olive oil
2 onions, skinned and
   chopped finely
1 garlic clove, skinned and
   chopped

1 × 2 lb/1 kilo tin of
   tomatoes
½ tsp sugar
salt and freshly ground
   black pepper

FOR THE TOPPING

6 oz/175 g mozzarella
   cheese

20 small black olives, stoned
   and quartered

Put the ½ pt/300 ml of hand-hot water into a bowl and stir in the sugar, then the dried yeast. Leave the bowl in a warm place till the yeast mixture is doubled in size, and has a deep frothy head to it. Sieve the flour into a bowl, with the salt, and put the bowl in a warm place. When the yeast is well risen, mix it into the flour and then mix in the beaten eggs, warm water and oil. Mix well, then knead on a floured work surface till you have a smooth, elastic dough. Rub oil inside the bowl (which held the flour) and put the kneaded dough into it; cover the bowl with a teatowel and leave in a warm place for the dough to rise. Once the dough has doubled in size, knead it again for several minutes, then divide into three even pieces and begin to make the pizza.

While the dough rises make the sauce for the pizza

233

covering. Heat the olive oil and cook the chopped onions and garlic in the oil for several minutes, stirring occasionally. Liquidize the tinned tomatoes and add them to the onions and garlic, season with sugar, salt and pepper and simmer, uncovered, till the sauce has reduced and thickened – about 40 minutes. Cool.

To assemble the pizza, take one piece of dough and pull and stretch it out to fit an oiled shallow baking tray about 10 × 12 in/25 × 30 cm, pulling the dough up the sides. Brush the dough with oil. Spoon some sauce over the surface of the dough but don't be tempted to make the layer too thick. Dot evenly with slivers of mozzarella, and lay the quarters of black olive in neat and even lines along the pizza. Bake in a hot oven – 425°F/220°C/Gas 7/top right oven in a 4-door Aga – for 15–20 minutes. While still very hot from the oven, with a sharp knife cut into approximately 2 in/5 cm squares. Use a small palette knife to lift the squares onto the serving tray or plate.

Mushroom and rice filo parcels

Makes approximately 50 triangles

These can be made up the day before, and baked on the afternoon of the party. For serving, arrange plates made up of half filo triangles and half crab profiteroles, thereby keeping hot items together rather than mixing up hot and cold items.

1 packet of filo pastry	*sunflower oil or melted butter, to brush each sheet of filo pastry and the finished triangles*

FOR THE FILLING

3 tbsp sunflower oil	*2 tsp cumin seed*
2 oz/50 g butter	*1 tbsp flour*
2 onions, skinned and chopped very finely	*¼ pt/150 ml medium sherry*
2 lb/1 kg mushrooms, wiped, stalks removed, and chopped finely	*salt and freshly ground black pepper*
	4 oz/100 g basmati rice, boiled till tender, then drained well

First make the filling. Heat the oil and melt the butter together in a wide saucepan or frying pan. Add the finely chopped onions and cook them for about 5 minutes, stirring so that they cook evenly. Add the very finely chopped (or shredded) mushrooms – you can do this in a food processor – and cook for a minute or two. Then stir in the cumin, and the flour, and cook for 2–3 minutes. Stir in the sherry, season with salt and pepper, and let the mixture bubble. Stir in the cooked rice, and mix all together thoroughly. Take the pan off the heat and cool the mixture.

Meanwhile, unwrap the filo pastry, and lay out one sheet – keep the rest of the filo pastry covered with a damp teatowel to prevent it from drying out while you work. Brush the sheet of filo with sunflower oil or melted butter, and lay another sheet of filo exactly on top of it. Brush the top sheet of filo with oil or butter and, with a sharp knife, cut it lengthways in 8 even-sized strips. Put a teaspoonful of mushroom mixture at the bottom of each strip, and roll each into a triangle shape till you get half way up the strip, then cut it in half and put another small teaspoonful of mushroom mixture on and make a second triangle with the top half of the strip. Repeat this, till all the filo pastry is used up. Put the triangles on baking trays well-brushed with oil or melted butter. Brush the finished triangles with melted butter and cover them with clingfilm till you are ready to bake them – this prevents them from drying out. Bake them for 10 minutes in a hot oven – 425°F/220°C/Gas 7/top right oven in a 4-door Aga – till they are golden brown and crispy.

Crab-stuffed profiteroles

Makes about 60

These hot cheesey profiteroles are filled with crabmeat in a creamy sauce. The profiteroles can be made and frozen then, when thawed, popped into a hot oven for a few minutes to refresh them before being filled, and reheated to serve.

FOR THE PROFITEROLES

6 oz/175 g butter, cut in
    pieces
¾ pt/450 ml cold water
9 oz/250 g plain flour, sieved
    twice
½ tsp salt

2 tsp mustard powder
5 large eggs, beaten
a dash of Tabasco
4 oz/100 g good Cheddar
    cheese, grated

FOR THE CRAB FILLING

2 oz/50 g butter
2 oz/50 g flour
1 tsp mustard powder
1 pt/600 ml milk

salt and freshly ground
    black pepper
3–4 gratings of nutmeg
1 tbsp dry sherry
2 lb/1 kg white crab meat

Put the butter and water into a saucepan over a moderate heat and let the butter melt as the water heats, but take care not to do this too fast – don't let the water boil before the butter has melted completely. When the liquid rolls to a good boil, add the twice-sieved flour all at once, and beat it hard, till the mixture comes away from the sides of the pan. Beat in the salt and mustard powder, let the mixture cool for 10 minutes, then beat in the eggs, a small amount at a time. I find this beating easiest done with a handheld electric beater. Beat in the Tabasco and the grated cheese.

Rinse baking trays with water, and pipe the cheesey choux pastry onto them in small, even-sized blobs about the size of a 5-pence piece. Bake in a hot oven – 400°F/200°C/Gas 6/top right oven in a 4-door Aga – for 20–25 minutes, or till the profiteroles are golden brown and well risen. If you are in any doubt that they are thoroughly cooked, give them a few more minutes' cooking time. If you are cooking more than one tray at a time, switch them around halfway through cooking time. Cool the profiteroles on a wire cooling rack.

To make the crab filling, first melt the butter and add the flour and mustard powder, and cook for 2–3 minutes. Then, stirring continuously, add the milk, stirring till the sauce boils. Season with salt, pepper and nutmeg and stir in the sherry. You can make the sauce in the morning, and reheat it, but don't add the crab to the sauce until you reheat it to stuff the profiteroles.

To stuff the profiteroles, slice each one in half but don't separate them – slice them just enough so that you can slip a teaspoonful of filling inside. Reheat the profiteroles, and fill with the hot sauce before arranging them on a serving plate or tray.

Smoked salmon and dill cream cheese spread

This makes a change from the endless triangles of smoked salmon which turn up at drinks parties. It is also much more convenient to make, and tastes so much better. The smoked salmon is cut into shreds and mixed into the flavoured cream cheese, which is spread on bread (I like to use granary bread) then each slice is cut into triangles.

---

1 lb/500 g smoked salmon	*1 good handful of dill fronds*
1 lb/500 g cream cheese	*plenty of freshly ground*
juice of 1 lemon	*black pepper*
	1 loaf of granary or other
	good brown bread

Slice the smoked salmon in thin strips, then chop these by slicing them the other way. Put the cream cheese into a food processor and whiz till smooth. Then whiz in the lemon juice, adding it slowly, and the dill, and season with the black pepper. Turn this cream cheese mixture into a bowl, and mix in thoroughly the shredded smoked salmon. Spread this on the sliced bread, cut off the crusts, and cut each slice into triangles. You can do this the morning of the party, providing you cover the serving plates with clingfilm till just before your guests arrive.

Crudités with avocado dip

Serves 30

Everyone loves crudités at a party like this, and an avocado dip is appreciated by all. If you like, you could make the *Tomato béarnaise dip* (see page 329) instead of or as well as the avocado dip.

Serve the crudités in stacks on a large serving dish or a wide shallow tray lined with foil. A good selection would be strips of red peppers, yellow peppers, celery, carrots, and cauliflower, but if you use cauliflower, blanch the florets for 2–3 minutes then rinse them under running cold water; it just takes the bitterness out of raw cauliflower. Put the dip in a pretty bowl in the centre of the dish surrounded by the stacks of crudités.

---

8 oz/250 g cream cheese
3 avocado pears – 4, if they are the small, dark, knobbly type
juice of 1½ lemons

salt and lots of freshly ground black pepper
½ tsp Tabasco
2 tbsp snipped chives

Put the cream cheese into a food processor and whiz till smooth. Cut each avocado in half and flick out the stone. With a spoon, scoop out all the flesh, scraping each half down to the skin because that is where the darkest green colour is, right next to the skin. Whiz the avocado flesh in with the cream cheese, and gradually add the lemon juice. Season with salt, pepper and Tabasco, and stir in the snipped chives. Put the avocado mixture into a bowl, and cover with clingfilm. You can make this dip in the morning, but when you take off the clingfilm, stir the dip before serving.

Sesame toast fingers with a curried dip

Enough for about 70 sesame toast fingers

My sister Livi Milburn gave me the idea for these toasts, and they are delicious served with soup or any first course. I think they also make a good and delicious carrier for a tasty dip, like this curried garlic mayonnaise.

FOR THE SESAME TOAST FINGERS

a loaf of firm-textured white
  bread, sliced thinly
softened butter for spreading

sesame seeds
salt
oil for greasing

FOR THE CURRIED DIP

1 whole egg plus 1 yolk
½ tsp salt
lots of freshly ground black
  pepper
1 tbsp honey (dip the spoon
  in hot water first)

1 large garlic clove, skinned
  and chopped
2 rounded tsp medium curry
  powder
½ pt/300 ml sunflower oil
3–4 tbsp wine vinegar

Butter the sliced white bread for the toast thinly on each side. Cut off the crusts and cut the slices neatly into strips about ½ in/1 cm wide and just under 1 in/2 cm long. Mix together sesame seeds with a small amount of salt, and press both sides of each buttered bread finger in the sesame seeds. Put the sesame fingers on a very lightly greased baking tray and bake them in a moderate oven – 350°F/180°C/Gas 4/bottom right oven in a 4-door Aga – for 10–15 minutes, till they are golden on one side, then carefully turn them over and cook for the same amount of time on the other side. Let them cool, and store them in an airtight container – they can be made 2–3 days ahead.

To make the dip, first put the whole egg, the egg yolk, salt, pepper, honey, garlic and curry powder into a food processor or liquidizer and whiz till all is well mixed. Whizzing continuously, add the oil, drop by drop at first, then in a thin trickle. Add the wine vinegar – taste after 3 tablespoons, and add more if you like a sharper taste. If you feel the mayonnaise is too thick, whiz in some near-boiling water, which will make it a creamier consistency.

Store in a covered bowl in the fridge. You can make this dip 3–4 days in advance.

A Fortieth Birthday Celebration

Following the twenty-first, the fortieth is the next real milestone – thirty is fun and of course well worth a party (so is every other birthday) but the fortieth is somehow momentous. Last November Godfrey was forty, and we had a houseful of great friends to stay, and others joined us for dinner on his actual birthday. We were about thirty for dinner that night, and as one or two of our friends are octogenarians I wanted to seat our guests. We had five tables, each with a seating plan, and every male guest moved to a different table for each course, which seemed to work very well. The suggested fortieth birthday menu I give here is what we had that night, 28 November 1987, here at Kinloch.

FORTIETH BIRTHDAY
CELEBRATION FOR TEN

Smoked salmon terrine with red pepper sauce
Roast fillet of beef with mushroom and madeira sauce
Purée of parsnips with toasted cashews
Steamed brussels sprouts
Lemon mousse with raspberry sauce
Dark chocolate truffle cake

Smoked salmon terrine with red pepper sauce

Serves 10

FOR THE TERRINE

about 6 oz/175 g smoked
  salmon slices
1¼ lb/600 g smoked salmon
  (pieces will do)
½ pt/300 ml single cream
¼ pt/150 ml cold water
2 sachets powdered gelatine
  (approximately 1 oz/
  25 g)

¼ pt/150 ml boiling water
juice of 1 lemon
freshly ground black pepper
½ pt/300 ml double cream,
  whipped
1 large egg white

FOR THE RED PEPPER SAUCE

3 red peppers, halved
  lengthways and deseeded
2 large garlic cloves
½ pt/300 ml oil (I use
  sunflower as I think olive
  oil would have too strong
  a flavour here)

salt and freshly ground
  black pepper
juice of ½ lemon, more if
  you wish

Trim the smoked salmon slices and use them to line a
10 in/25 cm long loaf tin or terrine as neatly as you can.

Put the smoked salmon pieces into a food processor
and whiz, pouring in the single cream as you do so. Whiz
till smooth.

245

Pour the cold water into a bowl, sprinkle over the gelatine, then pour on the boiling water and stir until the gelatine has dissolved. Mix the lemon juice into the dissolved gelatine, and when it is cool pour this into the processor, whizzing as you do so. Season with pepper to taste. Turn this smoked salmon mixture into a bowl and fold in the whipped cream. Whisk the egg white till very stiff then, with a metal spoon, fold it quickly and thoroughly through the smoked salmon mixture. Pour this into the smoked salmon-lined tin, cover with clingfilm and put in the fridge for several hours.

To turn out the terrine, run a knife down the sides, and invert it onto a board and slice. Serve with a good spoonful of the red pepper sauce.

To make the sauce, first put the halved peppers under a grill till the skin chars and curls up. Then put them into a polythene bag, tie it tightly and leave for 20 minutes; you will find the skin peels off easily. Put the skinned peppers into a food processor. Meanwhile, simmer the unpeeled cloves of garlic in water for 2–3 minutes. Take them off the heat and rinse under cold water. Snip off the end of each clove and squeeze – the contents will pop out of their skins. Put them into the food processor with the peppers and whiz together till you have a smooth purée then, still whizzing, very slowly add the oil, drip by drip at first then in a very steady trickle, till it is all used up. Season with salt and pepper and whiz in the lemon juice, taste, and adjust the seasonings. Serve a spoonful of sauce at the side of each slice of terrine.

Roast fillet of beef with mushroom and Madeira sauce

Serves 10

2 fillets of beef, each
  weighing about 3 lb/
  1.5 kg – 3 if they are
  smaller

good beef dripping (see
  below)
freshly ground black pepper

FOR THE SAUCE

1 pt/600 ml Madeira
2 onions, skinned and
  chopped very finely
1 tbsp beef dripping
1 lb/500 g mushrooms,
  wiped, destalked, and
  sliced thinly

1–1½ oz/25–40 g flour
1 pt/600 ml good beef stock
  – or, as a short cut, use
  good (Crosse and
  Blackwell) beef
  consommé
salt and freshly ground
  black pepper

Trim the beef fillets of obvious gristle, but leave as much fat in place as you can. Trim off the thinner end, and keep it for a beef stroganoff to have a night or two after the party, to cheer yourselves up. Melt a spoonful or two of good beef dripping (with this party in mind, it is worth having roast beef several days previously if only to get good beef dripping, for which there is no substitute) in the bottom of a roasting tin. Put the trimmed fillets into the hot fat and grind black pepper generously over the meat. Baste well, and roast in a hot oven – 425°F/220°C/ Gas 7/top right oven in a 4-door Aga – for 10–15 minutes

247

to the pound/½ kilo, depending on how rare you like your meat. During the cooking, baste the meat two or three times with the dripping in the roasting tin. When the cooking time is up, take the meat out of the oven, cover loosely with foil and let it stand for 5–10 minutes before carving. Meanwhile, make the sauce.

Put the Madeira and finely chopped onions in a saucepan and, over a moderate heat, simmer the Madeira till it has reduced down to approximately ¼ pt/ 150 ml of syrupy liquid; the onions will be soft and well cooked. In another saucepan, melt the dripping, and add the thinly sliced mushrooms. Cook over a high heat for several minutes, stirring occasionally, so that the mushrooms really brown. Then stir in the flour and cook for a further couple of minutes before pouring in the beef stock, stirring till the sauce boils. Stir in the Madeira and onion mixture, season to taste with salt and pepper and serve with the sliced roast beef fillet.

Purée of parsnips with toasted cashews

Serves 10

This is one of Godfrey's favourite vegetable dishes, and it goes so well with the fillet of beef. The toasted, slightly salted cashew nuts add a good contrasting crunch. The pale colour of the parsnip purée looks well against the dark rich Madeira sauce, the rare sliced beef, and the bright fresh green of the steamed brussels sprouts.

10 good-sized parsnips – a
few more if they are small
3 oz/75 g butter, cut in
pieces
salt and freshly ground
black pepper

freshly grated nutmeg
2 oz/50 g cashew nuts
1 tsp salt

Peel the parsnips, trim them, and slice quite thickly.
Cook them in boiling salted water till they are tender –
test by sticking a knife into a fat piece to see if it is
cooked. Drain very well, and steam over heat to remove
excess moisture. Put the cooked parsnips into a food
processor and whiz, adding the butter. Season with salt
and freshly ground black pepper, and a couple of gratings
of nutmeg.

Butter a vegetable dish and put the purée into it.
Cover, and keep warm in a cool oven till you are ready to
serve. Dry-fry the cashew nuts in a saucepan with a
teaspoon of salt, shaking the pan till the nuts are fairly
evenly golden brown. Sprinkle a few over each helping of
purée, or sprinkle all the toasted nuts over the dish of
parsnip purée if you intend to hand round the vegetables.
But don't sprinkle the nuts over the parsnip mixture till
just before you serve it, otherwise they soften in the
purée.

Steamed brussels sprouts

Allow 5–6 sprouts per person

Steaming brussels sprouts over water gives a much better
flavour than boiling in water. Steam till the sprouts are
just tender when stuck with a fork.

Lemon mousse with raspberry sauce

Serves 10

Lemon and raspberries seem made for each other, so well do their flavours complement each other. A really good lemon mousse tasting strongly of lemon is still the favourite way to end a dinner for many people. This mousse can be made a day or two in advance and kept, covered, in the fridge – but do remember to take it out of the fridge when your guests sit down to dinner, then it will be at room temperature by the time it is ready to be served. Serve the raspberry sauce in a bowl to go with the mousse.

FOR THE MOUSSE

8 large eggs, separated
8 oz/250 g caster sugar
finely grated rind of
    4 lemons, and the juice
    of 3

1½ sachets powdered
    gelatine (approximately
    ¾ oz/20 g)
¾ pt/450 ml double cream,
    whipped

FOR THE SAUCE

1½ lb/750 g raspberries

4 oz/100 g icing sugar –
    more if you like a less
    sharp sauce

Whisk the egg yolks, gradually adding the caster sugar and whisking till the mixture is very thick and pale in colour. Put the finely grated lemon rind and juice into a saucepan and sprinkle over it the gelatine. Over a gentle heat, dissolve the gelatine granules completely in the

Oatmeal biscuits

6 ozs Wholewheat flour
2 ozs Medium oatmeal
4 ozs Butter or marg
4 to 1/2 tsp soft brown sugar
1 — 1 tsp baking powder
1/2 tsp salt
A little cinnamon powder
A about 1 tablesp milk for binding

Pre-heat oven to 350 Watts, 350°F, 180°C

Combine all ingredients except milk
well in fat, and add milk to give you
a stiff glossy batter dough then you
gum into floured surface and roll
out to 1/2 inch thick. Use a 2 3/4 inch
cutter. Add drop of milk if dough dries
Bake 15 — 20 mins until firm and
lightly brown. Leave to cool on biscuits about 5 min
cool on wire rack.

lemon juice, then heat it to just before boiling point and, still whisking, pour it steadily but slowly onto the yolks. Whisk well, and when cold, fold the whipped cream into the lemon mixture. When the mixture is thick enough to coat the back of a metal spoon thickly, whisk the egg whites until very stiff and, with a metal spoon, fold them quickly and thoroughly into the creamy lemon mixture. Pour this into a glass or china serving dish, cover, and put the bowl in the fridge.

To make the sauce, liquidize together the raspberries and icing sugar, then sieve the purée, which is the only way to get rid of the woody pips. Serve in a bowl, to accompany the lemon mousse.

Dark chocolate truffle cake

Serves 10–12

This recipe is John Tovey's. Being the generous and kind friend that he is, he didn't – appear to! – hesitate when I asked him for his permission to use this recipe in this book. It is quite simply the best recipe for the most satisfying, densely chocolatey truffle-textured pudding I have ever come across, and I am a complete chocolate addict. As with all chocolate recipes, it is vital to use the best chocolate you can lay your hands on, don't for a moment consider using stuff like Cakebrand or Scotchoc chocolate flavouring (which isn't even chocolate) in any cooking; in a rich pudding like this it would be a total waste of all your other ingredients. John calls this pudding Chocolate Orange Gâteau, but when we put it on the menu for our guests here at Kinloch we call it

Dark chocolate truffle cake, because I think that more accurately describes the texture of the pudding. It is, needless to say, one of Godfrey's most favourite of all the puddings we make.

---

3 fl oz/85 ml liquid glucose
juice and finely grated rind
   of 1 orange
2½ fl oz/70 ml water
3 oz/75 g caster sugar

1 lb/500 g good dark
   chocolate, broken into
   pieces
8 tbsp orange curaçao
¾ pt/450 ml double cream
1 egg white
sieved cocoa powder to finish

Lightly oil a loose-bottomed, springform cake tin about 10 in/25 cm in diameter. Line the base with bakewell paper (siliconized greaseproof paper).

Heat the glucose, orange juice and rind, water and caster sugar together gently, to melt the sugar. When the sugar has melted, bring the liquid to the boil. Melt the broken-up chocolate in the orange curaçao in a bowl over a pan of barely simmering water – take care not to let the water touch the bottom of the bowl. Mix the glucose mixture into the melted chocolate and leave to cool for 10 minutes or so.

Whip the double cream till it forms soft peaks and fold this into the chocolate mixture. Whisk the egg white till it is very stiff and, with a metal spoon, fold this quickly and thoroughly into the creamy chocolate mixture. Put this into the prepared loose-bottomed springform tin. Leave in a cool place for several hours. Turn onto a serving plate, peel off the disc of paper from the (now) top of the cake, and dust with sieved cocoa powder (*not* drinking chocolate!). I personally think it needs no further embellishment, but for Godfrey we stuck a candle in the middle – a large one, rather than forty smaller ones.

A Seventieth Birthday Celebration

Any birthday is a special occasion, but the older one gets the more special they become! As I get older, I feel middle age starts later and later – now I'm forty, I feel that middle age starts round about the age of seventy . . .

Here is my suggested menu for a seventieth birthday dinner for ten.

SEVENTIETH BIRTHDAY CELEBRATION FOR TEN

Goat's cheese-stuffed crêpes with leek purée
Crab cakes with tartare sauce
Sautéed spaghetti courgettes
Steamed new potatoes with applemint
Layered chocolate and coffee bavarois
Vanilla sponge birthday cake with white icing

Goat's cheese-stuffed crêpes with leek purée

Serves 10

These parsley-flavoured crêpes have a filling of goat's cheese, and a purée of leeks is served with them. I think the flavour of goat's cheese and leeks is a wonderful combination. You can leave the chopped tomatoes out of the goat's cheese filling if it is winter – tomatoes simply aren't worth their exorbitant cost when there is no flavour to them at that time of year.

FOR THE CRÊPES

4 large eggs
8 oz/250 g plain flour
1 oz/25 g butter, melted
¾ pt/450 ml milk and ¼ pt/
   150 ml water, mixed

2 tbsp chopped parsley
salt and freshly ground
   black pepper
a little extra butter, or oil,
   for greasing

FOR THE FILLING

1½ lb/750 g goat's cheese,
   weighed before trimming
2 large egg whites

freshly ground black pepper
4 tomatoes, skinned,
   deseeded and chopped
   quite small

FOR THE LEEK PURÉE

8 medium-sized leeks,
   washed, trimmed and
   sliced
salt and freshly ground
   black pepper

freshly grated nutmeg
2 oz/50 g butter

Put the eggs into a food processor or liquidizer and whiz, gradually adding the flour, melted butter, the milk and water, parsley, salt and pepper. Whiz till all is very well blended. Leave this batter, in a jug, for at least half an hour – you can make up the batter the previous day and keep it in the fridge overnight, but give it a good stir before you make up the crêpes. To do this, melt a small nut of butter in a pancake pan; when it is very hot, pour in a small amount of parsley batter, swirling the pan with your right hand while you pour with your left – as you pour, a thin film of batter covers the bottom of the pan. The aim is to make the pancakes, or crêpes, as thin as possible. Cook for a minute or two, then, using your fingers and a palette knife, turn over the crêpe and cook it for a minute on the other side. Slip it onto a plate, and make a second crêpe. Put a disc or rectangle of bakewell paper (siliconized greaseproof paper) between each crêpe as you make them, which prevents them from sticking together. If you make pancakes often, it is well worth while investing in a second pancake pan, which halves the making time of a batch of crêpes such as this. Cover the finished crêpes with clingfilm, and keep them in the fridge – they keep for several days – before stuffing them. You should allow 2–3 per person.

To make the filling, first derind the goat's cheese, then put it into a food processor and whiz, gradually adding the egg whites. Season with black pepper. Take the cheese mixture out of the processor, put it into a bowl, then fold in the chopped tomatoes. Put a spoonful – a heaped teaspoon, or two if they are small – in the middle of each crêpe. You can stuff them in the morning ready for dinner that night. Fold over one side, then the next, clockwise till you have folded all the sides over to form a fat rectangular parcel. Butter an ovenproof dish and lay the stuffed crêpes in it. Brush the crêpes with melted butter or sunflower oil. Heat the crêpes in a moderate oven – 350°F/180°C/Gas 4/bottom right oven in a 4-door

256

Aga – for 25 minutes – they will puff up slightly. Serve them hot, accompanied by the following leek purée:

Steam the sliced leeks, and when tender liquidize or process them with the seasonings and the butter. If the blades in your liquidizer or food processor are blunt, you may need to sieve the purée to get rid of the fibres. Put the hot purée into a buttered serving dish, and keep it warm in a low oven until you are ready to dish up the first course.

Crab cakes with tartare sauce

Serves 10

This makes a most luxurious main course for a special occasion. My recipe for crab cakes was given to me by Ellice McDonald, a great friend of ours from Delaware, USA, but I have juggled about a bit with the ingredients. You can make up the crab cakes in the morning, for dinner that evening, putting them on a baking tray lined with bakewell paper (siliconized greaseproof paper) and covering them with clingfilm. The *Tartare sauce* (see below) served with them is a treat in itself – so few people bother to make it and it is such a delicious and convenient sauce, because you can make it a day or two in advance and keep it in the fridge.

2 lb/1 kg crab meat – I like
   to use a mixture of white
   and brown, but pick out
   any bits of shell
4 oz/100 g breadcrumbs –
   white or brown – plus
   another 4 oz/100 g set
   aside on a plate

4 rounded tbsp mayonnaise
1 tbsp made-up English
   mustard
1 tbsp Worcestershire sauce
2 eggs, well beaten, for
   coating
butter and sunflower oil for
   cooking

In a bowl mix together well the crabmeat, the first
4 oz/100 g breadcrumbs, mayonnaise, mustard and
Worcestershire sauce. Mix very well. Form into small
cakes (they are very filling) about 2 in/5 cm diameter.
Dip both sides of each into the beaten egg, then in the
breadcrumbs, and put them onto a bakewell paper-lined
baking tray. Fry in a mixture of butter and sunflower oil
till golden brown and crispy on each side. When cooked,
put the crab cakes on a serving dish lined with several
thicknesses of kitchen paper.

Tartare sauce

Serves 10

FOR THE FLAVOURED VINEGAR

½ pt/300 ml wine vinegar
½ onion, skinned
a bay leaf

a few black peppercorns
a small bunch of parsley

FOR THE TARTARE SAUCE

1 large whole egg, plus
  1 large yolk
½ tsp salt
1 rounded tsp mustard
  powder
1 rounded tsp caster sugar
1 garlic clove, skinned and
  chopped
freshly ground black pepper
½ pt/300 ml sunflower oil

the reserved flavoured wine
  vinegar
3–4 tbsp very hot water
2 hardboiled eggs, chopped
1 tbsp chopped black olives
2 tsp chopped capers
1 heaped tbsp chopped
  parsley
4 in/10 cm piece of
  cucumber, peeled,
  deseeded and diced

Put the wine vinegar, half onion, bay leaf, black peppercorns and parsley into a small saucepan. Simmer over moderate heat till reduced by more than half, then take off the heat, strain, and reserve this flavoured vinegar.

To make the mayonnaise, whiz together the egg, yolk, salt, mustard, sugar, chopped garlic and pepper in a food processor or liquidizer and very gradually add the oil – literally drop by drop to begin with, then in a steady but very thin trickle. Whiz in the flavoured wine vinegar, then the very hot water. Pour the mayonnaise into a bowl, and stir in the remaining ingredients. Cover the bowl with clingfilm till you are ready to serve it, with the *Crab cakes* (see above), fish or deep-fried shellfish.

Sautéed spaghetti courgettes

Serves 10

---

2 lb/1 kg small courgettes, washed, dried and trimmed	*salt and freshly ground black pepper*
olive oil for sautéeing	*very finely chopped garlic (optional)*

These courgettes can be sliced into very thin spaghetti strips with a mandolin or vegetable peeler on the morning of the dinner party, and they take literally only a minute to cook in a few spoonfuls of hot olive oil, seasoned with salt and freshly ground black pepper. If you wish, and you know that all your guests are garlic lovers, add some very finely chopped garlic to the oil, too.

Layered chocolate and coffee bavarois

Serves 10

This smooth, creamy pudding is set in a 9 × 5 × 3 in/

23 × 12.5 × 7.5 cm deep terrine or loaf tin, turned out and served in slices, with the *Caramel sauce* (see page 152). The coffee and chocolate creams taste so good together, enhanced by the caramel. For a birthday cake, I suggest a simple white-iced vanilla sponge cake (see recipe on page 262).

---

2 pt/1.2 L single cream
1 tbsp instant coffee
  granules
3 oz/75 g very good dark
  chocolate
8 large egg yolks
2 rounded tsp cornflour,
  sieved

6 oz/175 g caster sugar
2 sachets powdered gelatine
  (approximately 1 oz/
  25 g)
3 tbsp coffee liqueur, such as
  Tia Maria or Kahlua

Take two saucepans, and heat 1 pint/600 millilitres of cream in each. Sprinkle the coffee granules into one saucepan, and break the chocolate into the other.

Take two bowls and put in each 4 egg yolks, a rounded teaspoon of sieved cornflour and 3 oz/75 g of caster sugar. Pour a little of the hot cream from each pan into each bowl and mix very well. Pour the contents of each bowl back into its relevant saucepan and, over a gentle-to-moderate heat, stir each till the custard thickens enough to coat the back of the wooden spoon. Take the pans off the heat.

Take two small bowls. Measure 3 tablespoons of cold water into one, and sprinkle over a sachet (½ oz/15 g) of gelatine. Stir this into the chocolate custard. Into the other small bowl measure 3 tablespoons of coffee liqueur and sprinkle over a sachet (½ oz/15 g) gelatine. Let this sponge up, and stir it into the coffee custard, then stir both custards till the gelatine has dissolved in the heat of each. Let the custards cool, stirring from time to time to prevent a skin forming. When they are cold, pour half the chocolate custard through a sieve into the terrine or loaf tin. Leave in a cool place to set, then pour half the coffee custard through a sieve on top of the set chocolate layer. Let the coffee custard set in the terrine, repeat with the remaining chocolate custard (reheat it first very gently if it has set too much in the saucepan). Let this layer set in the terrine or loaf tin, then sieve the rest of the coffee custard on top of the second layer of chocolate. Leave for several hours in the fridge, or overnight.

Dip the tin in a bowl of warm (not hot) water for several seconds, to loosen it, then turn it out onto a serving dish or plate. Decorate, if you like, with piped rosettes of whipped cream round the base. Slice to serve.

Vanilla sponge birthday cake

This simple sponge cake can be made ahead and frozen, then thawed and simply iced on the day of the party, or it can be made and eaten on the same day – it is much the nicest when eaten fresh, whether frozen and thawed, or just made, rather than after sitting for a day or two.

---

3 large eggs	*3 oz/75 g self-raising flour,*
3 oz/75 g caster sugar	*sieved twice*
½ tsp vanilla essence	*white icing (see below)*

Line an 8 in/20 cm cake tin with a disc of bakewell paper (siliconized greaseproof paper), butter the sides of the tin and dust them with caster sugar.

Whisk the eggs, gradually adding the caster sugar, and whisk till the mixture is thick enough that you can trace a squiggle and the squiggle remains on the surface; this whisking takes time, about 10 minutes with a handheld electric beater. Beat in the vanilla essence and, with a large metal spoon, fold in the twice-sieved self-raising flour, folding thoroughly so that no pockets of flour remain. Pour this cake mixture into the prepared tin, and bake in a moderate oven – 350°F/180°C/Gas 4/bottom right oven in a 4-door Aga – for 25 minutes – the cake will be just coming away from the sides of the tin when cooked. Take it out of the oven, cool in the tin for a couple of minutes, then turn it out onto a wire cooling rack to cool completely.

Ice the cake with sieved icing sugar mixed with boiling water. If you like, you could pipe 'Happy Birthday' in chocolate on the cake. This cake is delicious eaten with the *Layered chocolate and coffee bavarois* (see page 260).

Christmas

I start anticipating Christmas round about the end of June. It is my most favourite time of the whole year, and one of the advantages of our house is that when it isn't being a hotel it has plenty of room to have lots of people to stay, and it really comes into its own at Christmas and New Year. I love having family and friends to stay, but after nineteen married Christmases I have learned over the years that the only way to be able to enjoy it as much as – hopefully! – the family and friends staying, is to Be Prepared. I've got Christmas and New Year preparation down to a fine art – this isn't meant to sound immodest, it's the truth! When I hear people moaning about how much work is involved in this great holiday I feel so cross, because much of it is geared to food and, with planning, a great deal can be done in advance. One of the pitfalls of this time of year is that people plan too-elaborate meals. The food we eat traditionally around Christmas time is rich and filling, and there are inevitably quite a few edible gifts of chocolate, crystallized fruits, etc., so I like to try and keep my menus simple. The other thing is to plan food which can be made ahead and preferably frozen. In this chapter I suggest menus and dishes which can be cooked ahead, and in some cases frozen.

As a family we have always had dinner on Christmas Day. I feel that the atmosphere of curtains drawn, candles lit would be sorely missed were we to eat lunch. In our family it has always been a tradition to have

Christmas dinner rather early, around 7.30, for the benefit of the younger children. This great family dinner must have originated in my grandparents' day, because both my maternal grandparents had their birthdays on Christmas Day, which made it even more of a special occasion. As far as the very young children are concerned, food doesn't mean much to them anyway, and by evening they are exhausted, what with the excitement of the inevitable early start to the day, opening their stockings and their presents, that they have always been more than happy to have just sausages and beans and go to bed. For the older children, it is of course a great thing to be deemed old enough to stay up for dinner on Christmas Night, having had their compulsory rest in bed during the afternoon.

Christmas dinner – for us, always turkey, fresh and free range – is punctuated between courses by various children singing carols or giving a short recital on a musical instrument. After dinner there are the inevitable charades, which is where the mixed generations present really come into their own, divided into teams. Christmas dinner, I reckon, is one of the easiest meals of the year, because I make and freeze both the turkey stuffings, the bread sauce, and the lime (or lemon) mousse, which is the alternative pudding for Christmas pud haters. The giblet stock for the gravy is made two days ahead, strained and stored in the fridge. The Christmas pudding and brandy butter are made in advance anyway, the pud only needing to steam for a couple of hours, but I do make a vanilla-flavoured sauce for my mother and me, neither of us particularly liking brandy butter. I peel the spuds and pick over the sprouts a day or two in advance, and I stuff and wrap the turkey on Christmas Eve, ready to be popped into the oven. It really is the easiest of meals, bar actually lifting the great bird out of the oven – we always have a large turkey because I do so love it cold for supper on Boxing Night.

In this chapter I give two possible other main courses for Christmas dinner – *Roast goose with apple, date and lemon stuffing*, or *Roast pheasant with mushroom stuffing* – the latter is particularly good when there are just a few people celebrating Christmas together. Around Christmas, I try not to serve chicken, or anything at all similar to turkey, just to avoid a sameness. I always wish there was another week between Christmas and New Year. Their very closeness, only a week apart, means that you have to plan for both festivities in one – and in planning, to remember the mundane but vital things of life like loo paper, milk, etc. The shops are closed for so long – depending, I suppose, on just where you live in Britain – that it is wise to check up on your store of light bulbs etc. then you can forget about them. Equally as important as a list of what you plan to eat and when, is another list, of what to take out of the freezer and when. I keep the two lists side by side, stuck on my fridge door. I love Christmas shopping, and try to buy, wrap, and send my presents early. There is so much work involved in this it could well be a full-time December occupation if left till then.

Dark Christmas cake

Makes 1 cake about 10 in/25 cm in diameter

Everyone has their own Christmas cake recipe, this is mine. I make several cakes each year – three large ones for the house, and the rest are presents for friends. If you don't like, say, the ginger in the recipe just leave it out but add another couple of ounces of raisins or sultanas. The same applies to the glacé cherries – in fact any fruit you don't like, but do be sure to make up the weight with other fruit ingredients. It is well worth the small amount

266

of trouble involved in toasting the flaked almonds, they add a wonderful flavour to the cake. Make the cake as soon as you like, and keep it on a shelf in a cool place, ideally a larder, until you are ready to marzipan and ice it.

Finally, a word on the finishing off of a Christmas cake; I have never found any cookbook (and I have searched on many an occasion) which tells you how early one can marzipan a Christmas cake. I realized that you see Christmas cakes for sale in shops long before Christmas, so I have deduced over the years that it is *not* a job one has to leave till the last week or two before Christmas, as I had previously thought. I now try to make my cakes by the end of September, and I marzipan them early in December, keeping them wrapped up to prevent the marzipan from drying out. I ice them about ten days before Christmas.

---

10 oz/275 g softened butter
10 oz/275 g soft dark brown sugar, or muscovado
1 lb/500 g sultanas
1 lb/500 g raisins
6 oz/175 g chopped candied peel
4 oz/100 g chopped glacé cherries
2 oz/50 g preserved ginger, chopped
12 oz/350 g currants
3 oz/75 g dried apricots, snipped

6 oz/175 g flaked almonds, toasted till golden brown
10 oz/275 g plain flour, sieved
1 rounded tsp mixed spice
½ tsp freshly grated nutmeg
2 rounded tsp powdered cinnamon
6 large eggs, beaten
grated rind of 2 oranges and 2 lemons
¼ pt/150 ml brandy, whisky or rum

Butter a 10 in/25 cm cake tin and line it with bakewell paper (siliconized greaseproof paper).

Beat together the butter and sugar till the mixture is

267

very well mixed and fluffy. In a large bowl (or saucepan) mix together all the dried fruits and the toasted flaked almonds. Sieve in about half of the flour and spices and mix in well, using your hands.

Beat the eggs into the butter and sugar mixture, alternating with the remaining flour and spices. Beat in the grated orange and lemon rinds. Mix in the flour-coated fruits and nuts, mixing really well, and lastly mix in the alcohol. Pour into the prepared cake tin, smoothing it even, and then hollow out the middle with the back of a wooden spoon. Bake for 30 minutes in a moderate oven – 350°F/180°C/Gas 4/bottom right oven in a 4-door Aga – then lower the temperature to 275°F/140°C/Gas 1/ top left oven in a 4-door Aga – and then bake for a further 2½ hours. The cake is cooked when it is just beginning to come away from the sides of the tin. Another way to test for doneness is to stick a skewer or knife into the middle of the cake – if any cake mixture sticks to it, give it a bit more cooking time. Take the cake out of the oven and cool it in its tin. When cold but still in its tin, stick a skewer right down through the cake in as many places as you can, evenly all over. Pour brandy, whisky or rum over the cake, leave for a few minutes, then tip it out of the tin and wrap it up well in foil and store it in a cool place until you are ready to marzipan and ice it.

Marzipan

Enough to cover a 10 in/25 cm cake

It really is worthwhile making your own marzipan; I am always one for taking the easy way out of anything if I can, but one year I experimented by buying three different brands of ready-made marzipan, and each was so truly disgusting that I threw them away and made my own. Marzipan (or almond paste) is so easy to make, the only thing to remember is that if you like it as much as I do make a bit more to allow for eating some as you go along.

1¼ lb/600 g ground
   almonds, sieved
10 oz/275 g caster sugar
10 oz/275 g icing sugar,
   sieved
4 tsp lemon juice

2 tbsp orange flower water
   or sherry (or more lemon
   juice)
4 large egg yolks

Mix all the above ingredients together well. Put the cake upside down on a cake board or serving plate – this gives you a good clear top and edge. Put half the marzipan on top of the cake and, with the palms of your hands, pat and smooth the paste over the top of the cake. When the surface is covered, roll it smooth and even with a rolling pin. Take the rest of the paste and work it round the sides of the cake, again using the heel of the palm of your hand. Hold the rolling pin upright and roll it round to get a smooth and even surface. Cover the cake and leave for a week before icing.

You will notice that I use no apricot jam or egg white to brush the cake before marzipanning – I've never done so, and see no need to.

Royal icing

Enough for 1 10 in/25 cm cake

This recipe makes enough icing for a 10 in/25 cm cake. You can make more and do some piped cake decoration if you like, but I usually rough up my Christmas cake icing, optimistically thinking it looks like snow! I then stick holly leaves on top. I have a horror of elaborately decorated Christmas cakes, always remembering a great friend of mine who, several years ago, was giving a demonstration on Christmas cake decorating to our local WRI. She was a bit thrown by the inevitable silence as she painstakingly and beautifully iced lovely decorations onto cakes. Her grand finale was a glistening white cake onto which she was piping in brilliant red HAPPY CHRISTMAS. She got to the end with a huge sigh of relief when a critical voice piped up from the audience, 'You've missed the R out of Christmas', and my friend Jo took a large palette knife and, with a flourish, swept all the red piping off the white surface, leaving a brilliant red sweep across the cake. If it had been me, I would have thrown the cake at the woman who drew attention to what I'm sure wouldn't have been noticed by anyone else!

1½ lb/750 g icing sugar,
  sieved
4 large egg whites, beaten to
  a froth

2 tsp glycerine
1 tbsp lemon juice

Mix the sieved icing sugar into the beaten egg whites, along with the glycerine and lemon juice. Beat it all really well, then cover the bowl with a damp teatowel and leave the icing for an hour or two.

Light Christmas cake

Makes 1 10 in/25 cm cake

This cake is a change from the traditional dark fruit cake which is the more usual Christmas fare. It is a rich cake, and I like to decorate it with glacé fruit arranged over the surface rather than with marzipan and icing.

---

12 oz/350 g softened butter
12 oz/350 g soft light brown sugar
2 oz/50 g preserved ginger, chopped
8 oz/250 g crystallized pineapple, rinsed, dried and chopped
4 oz/100 g crystallized apricots, rinsed, dried and chopped
4 oz/100 g crystallized orange and lemon peel, rinsed, dried and chopped

4 oz/100 g crystallized (glacé) cherries, rinsed, dried and chopped
8 oz/250 g plain flour, sieved
2 oz/50 g ground almonds
2 oz/50 g flaked almonds, toasted till golden
8 large egg yolks
4 tbsp brandy
4 egg whites, whisked till stiff

Butter and line a cake tin about 10 in/25 cm in diameter with bakewell paper (siliconized greaseproof paper).

Beat together the butter and sugar very well, till soft and fluffy. Mix together the chopped fruits, and mix into them the sieved flour, and the ground and flaked almonds. Beat the egg yolks into the butter and sugar mixture, one at a time. Then mix in the flour-coated fruit and nuts, mix in the brandy, and lastly, using a large metal spoon, fold in the stiffly beaten whites. Pour into the prepared tin and bake in a cool oven – 325°F/150°C/Gas 3/bottom of the bottom right oven in a 4-door Aga –

for 1½–2 hours. Stick a knife in to test for doneness. Cool in the tin.

Mincemeat

Makes about 6 lb/2.75 kg

Mincemeat takes so little time to make – really, all the time is spent assembling the ingredients, putting them together takes seconds. The flavour of homemade mincemeat is much superior to commercial mincemeat, well worth the minimal effort of making it. Over the years I have experimented with ingredients; for a while I made mincemeat without suet, but this is really rather dry so I now add a small amount. We have a large tub – more of a bucket really, with a well-fitting lid – and this is the container we use for mincemeat. From time to time I take the lid off and give a good stir, and I find the smell of deliciously boozy mincemeat most invigorating!

Make this at least three weeks in advance, but it is better made two or three months ahead.

---

12 oz/350 g raisins
12 oz/350 g sultanas
1 lb/500 g currants
6 oz/175 g chopped mixed peel
6 oz/175 g flaked almonds, toasted
2 lb/1 kg good eating apples (I use Cox's), cored and chopped, but not peeled
8 oz/250 g shredded suet

(I use Atora, but you can just as well use vegetarian suet)
2 tsp freshly grated nutmeg
1 tsp ground allspice
1 rounded tsp powdered cinnamon
grated rind and juice of 2 lemons and 2 oranges
¼ pt/150 ml brandy or whisky

Simply mix together all the ingredients. When well matured and stirred (see above) pot and seal in jars.

CHRISTMAS EVE DINNER
FOR EIGHT–TEN

*Chicken liver and pecan pâté with cranberry
Cumberland jelly
Scallops in saffron and white wine sauce
Basmati or brown rice
Cinnamon crêpes with Calvados butter and spiced
apple filling*

Christmas Eve Dinner

Chicken liver and pecan pâté
with cranberry Cumberland jelly

Serves 8

4 oz/100 g chopped pecan
    nuts
½ tsp salt
3 oz/75 g butter
1 small onion, skinned and
    chopped finely
2 lb/1 kg chicken livers,
    carefully picked over and
    any greenish bits removed

4 tbsp Madeira, or brandy
lots of freshly ground black
    pepper
¼ pt/150 ml double cream

Roast the pecan nuts by shaking them in a saucepan with the salt, over a moderate heat, for 5 minutes.

Melt the butter and add the finely chopped onion. Cook for about 5 minutes, stirring from time to time so that the onions don't burn. Then add the chicken livers, cook for a couple of minutes, then pour in the Madeira. (You can substitute brandy if you prefer, but the Madeira is, I think, much nicer.) Let the chicken livers and Madeira cook together for 2–3 minutes, then take the saucepan off the heat. Season with lots of freshly ground black pepper. Liquidize the mixture, adding the cream as you do so, then stir in the pecans. Pour into a serving dish. Cover with clingfilm when the pâté is quite cold, and store in the fridge for 3–4 days, or freeze. Serve with *Cranberry Cumberland jelly* (see below).

Cranberry Cumberland jelly

Makes about 1 lb/500 g jelly

This makes a perfect accompaniment to the *Chicken liver and pecan pâté* (see page 275). Any left over is delicious with the cold turkey on Boxing Night.

---

8 oz/250 g cranberries
1½ pt/1 L water
pared rind of 1 orange
8 oz/250 g redcurrant jelly
¼ pt/150 ml port

1 rounded tsp mustard
  powder
grated rind and juice of
  1 orange
grated rind and juice of
  1 lemon
2 tsp powdered gelatine

Put the cranberries into a saucepan with the water and the pared orange rind. Simmer for 10 minutes, till the cranberries burst. Then drain them.

Put the redcurrant jelly into a saucepan. Slake the mustard with a little of the port and put that into the pan with the jelly. Add the grated rinds and juice of the orange and lemon, and sprinkle over the gelatine. Over moderate heat, melt the jelly and mix together with the other ingredients. Stir in the cooked cranberries. Pour into warmed pots. Stir as it sets, to prevent the cranberries from sinking to the bottom.

Scallops in saffron and white wine sauce

Serves 8

This makes a delicious, fragrant main course. I allow 4 average-sized scallops per person.

---

32 scallops, with the tube at   2 oz/50 g butter
   the end of the coral
   trimmed away

FOR THE SAUCE

3 oz/75 g butter   ½ pt/300 ml dry white wine
1 onion, skinned and   1 pt/600 ml fish or vegetable
   chopped finely   stock
2 oz/50 g flour   salt and freshly ground
1 packet of saffron (not the   black pepper
   powder, the strands)   about 1 tbsp lemon juice

Make the sauce first – and this can be done in the morning for dinner that evening, or the day before, and kept in the fridge. Whichever way, if you make it in advance, wring out a piece of greaseproof paper in water and cover the surface of the sauce with it.

Melt the butter for the sauce in a saucepan, and add the finely chopped onion; cook for 5 minutes or so, giving the onion an occasional stir. Then stir in the flour, and let it cook in the butter for a minute, before stirring in the white wine and stock. Stir till the sauce boils, then take it off the heat, and season to taste with salt, pepper and lemon juice. Stir in the saffron.

Shortly before dinner, melt the 2 oz/50 g butter in a frying pan and gently cook the scallops, for a minute –

half a minute on each side. Pour them and the butter in which they cooked into the sauce, and reheat the sauce. Try not to let the scallops sit in the hot sauce for too long before eating, as they tend to toughen and shrink.

I like to serve these scallops with basmati rice, but brown rice is also delicious with them.

Cinnamon crêpes with Calvados butter and spiced apple filling

Serves 8

This recipe may sound a fiddle to make, but it really isn't. It is also quite delicious, and most convenient because the whole dish freezes very well, only needing a couple of hours of thawing at room temperature before the crêpes are reheated for 20 minutes in a moderate oven, then flamed with Calvados to serve.

FOR THE CRÊPES

4 oz/100 g plain flour
1 tsp powdered ground
  cinnamon
1 oz/25 g caster sugar
1 oz/25 g butter, melted

2 large eggs
just over ½ pt/325 ml milk
  and water mixed (¾
  milk, ¼ water)

FOR THE CALVADOS BUTTER

4 oz/100 g softened butter
4 oz/100 g sieved icing sugar

4 tbsp Calvados

FOR THE SPICED APPLE FILLING

2 oz/50 g butter
8 apples – Cox's if possible,
  and never the so wrongly
  named Golden Delicious
1 tbsp lemon juice

1 tsp cinnamon
a grating of nutmeg
2 oz/50 g soft brown sugar

Mix together all the ingredients for the crêpe batter, beating really well, then leave the batter for an hour at least (you can make it up and leave it in the fridge overnight, but give it a good stir before using) then make it up into crêpes. Making crêpes is so much easier (and less boring!) a job to do if you have two crêpe pans and, if you make a lot of pancakes, it is well worth while investing in a second one. Make them as thin as you can (follow the directions given on pages 98–9 if you are not sure how to cook crêpes) and as they are made stack them on a plate, with a piece of bakewell paper (siliconized greaseproof paper) between each. This amount of batter makes 20 crêpes.

Next make the Calvados butter. Put the butter for this

d, with a handheld electric whisk, beat it
dually adding the sieved icing sugar. Beat
los, a spoonful at a time, beating really well.
the filling, first peel, core and chop the apples
iem in the lemon juice. Melt the butter in a
pai.   dd the chopped apples, the spices and the soft
brown sugar. Cook over a moderate heat for about 20
minutes, or until the apples are soft when pressed against
the sides of the pan with the back of your wooden spoon.

To assemble the dish, spread each crêpe with some
Calvados butter, put a rounded teaspoon of apple
mixture in the middle of each, and fold into a fat parcel.
Butter a shallow ovenproof dish, and arrange the stuffed
crêpes in it. Cover with clingfilm and freeze. Thaw at
room temperature for a couple of hours, then reheat for
20 minutes in a moderate oven – 350°F/180°C/Gas 4/
bottom right oven in a 4-door Aga. Sieve a spoonful of
icing sugar over the crêpes, and warm 4 tablespoons of
Calvados. Ignite it in the saucepan and pour the flaming
Calvados over the crêpes before serving them.

Christmas Day breakfast

Fresh orange juice, *Lemon and cinnamon fruit bread*, coffee
and tea are all you need to see you through from
Christmas dawn to Christmas dinner! This bread can be
made and frozen two or three weeks before Christmas,
and needs only to be taken out of the freezer before you
go to bed on Christmas Eve. I like to warm it to serve,
but the icing tends to dissolve into the bread – this really
doesn't matter though, because it tastes so good! All
European countries have a traditional yeast fruity bread
at Christmas time – stollen in Germany, pannetone in
Italy – and I thought we should follow their good
example!

Lemon and cinnamon fruit bread

Makes 2 bread circles

FOR THE FRUIT BREAD

2 tsp sugar
½ pt/300 ml hand-hot water
2 oz/50 g dried yeast
2 lb/1 kg wholewheat flour
4 rounded tsp powdered
  cinnamon
6 oz/175 g raisins

3 oz/75 g chopped mixed
  peel
3 oz/75 g caster sugar
grated rind of 2 lemons
¼ pt/150 ml warm water
2 oz/50 g butter, melted
2 large eggs, beaten

FOR THE ICING

juice of 1 lemon
4 heaped tbsp sieved icing
  sugar

1 rounded tsp powdered
  cinnamon

Sprinkle the teaspoon of sugar into the ½ pt/300 ml of hand-hot water. Stir in the dried yeast, and leave this yeast mixture in a warm place until it has frothed up and nearly trebled in size.

Mix together the flour, cinnamon, raisins, chopped mixed peel, caster sugar and lemon rind in a bowl and put this in a warm place. When the yeast has all frothed up, mix it into the flour etc., along with the warm water, the melted butter and the beaten eggs. Mix well, then turn onto a floured work surface and knead very well – I count to 200 – till the dough feels pliable. Divide the dough in two pieces, and knead each for a further count of 100, or about 2 minutes. Form each piece of dough into a circle on a greased baking tray, and leave in a warm place, covered with a teatowel, till the dough has doubled in size – 20–25 minutes if it is a draught-free really warm place, longer if not. Bake in a hot oven – 425°F/220°C/Gas 7/top right oven in a 4-door Aga – for 20–25 minutes, then take it out of the oven, cool on a wire rack in a warm place (if you cool it too quickly in a cold place the dough toughens, I find).

When the fruit bread is quite cold ice it with the lemon and cinnamon icing. To make this, warm the lemon juice and mix it into the icing sugar and cinnamon. Pour over the top of each ring, and let the icing trickle down the sides. When the icing has set, cover the circles with clingfilm and freeze. Thaw for a couple of hours at room temperature, or, much more convenient, thaw overnight.

Christmas Day lunch

Lunch on Christmas Day can be as simple as you like. We begin with a good soup, made two or three weeks in advance and frozen. We finish with cheese – Stilton, and a creamy one at that, and mince pies. If you feel you need a bit more lunch, you could accompany the soup with garlic bread, but cheese and mince pies (and I like them together) are very filling, and the forthcoming dinner is something of a gastronomic onslaught.

Jerusalem artichoke soup

Serves 8

2 oz/50 g butter
2 tbsp oil (I use sunflower)
2 medium onions, skinned
  and chopped
1½ lb/750 g Jerusalem
  artichokes, scraped and
  chopped

2 pts/1.2 L good chicken
  stock
salt and freshly ground
  black pepper
2 tbsp finely chopped parsley
  (optional)

Melt the butter and heat the oil together in a saucepan, and add the chopped onions. Cook over a moderate heat for about 5 minutes, stirring from time to time to prevent them from burning. Then add the chopped artichokes, cook for a further 5 minutes, and pour in the stock. Half-cover the pan with a lid, and simmer the soup gently for half an hour. Liquidize and sieve the soup. Season to taste with salt and pepper.

I like to stir a couple of tablespoons of finely chopped parsley through the soup just before serving – it lifts the otherwise rather anaemic colour which belies its exquisite taste.

A SELECTION OF CHRISTMAS DINNERS

Roast turkey
with pork sausagemeat and chestnut stuffing
and lemon and parsley stuffing
Bread sauce
Roast or grilled chipolatas
Brussels sprouts with bacon bits
Roast potatoes
Giblet gravy

OR

Roast goose with rice, apple
and date stuffing
Braised celery

Roast pheasant with
mushroom stuffing
Port and redcurrant gravy
Purée of celeriac

Mrs Hill's Christmas pudding
Orange-flavoured brandy butter
Vanilla sauce

OR

Lime mousse

Christmas Dinner

Now for the easiest dinner in the year – providing you get ahead with the preparations! I am going to give you a choice of three possible main courses – we never have a first course at this dinner, because the food traditionally eaten is so filling I consider a first course quite unnecessary. As a family we have always had roast turkey on Christmas Day, but then there are turkeys and turkeys! A frozen turkey is a sorry sight, with its pallid slimy skin – and it's an even sorrier taste, with its soggy flesh. A fresh turkey, and preferably a free-range bird (and they *can* be found), is quite different, with its dark, coarse skin and its flesh which tastes of turkey – I honestly think that thanks to people like Bernard Matthews a large number of people in Britain have forgotten what the true flavour of turkey is like.

Because there are usually quite a number of us round the table at dinner on Christmas night, I get as big a bird as I can fit into my oven – about 22 lb/10 kg. I stuff it at either end, one has *Pork sausagemeat and chestnut stuffing*, the other *Lemon and parsley stuffing*.

Pork sausagemeat and chestnut stuffing

Enough for a 15 lb/6.75 kg turkey

This stuffing is even better if you use fresh chestnuts. They are undeniably a fiddle to skin but do have a delicious flavour.

2 oz/50 g butter
2 medium-sized onions, skinned and chopped finely
3 lb/1.5 kg good pork sausages – I use Marks and Spencer's Lincoln sausages
½ tsp mixed dried herbs
freshly ground black pepper
2 × 15 oz/450 g tins of whole chestnuts – or 1½ lb/675 g fresh chestnuts, cooked and skinned

Melt the butter and add the chopped onions. Cook for 7–10 minutes, stirring occasionally, then take them off the heat and cool completely. With the tip of a sharp knife, slit each sausage skin lengthwise, and remove each skin – they come off easily. Put each skinned sausage into a mixing bowl, and add the cold cooked onions, the mixed herbs, black pepper and chestnuts. With your hands – and this is the *only* way to do the job thoroughly – mix all together well. Pack into a large polythene bag and label – very important, at this stage you will think you will instantly know the contents of the poly bag but believe me, like all things frozen, it will assume total anonymity in the freezer so it is vital to label it clearly. Freeze. Take out of the freezer the night before you want to stuff the turkey.

Lemon and parsley stuffing

Enough for a 15 lb/6.75 kg turkey

This stuffing has to be made with a baked loaf, rather than a steamed sliced one.

3 oz/75 g butter	12 oz/350 g suet
2 medium onions, skinned and chopped finely	grated rind of 3 lemons
1 garlic clove, skinned and chopped finely	2 rounded tbsp chopped parsley
1½ lb/750 g day-old loaf, crusts cut off, made into crumbs	salt and plenty of freshly ground black pepper

Melt the butter in a saucepan and add the chopped onions. Cook for 7–10 minutes, stirring occasionally, adding the chopped garlic halfway through. Take the pan off the heat, and let the cooked onions cool completely.

Mix the rest of the ingredients with the cold cooked onions and garlic. Pack into a polythene bag, label and freeze. This stuffing takes a surprisingly long time to thaw, so I would take it out of the freezer two evenings before you want to stuff the bird, and thaw slowly in the fridge.

Cooking the turkey

All books tell you that a turkey needs 20 minutes' cooking time per lb/½ kg. If you are cooking a bird weighing about 10 lb/4.5 kg that is quite right, but if you cook a 20 lb/9 kg turkey for 20 minutes per lb, it would be quite uncarveable, the meat would drop off the bones. When cooking a large bird it is inevitable that the breast will be slightly overdone if the thighs are to cook thoroughly, but this is how I cook my turkey.

I stuff it with the two stuffings – one at each end. I make a cross out of two long, thick pieces of foil and place them in my largest roasting tin (foil is now so thin you have to be very careful not to tear it). I rub butter all over the turkey, sprinkle it with salt and grind black pepper over it. Then I put the turkey, *breast side down*, into the foil and wrap it well – this is a tip I learned from John Tovey several years ago, and I have followed it ever since. The juices run down during the cooking, preventing the turkey breast from drying out as the bird cooks. It does nothing for the shape of the bird when cooked, but who is going to look at it anyway? It's going to be carved and eaten! I leave the wrapped turkey in a cool place (outside, if the larder is full, but be careful of any marauding wild animals). I roast it in a hot oven – 400°F/200°C/Gas 6/top right oven in a 4-door Aga – putting it into the oven at about 2.30 in the afternoon for dinner aimed at around 7.30 p.m. Between 6.30 and 6.45 I stick a sharp knife into the thigh of the bird and the juices should run clear – if they are tinged with pink the bird must go on cooking. As I cook in an Aga and an elderly one at that, I am never too sure of its exact temperature. When the bird is cooked – after 3–4 hours – I take it out of the oven (luckily I am very strong!) and leave it sitting on top, wrapped in its foil, for 45 minutes or so. It won't get cold, and the resting makes it much easier to carve.

Testing the turkey to see whether it is cooked provides the ideal opportunity to scoop some of the fat from inside the turkey – I use a small ladle to put it into a saucepan for the gravy.

I find that it helps to remove all the stuffings from each end into two warmed serving dishes before carving the bird. If you are carving for any number of people, this makes the serving easier and therefore quicker.

Bread sauce

Serves 10–12

This is bread sauce as we like it – if you prefer it without the flavouring of cloves, leave them out of the recipe. As with so many things, bread sauce is very much a matter of personal taste.

---

2 pt/1.2 L milk
2 onions, skinned
about 24 cloves

1 lb/500 g white
    breadcrumbs from a day-
    old loaf, weighed when
    crumbed
salt and plenty of freshly
    ground black pepper
4 oz/100 g butter, cut in
    pieces

Put the milk into a saucepan with the 2 onions, stuck with the cloves, and warm it over a gentle heat till it forms a skin, then take the pan off the heat, and leave for a couple of hours, to infuse the milk well and truly with the onion and clove flavours. Then remove and discard the onions, stir in the breadcrumbs, salt and pepper, and the pieces of butter. The butter won't melt now, but don't worry, it will when the bread sauce is reheated to serve. Butter an ovenproof dish well, and pour the bread sauce into it. Cover, label, and freeze.

Take the bread sauce out of the freezer the day before you want to eat it, and reheat it in its dish (all ready to serve, you see – minimum effort, that's what I like!) in a moderate oven – 350°F/180°C/Gas 4/bottom right oven in a 4-door Aga – for 30 minutes. Stir it with a fork once or twice during reheating, to mix through the melting bits of butter.

Roast or grilled chipolatas

I like to buy twice as many chipolatas as we will need, then there will be enough for Boxing Night. I allow 3 per person, and I find the nicest we can buy are from Marks and Spencer. Put them on a baking tray, and either cook them in a moderate oven (the turkey will be in a hot oven, so if you have only one oven, grill the chipolatas). They will keep warm very satisfactorily for up to an hour.

Brussels sprouts with bacon bits

When calculating how many sprouts to cook, allow 5–6 per person, providing they are medium-sized sprouts. Pick over the Brussels sprouts and nick the base of each one at some point on Christmas Eve – this is a lengthy business, and best not left till Christmas Day itself. With any luck, you will find a member of the family or a friend willing to undertake the task. I serve crisp Canadian streaky bacon with the sprouts, grilled and broken into bits – you can do this in the morning while you are reheating the soup for lunch.

I like to steam the sprouts (and none of us really like them underdone), then I mix the bacon bits through them in their serving dish.

Roast potatoes

Many years ago I wrote how I peeled potatoes for

Christmas Dinner two days in advance, changing the water each day. I was castigated after this article appeared – by an unmarried male chef, who said that I would thereby ruin the flavour of the potatoes! But I think that roast potatoes taste of the fat in which they are roasted anyway, and besides if you are an unmarried chef you don't have to contend with the million things apart from the food which mothers have to over Christmas, especially on Christmas Day itself, which will probably have started at an unearthly hour in spite of dire warnings and threats (I once found Hugo sitting quietly in bed at 3 a.m. eating chocolate coins and garlic sausage, both of which F. Christmas had put in his stocking) and throughout the day busy mums will have been trying desperately to keep a check of presents, who gave what to whom. The last thing you want to do as well is to set to and peel potatoes in the middle of it all. So – I find they are perfectly fine when peeled two (and sometimes, three, but you MUST change the water each day) days in advance. When ready to cook them, drain the potatoes, pat them dry with a teatowel, and put in a roasting tin with hot fat. Dripping mixed with sunflower oil is good for roasting potatoes. Cook in a hot oven, turning them over every so often so that they brown evenly – they will take about 1½ hours if you have a full roasting tin. If you want to brown them more than they have done in cooking, pop them under a grill for a few minutes. Roast potatoes keep warm well for about three quarters of an hour.

Try to get everything cooked well in advance of the time you set to eat, so that you can have a drink with the rest of the household in comparative peace and calm!

Giblet gravy

Makes about 1–1½ pts

To make good-tasting gravy you need good stock. You can make giblet stock three days before Christmas, strain it and keep it in the fridge, boiling it up for 10 minutes on Christmas Eve.

FOR THE GIBLET STOCK

the turkey giblets
4 onions, skinned and halved
2–3 carrots, halved
2 sticks celery

2 leeks, chopped
a small handful of black peppercorns
2 tsp rock salt
a handful of parsley

FOR THE GRAVY

a little turkey fat
flour
the giblet stock

salt and pepper
gravy browning (optional)

Put the turkey giblets in a large saucepan with all the other ingredients. Pour in 4 pt/2.25 L cold water, bring to the boil, lower the heat, and let the stock simmer for 2½–3 hours. Cool completely, strain into a bowl or large jug and keep, covered, in the fridge.

To make the gravy, scoop out some of the fat (which will have the delicious flavours of turkey, pork, lemon etc, in it) into a saucepan. Stir in some flour, enough to take up the fat. Let it cook for a couple of minutes then, stirring all the time, pour in the giblet stock. Stir till the gravy boils, and let it boil for a few minutes. Taste, season with more salt and pepper if you like, and add a few drops of gravy browning if it looks too pallid. Reheat to serve.

Roast goose with rice, apple and date stuffing

Roast goose makes a delicious alternative to turkey for Christmas dinner. There are a couple of things to bear in mind, though, when contemplating goose; one most important fact is that goose has a broad breastbone, like domestic duck, and so although the bird looks big, don't be deceived into thinking that you will feed a large number of people off a 10–11 lb/4–4.5 kg goose – which is about their average size. There is no depth of meat to be carved off the breast and, apart from its two legs, there is nothing underneath to carve either. Against this, goose meat is very rich, as opposed to turkey which is not, and so you need not give your guests more than two or three slices each, along with a good spoonful of stuffing.

When you roast a goose you get a roasting tin full of fat. What you do with this fat depends on where you live in Britain – in the north-west of England, where I come from, they keep goose fat for rubbing into the chests of ailing cattle. But goose fat is the best fat for roasting or deep-frying potatoes, so it is worth keeping a bowlful if you plan to use it within two or three weeks.

Traditionally, goose has a sharp and fruity stuffing and I suggest here a stuffing made from rice, with apples, dates and lemon, which is delicious with the goose. I also think that braised celery goes very well with roast goose, so I give a recipe for it as I cook it. You can, of course, eat any vegetable you like with it as well as or instead of the suggested celery.

293

Rice, apple and date stuffing

Enough for a 10–11 lb/4.5–5 kg goose

2 oz/50 g butter
2 medium-sized onions,
  skinned and chopped
4 cooking apples, peeled,
  cored and chopped
6 oz/175 g dates, stoned and
  chopped

½ tsp dried thyme
½ tsp salt
freshly ground black pepper
2 lb/1 kg brown rice, boiled
  in salted water till nearly
  cooked, then drained
grated rind of 2 lemons

Melt the butter in a saucepan and add the chopped onions. Cook for about 5 minutes, then add the peeled, cored and chopped cooking apples. Cook till the apples are soft and falling into pulp, then add the chopped dates, thyme, salt and pepper. Let it cook for about 5 minutes, then take the pan off the heat, and stir the apple and date mixture into the drained cooked rice, together with the grated lemon rind. Leave to cool completely, pack into a strong polythene bag, label and freeze. Allow the stuffing to thaw overnight at room temperature.

Braised celery

Serves 8–10

---

2 oz/50 g butter
1 onion, skinned and
    chopped
3 heads of celery

½ pt/300 ml white wine
salt and freshly ground
    black pepper

Melt the butter in a casserole and add the chopped onion. Cook for about 5 minutes, till the onion is soft and transparent-looking. While the onion is cooking, wash the celery well, trim it and cut it into slices about 2 in/5 cm long. Add these to the onions in the casserole and pour on the white wine. Season with salt and pepper, cover with a lid or a piece of foil pressed down over the vegetables, and cook gently for 40–45 minutes.

Roast pheasant with mushroom stuffing and port and redcurrant gravy

If you don't want to be bothered with turkey or goose, roast pheasant makes a delicious alternative for dinner on Christmas Day – you will need two to serve four people. Pheasant is widely available these days, and as it hasn't a very pronounced gamey flavour it is enjoyed by nearly all who like chicken. The one thing to beware of when cooking pheasant is not to overcook it because it can tend to be dry in texture. I particularly like this mushroom and rice stuffing, which can be made two or three weeks in advance, like the stuffing recipes for the turkey and goose, and frozen. If you prefer, the sausage-meat and chestnut stuffing (see pages 285–6) is equally good with pheasant as well as turkey. The gravy, with its flavourings of port and redcurrant jelly, is a special occasion gravy-cum-sauce. I love to serve a purée of root vegetables with pheasant – in this case, my favourite, purée of celeriac. And, of course, no pheasant would be properly dressed without bread sauce, game chips and roast potatoes.

The carcasses make excellent stock.

Roast pheasant with mushroom stuffing

Serves 4 if both are hen pheasants, 5 if one is a cock

---

2 pheasants

6–8 rashers smoked streaky
    bacon

FOR THE STUFFING

3 oz/75 g butter
2 medium onions, skinned
    and chopped quite finely
1 lb/500 g mushrooms,
    wiped and chopped

2 oz/50 g wholemeal
    breadcrumbs
½ tsp thyme
salt and freshly ground
    black pepper

FOR THE PORT AND REDCURRANT GRAVY

½ pt/300 ml port
1 tbsp redcurrant jelly
1 oz/25 g butter
juices from the pheasant
    roasting tin
1 tbsp flour

1 pt/600 ml stock – game,
    chicken or vegetable
salt and freshly ground
    black pepper
a few drops of gravy
    browning

Melt the butter in a saucepan and add the chopped onions. Cook for about 5 minutes, stirring occasionally so that the onions cook evenly. Then add the chopped mushrooms, and cook for 2–3 minutes. Stir in the breadcrumbs, thyme, salt and pepper, take the saucepan off the heat, and cool completely. Either stuff the pheasants with the cooled stuffing right away, or put it into a polythene bag, label it clearly and freeze. Thaw at room temperature for about 6 hours before using.

To roast the stuffed pheasants, wipe them first inside

with a wad of absorbent kitchen roll, then divide the stuffing between each bird. Cover each bird with smoked streaky bacon, and put them into a roasting tin. Roast the pheasants in a hot oven – 400°F/200°C/Gas 6/top right oven in a 4-door Aga – for 15–20 minutes (15 if it is in an Aga); then lower the temperature to 350°F/180°C/Gas 4/bottom right oven in a 4-door Aga, for a further 45–55 minutes. Stick the point of a sharp knife into the thigh of the larger pheasant – if the juices run pink give it a few more minutes' cooking time. When the juices run clear, the pheasant is cooked.

Put the port and redcurrant jelly for the gravy into a small saucepan and simmer together till the port has reduced by half. Put the ounce/25 g of butter and the pheasant juices into another saucepan and stir in the flour. Let it cook for a couple of minutes, then stir in the pint/600 ml of stock, stirring all the time till the sauce boils. Stir in the reduced port and redcurrant liquid, season to taste with salt and pepper. Game gravy is traditionally thin, but if you like a slightly less thin gravy, use less stock to make the gravy. Add a few drops of gravy browning if you wish. Any leftover gravy can be put into the pheasant carcass stock pot.

Purée of celeriac

Serves 4

---

1 medium-sized celeriac	*2 oz/50 g butter, cut in*
1 good-sized potato	*pieces*
½ tsp salt	*1 egg yolk*
	salt and pepper

Peel the celeriac and cut it into chunks. Peel the potato and cut it into chunks too. Put the cut-up celeriac and potato into a saucepan and cover with water. Add the salt and boil the vegetables together till they are tender when you stick a knife into them. Drain, and steam to get rid of any excess moisture. Then mash well, and beat the purée well with a wooden spoon, adding the pieces of butter and the egg yolk, with salt and pepper to taste. Butter an ovenproof dish, and put the purée into the dish. Cool, cover and freeze, or if you are not intending to freeze it, keep it in a warm oven till you are ready to serve it. If you freeze it, allow it to thaw overnight, and reheat in a moderate oven for 20–30 minutes, with small bits of extra butter dotted over the surface.

Mrs Hill's Christmas pudding

Makes 1 large pudding, or 2 small

This recipe has been printed in two books I have written already, but it is simply unique and it belongs here, so here it is again, with apologies to those who already know it. It is unique because it contains no flour or breadcrumbs whatever, and I have never seen another recipe for Christmas pudding which contains neither. Mrs Hill was the wife of a vicar in my home village of Tunstall, in Lancashire, many, many years ago. We have made it every Christmas ever since she gave my mother the recipe. This amount makes one large pudding, or two smaller ones.

12 oz/350 g raisins
12 oz/350 g sultanas
6 oz/175 g currants
12 oz/350 g shredded suet,
    beef or vegetarian
6 oz/175 g chopped
    crystallized peel
3–4 oz/75–100 g flaked
    almonds, toasted

grated rind of 1 lemon
about ½ tsp freshly grated
    nutmeg
6 large eggs, beaten
¼ pt/150 ml brandy
7 fl oz/200 ml milk
6 oz/175 g soft brown sugar
    (optional)

Mix all the ingredients together very well, then put it into a buttered 3 pt/1.75 L pudding bowl – I use the boilable plastic ones with the snap-on lids. Put a disc of bakewell paper (siliconized greaseproof paper) over the top of the mixture before snapping on the lid. Cook the pudding by steaming it in a saucepan with simmering water coming halfway up the sides of the pudding bowl, and with the lid on the saucepan. Steam for 5–6 hours, but do keep an eye on the level of the water in the pan, it will need regular topping up. Boiling a pudding dry is a thing you do only once! After it has cooked, keep it in a cool place – ideally a larder, and reheat before serving by steaming again for 1½–2 hours.

To serve, turn the pudding onto a warmed serving plate – it will turn out easily. Warm some brandy, whisky or rum in a small saucepan – take care, though, not to let it boil. Ignite the alcohol in the saucepan, then pour over the pudding. This is much easier to do than pouring the alcohol over and then trying to ignite it. Stick a sprig of holly in the top of the pudding, and bring to the table. Accompany with *Orange-flavoured brandy butter* and/or *Vanilla sauce*.

Orange-flavoured brandy butter

Serves 10–12

This keeps very well in the fridge for three or four weeks, so you can make it well in advance, but do keep it in a covered container.

---

8 oz/250 g softened butter
8 oz/250 g icing sugar,
  sieved

grated rind of 1 orange
5 tbsp brandy

Put the butter into a bowl and beat it well – I find a handheld electric beater ideal for doing this. Gradually beat in the sieved icing sugar, and the grated orange rind. Then, still beating, add the brandy a spoonful at a time. (If you add the brandy all at once, you are in danger of curdling the brandy butter.) Scoop into a bowl, cover, and store in the fridge.

Vanilla sauce

Serves 6, allowing for those who prefer brandy butter

This also is a delicious accompaniment to Christmas pudding, particularly for those who don't like brandy butter with it – which I don't, and neither does my

er. This is a rich vanilla-flavoured creamy custard
.ce, and any left over is delicious with mince pies.

½ pt/300 ml double cream   2 oz/50 g caster sugar
4 egg yolks   a few drops of vanilla
                                 essence

Put the cream into a heavy-bottomed saucepan over
gentle heat, and heat till it forms a skin. Meanwhile, in a
bowl, beat together the egg yolks, caster sugar and
vanilla essence. Pour some of the hot cream onto the egg
yolk mixture, then pour this back into the saucepan with
the rest of the hot cream. Over gentle heat (and don't try
to hurry it, or the sauce will curdle), stir till the sauce
thickens enough to coat the back of the wooden spoon so
that when you trace your finger down the back of the
spoon it leaves a discernible path in the sauce. Take off
the heat, cool for a while in the pan, then sieve into a
serving bowl or jug. You can serve this sauce warm or
cold. You can also make it the previous day and keep it,
covered, in the fridge.

Lime mousse

Serves 6–8

There are some who don't like Christmas pudding at all,
and I always serve an alternative pudding for them. I
make a sharp fruity mousse, which used to be lemon but
in recent years I've switched to limes, because they are
even nicer, I think. This mousse can be made a week
ahead and frozen. If it's frozen for much more than a

week, the gelatine in the mousse tends to toughen up the texture.

There is no cream in this recipe; if you like, you can add ¼ pt/150 ml whipped double cream before the egg whites are folded in, but I prefer it as it is.

1½ sachets powdered
   gelatine (approximately
   ¾ oz/20 g)
3 tbsp cold water
grated rind and juice of
   4 limes

6 large eggs, separated
8 oz/250 g caster sugar

In a small pan, sprinkle the gelatine over the cold water and leave till spongy – about 5 minutes. Then heat gently till the gelatine granules have dissolved.

Put the grated lime rind and juice into a saucepan and heat till nearly boiling. Meanwhile, beat the egg yolks, gradually adding the sugar. Beat till the mixture is very thick and pale. Still beating (this is easiest done in a Kenwood), pour the nearly boiling lime juice and rind in a steady trickle into the yolks mixture. Mix in the dissolved gelatine, and leave till the mixture is thickening – enough to coat thickly the back of a large metal spoon. Whisk the egg whites till they are very stiff and, using the large metal spoon, fold them quickly and thoroughly through the mixture. Freeze in the serving dish.

BOXING DAY

When I was a child, Boxing Day felt like the dreariest day of the year. All the excitement and build-up to Christmas Day over! And what felt like eternity till next Christmas. One of our children remarked last year that on Boxing Day when she wakes up she feels about with her feet at the bottom of her bed hoping that Father Christmas may have slipped up and visited her again by mistake – wishful thinking! Now I'm grown-up (in age, anyway) I rather love the contrast of Boxing Day. We always seem to have people for lunch, which is great fun providing I have made the lunch well before Christmas, and frozen it. In the evening on Boxing Day, we are all very lazy and help ourselves to supper which I set out as a sort of buffet consisting entirely of cold leftovers from the previous evening accompanied by a salad based on grated carrots. How delicious cold roast turkey is – both the stuffings are so good eaten cold, too. As for cold bread sauce, I have a cousin who feels so passionately about it that he even takes bread sauce sandwiches out shooting! But, back to Boxing Day supper; if anyone feels like pudding of any sort, there are always the mince pies and brandy butter.

BOXING DAY LUNCH
FOR TWELVE

Cheese sablés
Game pie with forcemeat balls
Leek and carrot ragoût
Spiced bramble and lemon jelly
Iced Nesselrode pudding

Boxing Day Lunch

Cheese sablés

Have these as a pre-prandial appetizer, with mulled wine. This amount makes about 30, but if you cut them smaller, it makes more!

---

6 oz/175 g grated Cheddar cheese
6 oz/175 g chilled butter, cut in pieces

6 oz/175 g plain flour
1 tsp mustard powder

Put the grated cheese, pieces of butter, flour and mustard powder into a food processor. Whiz till the mixture forms a ball. Take it out of the processor and divide in two. On a floured surface, form the rich pastry dough into a long, thin oblong shape. Roll out with a floured rolling pin to about 4 in/10 cm wide, cut with a sharp knife in two lengthways, and cut on the slant then straight across, to form triangles. With the help of a palette knife, put the triangles onto a baking tray. Bake in a hot oven – 400°F/ 200°C/Gas 6/top right oven in a 4-door Aga – for 10 minutes. Set a pinger, because they burn easily. On the other hand, if you cook them in a cooler oven, they spread their shape, so just be vigilant! Carefully lift the cooked sablés off the tray with a palette knife, onto a wire cooling rack and, when quite cold, store in an airtight tin. You can make these before Christmas, and freeze them if you make them much more than 10 days in advance.

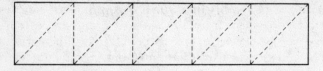

Shape of pastry and how to cut into triangles.

Game pie with forcemeat balls

Serves 12

FOR THE PIE

*a mixture of game – for
    example, 4 pheasants,
    4 pigeons, 1 hare*
*seasoned flour made from
    3 oz/75 g plain flour,
    plenty of freshly ground
    black pepper, and ½ tsp
    salt*
2 oz/50 g butter
4 tbsp sunflower oil
*3 medium onions, skinned
    and chopped*

*3 pt/1.75 L game stock
    (see below)*
¼–½ pt/150–300 ml port
1 tbsp redcurrant jelly
*grated rind of 2 oranges and
    1 lemon*
4 juniper berries, crushed
1 lb/500 g puff pastry

FOR THE GAME STOCK

the game carcasses
4 onions
3 carrots

3 sticks of celery
about 12 peppercorns
2 tsp rock salt

With a very sharp knife, which makes the task effortless, cut all the flesh from the carcasses, and try to cut it into pieces as even in size as possible. Put the carcasses into a large pan with the other stock ingredients. Cover with water, bring to the boil, simmer for 2½–3 hours then strain.

Coat the pieces of game with the seasoned flour. Melt the butter and heat the oil together in a large, heavy-bottomed casserole and brown the floured pieces of game all over, a few at a time, removing them with a slotted spoon to a dish where they can keep warm as you cook the rest. When all the game is browned, put the chopped onions into the casserole, and cook them for about 5 minutes, stirring occasionally to prevent them sticking. Dust in any of the leftover seasoned flour to take up any excess fat, cook for a minute or two, then gradually add the game stock and, stirring continuously, bring to the boil. Stir in the port, redcurrant jelly, grated orange and lemon rinds and crushed juniper berries. Replace the browned game in the sauce, cover the casserole with a lid, and cook in a moderate oven – 350°F/180°C/Gas 4/ bottom right oven in a 4-door Aga – for 1½ hours. Take it out of the oven, put the contents into one large pie dish or two smaller ones, let it cool completely, then cover, label and freeze. Take it out of the freezer on Christmas Eve and leave it in the fridge. On Boxing Day morning just roll out the puff pastry and cover the pies, brushing each with beaten egg, before baking them in a hot oven – 425°F/220°C/Gas 7/top right oven in a 4-door Aga – for 30–40 minutes, till the pastry is deep golden and well puffed up.

Forcemeat balls

Serves 12

These are so delicious, complement game perfectly, and freeze beautifully. Because the pie is pastry-topped and the forcemeat balls are fairly filling in themselves, I have skipped the potatoes in this lunchtime menu.

---

2 oz/50 g butter
2 medium onions, skinned and chopped as finely as possible
8 oz/250 g day-old loaf, made into breadcrumbs
4 oz/100 g suet

2 tbsp chopped parsley
grated rind of 2 lemons
salt and pepper
1 egg, beaten
oil for frying (I use sunflower)

Melt the butter and cook the finely chopped onions in it for about 5 minutes, till they are transparent and soft. Take them off the heat, and mix well with the breadcrumbs, suet, parsley, grated lemon rinds, salt, pepper and beaten egg – add more egg if the mixture is too dry. Form into walnut-sized balls, and fry till golden brown. Drain them on several thicknesses of kitchen paper, to absorb any excess oil. When they are quite cold, freeze them on an open baking tray, then pack them into a polythene bag and stick them back in the freezer till you want to thaw them. Allow about 3 hours' thawing time, with the forcemeat balls flat on a baking tray, then reheat in a moderate oven – 350°F/180°C/Gas 4/bottom right oven in a 4-door Aga – for 10–15 minutes to serve.

Leek and carrot ragoût

Serves 12

This can be made at some point during the morning – it can cook slowly in a moderate oven, and will keep warm satisfactorily for about an hour.

---

2 oz/50 g butter
2 tbsp oil (I use sunflower)
2 medium onions, skinned and sliced finely

8 good-sized leeks, trimmed, washed, and sliced about ½ in/1 cm thick
12 carrots, peeled, and sliced quite thinly
salt and freshly ground black pepper

Melt the butter and heat the oil together in a heavy casserole. Add the chopped onions, and cook them for about 5 minutes, stirring occasionally. Then add the leeks and carrots and season with salt and pepper. Cook on the heat for about 5 minutes, stirring from time to time, then cover the casserole with a lid, and cook in a moderate oven – 350°F/180°C/Gas 4/bottom right oven in a 4-door Aga – for ¾ hour. Keep the ragoût warm till you are ready to serve.

Spiced bramble and lemon jelly

This is delicious, and goes very well with the game pie. It doesn't take more than a few minutes to make, but if you haven't got even a few minutes you can serve redcurrant jelly with the game pie, instead.

1 jar of bramble jelly – either your own, homemade, or bought juice of 1 lemon	1 cinnamon stick 6 cloves

Put the bramble jelly into a saucepan with the lemon juice, the cinnamon stick and the cloves. Over a moderate heat, melt the jelly then let the pan sit on a low heat for 10 minutes. Strain through a sieve into a clean, warmed jampot, cover and store in a cool place.

Iced Nesselrode pudding

Serves 12

This is a delicious sort of Christmas pudding-ice-cream, very good to eat, and convenient too because it can be made two or three weeks in advance. This recipe will serve twelve – halve the quantity if there are fewer of you.

8 oz/250 g raisins 6 tbsp orange liqueur, such as Cointreau 1 pt/600 ml double cream 8 large egg yolks	4 oz/100 g caster sugar 1 × 8 oz/250 g tin of whole chestnuts, chopped 4 oz/100 g flaked almonds, toasted till golden 4 oz/100 g crystallized apricots, rinsed under warm water, dried with kitchen paper and chopped

Soak the raisins overnight in the orange liqueur.

Put half the cream into a saucepan and heat till it forms a skin. Beat the egg yolks, gradually adding the caster sugar and continue beating till the mixture is thick and pale. Pour in a little of the hot cream, mix well, then pour the egg yolks and cream mixture into the pan with the rest of the cream. Stir over a gentle heat till the custard has thickened. When it coats the back of your wooden spoon, take the pan off the heat. If the mixture looks as though it is about to curdle, take it off the heat at once and whisk it. Let it cool, then pour it into a mixing bowl and stir in the chopped chestnuts, toasted flaked almonds, chopped apricots, and drained raisins. Meanwhile, whip the remaining half pint/300 ml of cream, adding the strained liqueur from the raisins. Fold this into the fruit and custard mixture, pour into a serving bowl and freeze. Allow to stand for 20–30 minutes at room temperature before serving.

St. Stephen's Day/Boxing Day Supper

This is a supper I really enjoy. I usually serve some cold turkey and stuffings, with the remaining cold chipolatas and some home-made chutney and a salad. This is one I find particularly delicious.

Grated carrot, orange and red pepper salad with French dressing

Serves 12

If you have a food processor with a grater attachment, this salad doesn't take minutes to prepare.

8 carrots, peeled and grated   2 red peppers
4 oranges

Peel the oranges and slice them into chunks with a serrated knife. Cut each pepper in half, and remove the seeds. Chop each pepper into small bits. If you are tempted to use green instead of red peppers, I would blanch them for 3 minutes, then drain them in a sieve, and rinse them under cold water. This makes them altogether more digestible, whereas red peppers never seem as indigestible raw as do green ones.

Mix together the grated carrots, chopped oranges and peppers with *French dressing*.

2 tsp caster sugar   ¼ pt/150 ml oil
1 tsp salt   3–4 tbsp wine vinegar
1 rounded tsp mustard
  powder

Mix all the ingredients together well. This makes ¼ pt/ 150 ml dressing.

DECEMBER 27TH/
BOXING DAY DINNER
FOR EIGHT

Dill roulade with Gravlax cream
Wild duck with grapes and paprika
Sautéed turnips and onions
Creamy mashed potatoes
Clementine sorbet
Stilton and celery soufflé

December 27th Dinner Party

Dill roulade with Gravlax cream

Serves 8

Because I love Gravlax so much I have devised this roulade, spiked with a little extra dill. It makes an ideal first course, being easy to slice and serve, and convenient because it is made in the morning for dinner that evening. The flavouring of the milk is all-important to the success of the end result, so please don't be tempted to skip it.

FOR THE FLAVOURED MILK

1 pt/600 ml milk
1 onion, skinned and halved
2 celery sticks

a few parsley stalks
1 tsp rock salt
about 12 peppercorns

FOR THE ROULADE

2 oz/50 g butter
2 oz/50 g flour
the strained flavoured milk

2 tsp dried dill weed
freshly ground black pepper
freshly grated nutmeg
4 large eggs, separated

FOR THE FILLING

½ pt/300 ml double cream
juice of ½ lemon
*8 oz/250 g Gravlax, cut into
  dice*

1 tsp honey
*1 rounded tsp grainy
  mustard*

First flavour the milk: put it into a saucepan with the halved onion, celery sticks, parsley stalks, salt and peppercorns. Heat till the milk forms a skin, then take the pan off the heat and leave for 1–1½ hours, to infuse the milk with the flavour of the other ingredients. Strain the milk into a jug.

Next make the roulade. Melt the butter in a saucepan and stir in the flour; let it cook for a couple of minutes before stirring in the strained flavoured milk, stirring continuously till the sauce boils. Let it bubble for a moment, then stir in the dried dill weed, season with a little more salt if you think it needs it, pepper and nutmeg, and beat in the egg yolks one by one. Whisk the egg whites and, with a large metal spoon, fold them quickly and thoroughly into the dill sauce. Put a piece of bakewell paper (siliconized greaseproof paper) onto a baking tray or swiss roll tin measuring about 14 × 16 in/ 35 × 40 cm and pour this mixture onto the paper-lined tray. Smooth it even, and bake in a moderate oven – 350°F/180°C/Gas 4/bottom right oven in a 4-door Aga – for 20–25 minutes. When it is golden brown and puffed up take it out of the oven, cover with a piece of bakewell paper and put a damp teatowel over the paper – the roulade will sink but don't worry, it's meant to. Leave for an hour or two to cool completely.

For the filling, whip the double cream with the lemon juice and fold in the diced Gravlax, along with the honey and mustard.

Lay a fresh piece of bakewell paper on a work surface or table. Remove the teatowel and bakewell paper from the top of the cooked roulade and, taking the short sides of the paper underneath the roulade in both hands, flip it over face down onto the paper on the table. Carefully peel off the paper in strips parallel to the roulade – that way the roulade won't tear. Cover the surface with the cream and Gravlax mixture, spreading it evenly right up to the edges. Roll up the roulade, away from you, and slip it onto a serving dish or tray. Leave in a cool place for several hours before slicing. Place a slice on each serving plate, and dust with finely chopped parsley, if you like, to add a contrasting colour.

Wild duck with grapes and paprika

Serves 8

This can be made in advance and reheated to serve – it is quick and delicious. You can freeze it, but don't add the grapes till it is thawed and about to be reheated, then add them along with the soured cream.

---

4 wild duck – mallard
2 onions, skinned and halved
1 pt/600 ml dry cider

½ pt/300 ml water
salt and freshly ground
   black pepper

FOR THE SAUCE

3 oz/75 g butter
2 medium onions, skinned
   and sliced thinly
1 tbsp flour
4 tbsp paprika

the duck cooking liquid
salt and freshly ground
   black pepper
10 oz/275 g grapes, halved
   and deseeded
¼ pt/150 ml soured cream

Put half an onion inside each duck. Put the ducks into a roasting tin, and pour the cider and water around them. Season with salt and freshly ground black pepper. Cover the ducks with foil and cook in a hot oven – 400°F/200°C/ Gas 6/top right oven in a 4-door Aga – for 1–1½ hours, till the duck meat is tender. Take the tin out of the oven, and let the duck cool. Then strain off the cooking liquid around them, and keep it for making the sauce. Strip the meat off the ducks, as neatly as you can.

For the sauce, melt the butter, add the finely sliced onions, and cook for several minutes till the onions are soft and transparent. Stir in the flour and paprika, and cook for a minute, then stir in the duck cooking liquid, stirring till the sauce boils. Take the saucepan off the heat, season to taste with salt and pepper, cool the sauce and when cold add the pieces of duck meat. Freeze at this stage. Thaw, and reheat in a moderate oven till the sauce is bubbling, then shortly before serving stir through the grapes and the soured cream.

This dish is excellent served with *Sautéed turnips and onions* (see below). Other good accompaniments would be creamy mashed potatoes, and spicy red cabbage.

Sautéed turnips and onions

Serves 8

The sweetness of the turnips and onions go together very well, and they complement the duck ideally. I like to serve creamy mashed potatoes as the other vegetable.

3 medium-sized onions	*1½–2 turnips, depending on*
2 oz/50 g butter	*their size*
2 tbsp sunflower oil	*salt and freshly ground*
	black pepper

Skin and chop the onions. Melt the butter and heat the oil together in a casserole, add the onions and cook over a moderate heat for 5 minutes. Meanwhile, cut the skin off the turnips, and slice them into ½ in/1 cm dice. Add the diced turnip to the onions in the casserole, season with salt and pepper, and cook over a moderate heat, stirring from time to time to prevent them from sticking and to make sure that they cook evenly. Stick a knife into a bit of turnip to test whether it is soft and cooked. This vegetable dish can be cooked, then the casserole covered with a lid, and kept warm for up to an hour before serving; it really comes to no harm being kept warm for such a comparatively long time.

Clementine sorbet

Serves 8

This is a refreshing finale to a dinner which has cream in its first course and in its main course. Clementines taste wonderful – their flavour and smell really is the essence of Christmas and New Year time, I think. Dreary satsumas just are no substitute – and besides, they are utterly tasteless and you can't grate their skin! The lemon in the sorbet recipe is vital to bring out the flavour of the clementines.

---

2 pt/1.2 L water
12 oz/350 g granulated
sugar
pared rind of 3 lemons

pared rinds of 6 clementines
(a potato peeler does the
job perfectly, removing
the rind with none of the
pith)
juice of 2 of the lemons and
all 6 clementines

Put the water into a saucepan with the granulated sugar. Over a gentle heat dissolve the sugar in the water – don't let it boil till the sugar has dissolved completely. Then add the pared lemon and clementine rinds, and leave the syrup to cool completely. Remove and discard the strips of peel, stir in the juice, pour the syrup into a plastic container, and freeze it. After 2–3 hours' freezing, take the container out of the freezer and beat the half-frozen syrup very well, with an electric whisk – you will find the syrup is frozen round the edges, so beat the frozen and the semi-frozen together well. Refreeze, and repeat the beating process twice more. If you have an ice-cream machine, you can freeze-churn the mixture. The more you beat it, the softer the sorbet and the greater the volume. The less you beat it, the more it will resemble ice lollies, with its frozen crystals!

Stilton and celery soufflé

Serves 8

4 oz/100 g butter	*freshly ground black pepper*
1 small onion, skinned and	*– about 15 grinds*
chopped finely	*about ¼ tsp freshly grated*
4 sticks of celery, washed	*nutmeg*
and sliced very finely	*6 oz/175 g Stilton cheese,*
4 oz/100 g plain flour	*crumbled*
1½ pt/1 L milk	*8 large eggs, separated*

Butter two soufflé dishes, each about 6 in/15 cm in diameter.

Melt the butter in a saucepan and add the finely chopped onion and the finely sliced celery. Cook over a moderate heat for about 5 minutes, stirring occasionally. Then stir in the flour, and cook for a further couple of minutes. Stir in the milk, adding it gradually and stirring continuously till the sauce boils. Take the pan off the heat, season with the pepper and nutmeg – the Stilton will add enough saltiness – and stir in the crumbled Stilton. Beat in the egg yolks, one at a time. Cool the sauce. Whisk the egg whites till they are very stiff and, with a large metal spoon, fold the whites quickly and thoroughly through the Stilton sauce. Divide between the two prepared soufflé dishes, cover each with clingfilm; you can then leave them for 3–5 hours before baking. Remove the clingfilm and bake in a hot oven – 425°F/220°C/Gas 7/top right oven in a 4-door Aga – for 45–50 minutes. Serve immediately.

New Year

The thing about New Year is that it follows so fast upon
the heels of the Christmas festivities there is scarcely time
to draw breath. The only thing to do is to prepare for
Christmas and New Year in one. It is vital to plan food
which, for the most part, can be made ahead and frozen.

New Year's Eve is the perfect night for a party, in
many houses for a combination of age groups. I am
always so glad we live in Scotland, where the mixed-
generation gathering is the norm, and where reels can be
danced by anyone, no matter what their age. Perhaps
wrongly, I feel that further south in Britain one notices
the generation gap far more. For dinner on New Year's
Eve I recommend sitting everyone down to eat; it is
invariably a late evening, and it's vital to preserve
everyone's strength, even if it means seating your guests
at a variety of tables. I would also advise you to dispense
with a first course, and get round this by having a choice
of two delectable eats, and a communal dip which goes
well with either, to pass around with drinks before
dinner.

For dinner itself, I suggest *Smoked pork loin and mushroom
goulash*, served with baked potatoes and onions, and a
large, colourful and good-tasting salad. To follow, I give
a choice of two puddings, both of which can be frozen:
Egg nog and chocolate pie, and *Hazelnut mocha torte*. On New
Year's Day I suggest a brunch, which caters for those
who feel no urge to get up in a hurry, and dispenses with
the need to provide lunch. For dinner that evening, there
is a delicious menu to herald the first day of the new year:
Mushroom and marsala soup (which can be frozen),
accompanied by *Leek and cheese filo parcels*, then *Lamb
ragoût* in red wine (which also freezes) as a main course,
and *Blackcurrant, raspberry and lemon suédoise* with tiny
vanilla meringues for pudding.

NEW YEAR'S EVE DINNER FOR TWENTY

Spinach-stuffed filo triangles
Rich cheese sticks
Tomato béarnaise dip
Smoked pork loin and mushroom goulash
Baked sliced potatoes and onions
Tomato, avocado, orange and sunflower-seed salad
Egg nog and chocolate pie
Hazelnut mocha torte

New Year's Eve Dinner

Spinach-stuffed filo triangles

Makes approximately 50 triangles

---

1 packet of filo pastry

sunflower oil, or melted butter, to brush each sheet of filo

FOR THE FILLING

3 tbsp sunflower or olive oil
2 onions, skinned and chopped
2 garlic cloves, skinned and chopped

1½ lb/750 g frozen spinach, thawed and well drained
salt and freshly ground black pepper
about ½ tsp freshly grated nutmeg

Heat the oil in a saucepan and add the chopped onions. Cook for about 5 minutes, giving an occasional stir to make sure that the onions cook evenly, then add the chopped garlic and the spinach – don't be tempted to add the garlic at the start with the onions, because it loses its pungency in cooking. Season with salt, pepper and nutmeg, and cook, stirring from time to time, over a moderate heat for about 10 minutes. Take it off the heat, and purée it in a food processor.

On a work surface, lay out a sheet of filo pastry – cover the rest of the filo pastry with a damp teatowel, to prevent it from drying out as you make up the triangles. Brush the sheet with sunflower or olive oil (or with melted butter if you prefer) and lay a second sheet of filo on top of the first; brush this, too, with oil or butter. Cut the double sheet of filo lengthways in eight even strips with the rectangle of filo laid widthways in front of you. Put a teaspoon of the spinach mixture in the bottom right corner of each strip, and fold each up the strip to form a triangle shape. Put these on a baking tray brushed with oil.

You can freeze the triangles at this stage, or you can make them up two days in advance, brush them with oil and cover with clingfilm, and keep them in the fridge till you are ready to bake them. Cook them in a hot oven – 425°F/220°C/Gas 7/top right oven in a 4-door Aga – for 10 minutes or until they are golden and crisp.

Rich cheese sticks

Makes about 48

These are easy to make, but they burn easily in cooking so do set a pinger to remind you when their cooking time is up. They freeze beautifully, and keep well in a tin for several days.

---

8 oz/250 g chilled butter, cut
  in pieces
8 oz/250 g plain flour
2 rounded tsp mustard
  powder
8 oz/250 g good Cheddar
  cheese, grated

pinch of salt
freshly ground black pepper
a dash of Tabasco

Put all the ingredients into a food processor and whiz till they are well combined and the mixture has formed a ball. Take out of the processor and divide into three – this is just because I find it easier to work in smaller amounts.

Sieve some flour onto a work surface. and flour your hands too. Take one piece of the cheese dough and, with the heel of your hand, push it into a long rectangle shape, about ¼ in/½ cm thick. Flour a rolling pin, and gently roll the dough to get an even shape. With a small, sharp knife, cut the rectangle in two lengthways, then cut it in short lengths. Lift them carefully onto a baking tray with a palette knife – there is no need to butter the tray, the mixture is quite buttery enough and they won't stick. Bake in a hot oven – 425°F/220°C/Gas 7/top right oven in a 4-door Aga – for 10 minutes, or till they are pale golden brown. Take them out of the oven, cool for a few seconds on the tray, then carefully lift them onto a wire cooling rack, again using a palette knife to lift them. Cool completely, then store in an airtight tin, or freeze them.

Tomato béarnaise dip

Makes ¾ pt/450 ml

You can make this dip and keep it in a bowl for several days in the fridge. It is well worth the small bother of reducing the flavoured wine vinegar to make the mayonnaise – hence the word Béarnaise in the name of the recipe. It is delicious!

Make this dip in two lots; that is, make the following amount twice over. But make the vinegar reduction in one go, so remember to divide it in two before using.

FOR THE VINEGAR REDUCTION

½ pt/300 ml red or white
  wine vinegar
½ onion, skinned
1 bay leaf

about 12 peppercorns
a few parsley stalks

FOR THE TOMATO DIP

1 large egg plus 1 large yolk
1 garlic clove, skinned and
  chopped
½ tsp salt
a good grinding of black
  pepper
1 tsp sugar

1 tsp mustard powder
½ pt/300 ml sunflower oil –
  or a mixture of olive and
  sunflower oil
half the wine vinegar
  reduction
2–3 tbsp boiling water, to
  thin down the mayonnaise
  slightly
1 tbsp tomato purée

Put the ingredients for the vinegar reduction in a saucepan and simmer until reduced by between half and two-thirds. Cool, strain, and discard the flavourings.

Make the tomato dip. Put the egg, yolk, garlic, salt, pepper, sugar, and mustard into the food processor or liquidizer and whiz. Then, still whizzing, gradually add the oil, drop by drop to start with, then in a steady trickle. When the oil is all incorporated, whiz in the vinegar, and the boiling water to thin down the mayonnaise. Whiz in the tomato purée, taste, adjust the seasoning to your own taste, and store in a covered bowl till you are ready to serve it.

Smoked pork loin and mushroom goulash

Serves 18–20

This is delicious, easy, and can be frozen, although not
for much longer than three weeks as then the smoked
pork loin tends to become salty.

---

5 smoked pork loins
3 pt/1.75 L milk
2 pt/1.2 L water

3 onions, skinned and
    quartered
6 cloves

FOR THE MUSHROOM SAUCE

4 oz/100 g butter
3 onions, skinned and
    chopped finely
4 oz/100 g flour
the strained pork cooking
    liquid
2 lb/1 kg mushrooms, wiped
    and sliced

a little oil and butter for
    sautéeing
freshly ground black pepper
a grating of nutmeg
½ pt/300 ml double cream

Take the smoked pork loins out of their wrappings, and
rinse each well in cold water. Put them in a roasting tin,
and pour in the milk and water. Add the onions, stuck
with the cloves, and cover the roasting tin with foil. Bake
in a moderate oven – 350°F/180°C/Gas 4/bottom right
oven in a 4-door Aga – for 2 hours. Take them out of the
oven, and let them cool completely in the liquid in which
they cooked. Then strain off the liquid and reserve it for
the mushroom sauce.

Next make the mushroom sauce. Melt the butter and
add the finely chopped onions. Over a moderate heat

cook the onions in the butter for about 5 minutes, stirring occasionally to make sure they cook evenly. Stir in the flour, and cook for a further couple of minutes then, stirring continuously, add about 3 pt/1.75 L of the strained cooking liquid, and heat till the sauce boils; then, if you like a thinner sauce, add more of the liquid. In a frying pan, sauté the sliced mushrooms in a small amount of oil and butter, over a high heat. Cook small amounts of the mushrooms at one time – this prevents the mushrooms from shrinking as they stew in the juices which come from them, which is what happens when they are cooked in too large quantities over too low a heat. Stir the sautéed mushrooms into the sauce, and season with the pepper and nutmeg – don't be tempted to add salt, the meat is usually sufficiently salty for most people's tastes. As the sauce cools, cut the meat into fat matchsticks about ½ in/1 cm thick – this doesn't take a minute providing you have a sharp knife. Stir the cut-up meat into the cool sauce along with the cream, and pour into serving dishes; cover and freeze.

Take the goulash out of the freezer the evening before, and reheat in a moderate oven – 350°F/180°C/Gas 4/ bottom right oven in a 4-door Aga – till the sauce is bubbling, about 20–30 minutes depending on the size of dish. If you cover the dish with foil, allow more time for the contents to reheat, as foil slows the cooking down. If you don't cover the goulash as it reheats, fork it through from time to time, to prevent a skin forming on the surface. Sprinkle with parsley, if you like, before serving.

Baked sliced potatoes and onions

Serves 20

You may very well prefer to serve boiled brown or basmati rice with the smoked pork dish, but I like it with a dish of baked sliced potatoes and onions. They are so easy to make, so good to eat, and I think they go so well with the goulash. They are very convenient too; you can make and cook them in the morning – or, if you have an Aga or Rayburn, you can cook them in a slow oven all day. I have made and cooked them the day before, and they have been reheated with little obvious detriment to the end result. Another thing: you need half the amount of potatoes for this dish that you would otherwise for the same number of people if you were going to serve mashed or roast potatoes. An extra point in its favour!

---

30 medium-to-large potatoes, peeled and sliced thinly (a mandolin is ideal for this)
6 medium onions, skinned and sliced thinly

salt and freshly ground black pepper
freshly grated nutmeg
8 oz/250 g butter
1 pt/600 ml milk

Butter a large, fairly shallow ovenproof dish. Arrange the thinly sliced potatoes in layers, with a scattering of sliced onions between each; dot each layer with butter and sprinkle with salt, pepper and nutmeg. When you get to the top, be generous with the dots of butter over the surface, and pour in enough milk to come up to the level of the top layer of potatoes. Bake in a moderate oven – 350°F/180°C/Gas 4/bottom right oven in a 4-door Aga – for 2½–3 hours, or for 45 minutes in the moderate oven then for 5–7 hours in a cool oven.

Tomato, avocado, orange and sunflower-seed salad

Serves 20

This salad both looks pretty, being very colourful, and tastes good. The toasted sunflower-seeds add a slightly contrasting texture, and the port vinaigrette is just a bit different from the more usual dressing.

FOR THE SALAD

4 Iceberg lettuces, sliced
   finely into shreds
12 tomatoes, skinned,
   deseeded and halved, and
   each half cut in 4 wedges
8 oranges, peeled with a
   serrated knife, and each
   cut in segments

8 avocados, flesh chopped
   and tossed in lemon juice
4 tbsp sunflower-seeds,
   toasted till golden brown,
   in a dry saucepan over
   moderate heat

FOR THE PORT VINAIGRETTE

¾ pt/450 ml sunflower oil
2 medium onions, skinned
   and chopped finely
2 tbsp honey
½–1 tsp salt

freshly ground black pepper
2 tbsp lemon juice
¼ pt/150 ml port
3 tbsp red wine vinegar

Make the port vinaigrette first. Put the oil in a saucepan and add the finely chopped onions. Gently simmer for about 5 minutes.

In a bowl, mix together the honey, salt and pepper, lemon juice, port and vinegar, and then mix in the hot oil and onions. Cool, then store in a jar in the fridge till required.

Mix all the salad ingredients together in a large bowl and toss gently with the vinaigrette before serving.

Egg nog and chocolate pie

Serves 20, with another pudding

This pie freezes beautifully. If you are feeding 20, I suggest you make two pies, each about 9 in/23 cm in diameter.

FOR THE PASTRY (FOR ONE PIE)

4 oz/100 g chilled butter, cut in pieces
5 oz/150 g plain flour

1 oz/ 25 g icing sugar
a few drops of vanilla essence

FOR THE FILLING (FOR BOTH PIES)

1 pt/600 ml milk
¼ pt/150 ml rum – white or dark
2 sachets powdered gelatine (approximately 1 oz/ 25 g)
6 large eggs, separated
6 oz/175 g caster sugar

1 rounded tsp cornflour, sieved
1½ tsp freshly grated nutmeg
¾ pt/450 ml double cream, whipped
6 oz/175 g dark chocolate, grated (easiest done with the grater of a food processor, or by hand if the chocolate is cold from the fridge)

I suggest you make this amount of pastry twice, rather than double the quantities and make it all in one go.

Put all the pastry ingredients together into a food processor and whiz till they are like crumbs. Pat round the sides and base of a 9 in/23 cm flan dish, and put the flan into the fridge for at least half an hour – preferably longer – before baking in a moderate oven – 350°F/180°C/Gas 4/bottom right oven in a 4-door Aga – for 20–25 minutes, until the pastry is golden brown. Take it out of the oven and cool.

While the pastry cases are baking, make the pie fillings. Heat the milk in a saucepan large enough to make the following custard in as well. Measure the rum into a small saucepan and sprinkle over it the gelatine, heat over a gentle heat till the granules have dissolved completely, but do take care not to let it boil. Beat together the egg yolks, caster sugar and sieved cornflour, beating really well. Beat in the grated nutmeg, and pour on a little of the hot milk; mix well, then pour this mixture back into the saucepan with the rest of the hot milk, stir well and, over a gentle-to-moderate heat, stir until the sauce thickens enough to well coat the back of your wooden spoon. Take the pan off the heat, stir in the dissolved gelatine and rum, and leave the rum custard to cool completely, stirring it occasionally to prevent a skin forming. When it is quite cold, fold in the whipped cream and the grated dark chocolate. Whisk the egg whites till they are very stiff and, with a large metal spoon, fold them quickly and thoroughly through the chocolate-flecked creamy rum and nutmeg custard. Pour into each of the baked pastry cases. Freeze, uncovered, then carefully cover each with clingfilm. Thaw for 3–4 hours before serving.

Hazelnut mocha torte

Serves 20, with another pudding

This is a heavenly, rich cake, and it freezes beautifully.

FOR THE CAKE

2 rounded tbsp cocoa (not drinking chocolate!)
12 oz/350 g ground hazelnuts, toasted till golden brown

12 large eggs, separated
12 oz/350 g caster sugar

FOR THE COFFEE AND CHOCOLATE BUTTERCREAM

4 tbsp boiling water
2 tbsp good instant coffee granules
6 large egg yolks
4 oz/100 g granulated sugar

3 oz/75 g good dark chocolate, broken in pieces
4 tbsp rum, white or dark
1 lb/500 g softened butter
6 oz/175 g icing sugar, sieved

Line two 12 in/30 cm diameter cake tins with bakewell paper (siliconized greaseproof paper).

With a fork, mix the cocoa through the toasted hazelnuts – I find a fork does this better than anything.

In a large bowl, beat the egg yolks well, gradually adding the caster sugar, and continue beating till the mixture is very thick and pale. Whisk the whites till they are very stiff and, with a large metal spoon, fold the hazelnut and cocoa mixture through the egg yolk mixture, alternating with spoonfuls of the stiff egg whites. Divide the mixture between the prepared cake tins, and bake in a moderate oven – 350°F/180°C/Gas 4/ bottom right oven in a 4-door Aga – for 40–45 minutes – the cakes will be just coming away from the sides of the tins. Take them out of the oven, cool for 10 minutes in their tins, then turn them onto wire cooling racks to cool completely.

Meanwhile, make the rich buttercream. Put the boiling water and coffee into a heatproof bowl, with the egg yolks, granulated sugar, broken-up dark chocolate and rum. Place the bowl over a saucepan of gently simmering water – take care not to let the bottom of the bowl touch the water. With a balloon whisk, stir (don't whisk) the mixture till the sugar has dissolved, and the coffee and rum custard mixture thickened – this takes about 10 minutes. Take the bowl off the heat, and cool the custard. Meanwhile, put the butter into a bowl and beat it with a handheld electric whisk. Gradually beat in the cooled custard. Beat in the sieved icing sugar, then put the bowl of buttercream into the fridge to let the mixture firm up – it will by now be quite soft.

Put one cake on a serving plate, and spread a layer of the buttercream over it. Put the other cake on top, and cover the top and sides with the remaining buttercream. Freeze, then when frozen cover with clingfilm. Thaw for 3–4 hours before serving. Decorate, if you like, with dark chocolate coffee beans around the edge of the cake, or lay strips of greaseproof paper in a diagonal pattern across the top, and sieve icing sugar over – when the strips of paper are carefully removed, you get a striped effect! Or just don't garnish at all; it is a case of gilding the lily anyway, the cake is so good!

NEW YEAR'S DAY BRUNCH FOR EIGHT

Warm dried fruit salad
Smoked haddock kedgeree
Oat pancakes

New Year's Day Brunch

Warm dried fruit salad

Serves 8

This can be made a day or two in advance and kept, in a covered container, in the fridge. Warm it up before serving. I like to serve it with Greek yoghurt. You can leave out the chopped preserved ginger from the list of ingredients if you don't like ginger.

---

4 oz/100 g dried peaches, each cut in half
4 oz/100 g dried apricots
4 oz/100 g prunes
4 oz/100 g dried apples or pears
1 small pineapple, skin cut off, core cut out, and the flesh cut in chunks

6 pieces preserved ginger, drained and chopped
1 pt/600 ml orange juice – freshly squeezed if possible
1 pt/600 ml water
2–3 oz/50–75 g soft brown sugar

Put everything into a heatproof dish, cover with a lid or foil, and bake in a low-to-moderate oven for 2–2½ hours.

Smoked haddock kedgeree

Serves 8

This must be the most convenient of all breakfast or

brunch dishes, because it freezes well for a fairly short time – not much more than three or four weeks. Once thawed, all you need to add to the kedgeree are chopped hardboiled eggs (which become rubbery if frozen), melted butter and chopped parsley. In a covered dish it keeps warm well without spoiling, which makes it ideal for serving to people who may eat at different times depending on when they arise in the morning! Do try and make it with good, undyed smoked haddock – now so much easier to find. Better still, if you can get it, is finnan haddock.

---

2 lb/1 kg smoked haddock, filleted

water and milk mixed in equal parts to cover the fish in a saucepan

3 oz/75 g butter

1 onion, skinned and chopped finely

2 rounded tsp medium curry powder

1 lb/500 g rice (I like to use basmati)

freshly ground black pepper

FOR FINISHING THE KEDGEREE

4 hardboiled eggs, shelled and chopped

3 oz/75 g butter, melted

2 tbsp finely chopped parsley

Put the fish into a saucepan with milk and water to cover. Over a medium heat, bring the liquid to a gentle simmer, and simmer for 3 minutes. Take the pan off the heat, and let the fish cool in the liquid. Then strain the liquid and keep it to cook the rice in. Flake the fish, throwing away all bones and skin, and set the flaked fish on one side.

Melt the butter in a saucepan and add the finely chopped onion. Cook for 3–4 minutes, then stir in the curry powder and rice. Cook for a couple of minutes, then pour in the reserved fish cooking liquid. Bring to simmering point and simmer gently till the rice is cooked, about 18 minutes. Pour the cooked rice into a sieve and run cold water through it. Drain well, then put the cooked rice and onion into a buttered ovenproof dish. Fork the flaked fish through it, cover the dish, and freeze.

Remove the rice mixture from the freezer the morning before it is required – rice takes a surprisingly long time to thaw. Put the covered dish into a moderate oven – 350°F/180°C/Gas 4/bottom right oven in a 4-door Aga – for 40–45 minutes to heat through, and half way through reheating, fork into the rice the chopped hardboiled eggs and the melted butter. Just before serving fork through the chopped parsley.

Oat pancakes

Makes about 16–20 pancakes

These are so good to eat, and you can cook some crispy bacon and serve them with the bacon and maple syrup, American-style, or just make the pancakes and serve them with butter and marmalade. You can weigh out and mix together the dry ingredients the night before, and beat in the eggs, milk and melted butter and syrup mixture in the morning – just let the mixture stand for 10 minutes before you make it up into pancakes. Pancakes are known as drop scones south of the Scottish-English border.

8 oz/250 g plain flour	3 oz/75 g butter
½ tsp salt	3 tbsp golden syrup (dip the
1 rounded tbsp baking	spoon into very hot water
powder	first)
1 rounded tsp bicarbonate of	2 large eggs, beaten
soda	7 fl oz/200 ml milk
4 oz/100 g porridge oats	oil or butter for greasing

Sieve the dry ingredients into a bowl and add the porridge oats. Melt together the butter and golden syrup and beat this, the beaten eggs, and the milk into the dry ingredients. Let the mixture stand for 5–10 minutes then heat a griddle or a frying pan. Grease it lightly, and drop spoonfuls of the pancake mixture onto the heated surface. Cook for 2–3 minutes each side, turning them over with a palette knife. As the pancakes cook, keep them warm on a plate, with a teatowel over them.

NEW YEAR'S DAY DINNER FOR EIGHT

Mushroom and Marsala soup
Leek and cheese filo parcels
Lamb ragoût
Purée of turnip, artichoke and potato
Blackcurrant, raspberry and lemon suédoise
Vanilla meringues
Pear and Poire William mousse
Chocolate sauce

New Year's Day Dinner

Mushroom and Marsala soup

Serves 8

This soup freezes very well. It is a really good soup, but, as with *all* soups, is only as good as the stock used in its making. I feel I am in danger of becoming a real bore in my crusade against stock cubes, but it really makes such a difference to the soup. The taste of Marsala complements that of the mushrooms, and the *Leek and cheese filo parcels* (see below) to eat with the soup make a delicious change from bread or rolls, the more usual accompaniment to soups. The filo parcels can be frozen, or made a couple of days in advance and kept, covered with clingfilm, in the fridge.

---

3 oz/75 g butter
2 medium onions, skinned and chopped
1 garlic clove, skinned and chopped
2 medium potatoes, peeled and diced quite finely
1 lb/500 g mushrooms, wiped and chopped

2 pt/1.2 L good chicken or vegetable stock
salt and freshly ground black pepper
¼ pt/150 ml Marsala
chopped parsley (optional)

Melt the butter in a saucepan and add the chopped onions, garlic and diced potato. Cook over moderate heat for 7–10 minutes, stirring occasionally to prevent them from sticking. Add the chopped mushrooms, cook for 2–3 minutes then pour in the stock. Simmer the soup till you can crush the bits of potato against the sides of the pan with your wooden spoon, then take it off the heat and cool for half an hour. Liquidize the soup, taste, and season with salt and pepper. Stir the Marsala into the soup as it is reheating. If you like, sprinkle chopped parsley over the surface to serve. Personally, I'm not a great garnisher, and this mushroom-flecked soup looks, to me, quite attractive served just as it is.

Leek and cheese filo parcels

Makes 24 parcels serving 8

---

4 sheets of filo pastry

melted butter, sunflower or olive oil

FOR THE FILLING

1 oz/25 g butter
2 tbsp sunflower or olive oil
6 medium-sized leeks, washed, trimmed, and cut in 1 in/2.5 cm slices
1 garlic clove, skinned and very finely chopped

salt and freshly ground black pepper
freshly grated nutmeg
3 oz/75 g cream cheese, such as Philadelphia

Start by making the filling. Melt the butter and heat the oil together in a saucepan, and add the sliced leeks and finely chopped garlic. Cook till the leeks are soft, about 10 minutes over a moderate heat. Season with salt and pepper, and freshly grated nutmeg. Take the pan off the heat and liquidize the cooked leeks to a smooth purée, adding the cream cheese. How smooth a purée you get depends on the sharpness of the blades of your food processor or blender; if you feel the purée is a bit stringy (leeks do vary) sieve the purée, but if you keep whizzing you should get it smooth enough.

Lay a sheet of filo pastry on a work surface; brush it all over with melted butter or sunflower or olive oil. Put a second sheet of filo exactly over the first, and brush this too with butter or oil. With a sharp knife, cut the filo in half, then cut each half into three even-sized strips. Cut each strip in half widthways. Put a teaspoonful of leek and cheese purée on each piece of filo, and fold into a parcel, brushing each with oil or butter. Repeat the process with the remaining pastry. Put the parcels on an oiled baking tray, cover the baking tray with clingfilm, and put the tray into the fridge until you are ready to bake the filo parcels. Bake them in a hot oven – 425°F/220°C/Gas 7/top right oven in a 4-door Aga – for 7–10 minutes, till they are golden brown and crisp. Serve, warm, on a plate or in a basket, to accompany the soup.

Lamb ragoût

Serves 8

I much prefer casseroled lamb to beef, the only drawback is that it tends to be a fiddle to prepare. This ragoût freezes beautifully, you can make it up to a couple of months in advance, which for me counterbalances the bother of cutting up the meat! This is a variation on a recipe given to me by my mother several years ago.

3 lb/1.5 kg boneless leg of
  lamb, trimmed weight
12 oz/350 g unsmoked
  bacon, as lean as possible
3 rounded tbsp plain flour
1 tsp salt
lots of freshly ground black
  pepper
3 oz/75 g butter

2 tbsp sunflower oil
3 medium-sized onions,
  skinned and chopped
  finely
1 pt/600 ml red wine
1 pt/600 ml water
bouquet garni: parsley,
  thyme, bay leaf, garlic
  clove

Cut the lamb into 1 in/2.5 cm cubes. Slice the bacon into 1 in/2.5 cm pieces.

Mix together the flour, salt and pepper, and turn the lamb and bacon in the seasoned flour till all the bits are evenly coated. In a heavy casserole melt the butter and heat the oil together, and, a few pieces at a time, brown the meats well, removing to a dish to keep warm while you continue browning the rest. When all the meat is browned, lower the heat under the casserole a little, and add the finely chopped onions. Cook them for 5–7 minutes, stirring occasionally to prevent them from sticking. Pour in the wine and the water, and stir continuously till the sauce comes to the boil. Put in the *bouquet garni*, and replace the browned meat. Cover with a lid, and cook in a moderate oven – 350°F/180°C/Gas 4/ bottom right oven in a 4-door Aga – for an hour. Take the dish out of the oven, cool it completely, and freeze it. When required, thaw overnight, and before serving cook it for a further 35–40 minutes from room temperature in a moderate oven – the sauce should be bubbling and the meat tender when you stick a knife into a bit.

Purée of turnip, artichoke and potato

Serves 8

The sweetness of these combined root vegetables goes extremely well with the lamb ragoût. This dish too can be frozen.

---

1 small turnip, peeled and cut in chunks
8 potatoes, peeled and cut in half
1½ lb/750 g artichokes, peeled and cut up if they are large

salt, pepper and grated nutmeg
3 oz/75 g butter, cut in pieces
2 large egg yolks

Put all the peeled and cut-up vegetables together in a saucepan, cover them with cold water and bring the water to the boil. Add ½ tsp salt, and simmer till the vegetables are tender when a knife is stuck into them. Drain them really well, steam them off over heat, then mash well. When you have mashed them as well as you can, beat the purée with an electric, handheld beater, beating in the pieces of butter and the egg yolks. Season to taste with salt, pepper and nutmeg. Butter an ovenproof dish and pile the vegetable purée into it. Cool completely, cover, and freeze. Thaw overnight, and reheat in a moderate oven – 350°F/180°C/Gas 4/bottom right oven in a 4-door Aga – uncovered, for 20–30 minutes to serve.

Blackcurrant, raspberry
and lemon suédoise

Serves 8

A suédoise is really just a set purée of fruit, in this case a refreshing combination of blackcurrants and raspberries, with lemon to enhance their flavour. I like to serve small vanilla meringues, sandwiched together with whipped cream, to accompany the suédoise.

---

*1 lb/500 g each frozen
    blackcurrants and
    raspberries
pared rind and juice of
    2 lemons
6 oz/175 g granulated sugar*

*1½ pt/1 L water
4 sachets powdered gelatine
    (approximately 50 g/
    2 oz)*

Put the blackcurrants, raspberries, pared lemon peel (I use a potato peeler for this job to avoid getting any pith with the rind) and juice into a saucepan with a pt/600 ml water. Bring the liquid to simmering point, then stir in the sugar. Simmer for a minute, take the pan off the heat, cool, and liquidize. While the fruit is cooling, sprinkle the gelatine over the remaining ½ pt/300 ml water in a saucepan, then warm it over a gentle heat, shaking the pan to dissolve completely the gelatine granules. Add this to the fruit purée as it cools. Sieve the liquidized purée – it's the only way to get rid of all the little woody pips – into a serving dish, and cover with clingfilm. Put in the fridge till you want to serve it – you can make the suédoise three days in advance. Serve with *Vanilla meringues* (see below).

Vanilla meringues

Serves 8

These can be made two or three weeks in advance, and kept in an airtight tin till required. Sandwich them together with whipped cream to serve with the suédoise (see above).

---

3 large egg whites

6 oz/175 g vanilla sugar (caster sugar, kept in a jar with a vanilla pod or two)

Lay a sheet of bakewell paper (siliconized greaseproof paper) on a baking tray.

In a clean bowl, whisk the egg whites till stiff then, still whisking, add the caster sugar a spoonful at a time, and continue to whisk till the sugar is all incorporated. With a star-shaped nozzle, pipe the meringue in even-sized blobs the size of a 10-pence piece onto the bakewell paper-lined tray. Bake in a low-to-moderate oven – 250°F/120°C/Gas ½/top left oven in a 4-door Aga – for 1½–2 hours, until the meringues lift easily off the paper.

Pear and Poire William mousse with warm chocolate sauce

Serves 8

This mousse doesn't freeze, but it can be made a day ahead and kept in a covered bowl in the fridge, and taken out and left to come to room temperature a couple of hours before being served. This is a fault you often come across with desserts containing gelatine – they are left in the fridge till the moment before they are brought to the dining-room, and therefore they tend to be rubbery in texture. The flavour of this mousse is deliciously boozy, and the pieces of pear don't discolour because they are tossed in lemon juice before being folded into the mousse. The *Chocolate sauce* is perfect with it.

---

4 pears, preferably Comice, peeled, cored and chopped
2 tbsp lemon juice
5 large eggs, separated
6 oz/175 g caster sugar

4 tbsp Poire William liqueur
2 tbsp cold water
1 sachet powdered gelatine (approximately ½ oz/ 15 g)
½ pt/300 ml double cream, whipped

Toss the chopped pears in the lemon juice.

In a bowl, whisk the egg yolks, gradually adding the caster sugar, and continue whisking till the mixture is very thick and pale. Measure the Poire William and water into a saucepan, and sprinkle over the gelatine. Let it sponge up into the liquid, then dissolve the gelatine over a gentle heat – take great care not to let the liquid boil. Whisk this into the egg yolk mixture, then fold the whipped cream into this. Let the egg yolk and cream combination set to the point where it thickly coats the back of a large spoon. Then whisk the egg whites till they are very stiff, and, with a large metal spoon, fold the whites quickly and thoroughly into the mousse. Pour into a serving dish, and fold through the chopped pears. Decorate with more whipped cream, or with grated dark chocolate.

Chocolate sauce

¼ pt/150 ml water
6 oz/175 g soft brown or
   caster sugar
1 tsp vanilla essence

3 rounded tbsp sieved cocoa
   powder (not drinking
   chocolate)
3 tbsp golden syrup (dip the
   spoon in very hot water
   first)

Put all the ingredients together in a saucepan and, over a moderate heat stir till the sugar dissolves completely. Then boil the sauce fast for 5 minutes – the longer you boil it the thicker and stickier it will become. This sauce keeps well in a jar in the fridge.

SUNDAY NIGHT SUPPERS FOR SIX–EIGHT

Parsnip, lemon and ginger soup
Fresh asparagus soup
Cheese and garlic granary bread
Cheese, mushroom and bacon soufflé
Crab soufflé
Cheese, tomato, bacon and parsley omelettes
Pipérade with garlic croûtes
Onion and pepper tart
Avocado, bacon and egg salad

Sunday Night Suppers

However much you love having people to stay, somehow I find that what to have for supper on Sunday evening presents one of the biggest problems of the lot – not that my affection for our guests is on the wane, it's just that Sunday evening finds me at my all-time culinary low. So this chapter gives you a few suggestions: none of them takes long to make (a vital ingredient for supper on a Sunday!) and they constitute a 'light' meal, which is intended to be supplemented by fruit and cheese.

Parsnip, lemon and ginger soup

Serves 8

Soup is wonderful Sunday night supper food. Easy to prepare, it can be made a couple of days in advance and kept in a covered container in the fridge. It combines with bread, cheese and fruit to make a light but satisfying meal, ideal at the end of a few days of probably rather rich food, during which one has very likely eaten more than one normally does during an ordinary family weekend. This parsnip soup has all the things I like in a

357

soup – I love the flavour of parsnips, and here it is complemented very well by the lemon and fresh ginger in the recipe. Soup – any soup – is elevated to being something really special if good stock is used to make it; personally, chicken stock is the one for me, but a good vegetable stock (remember not to include any potato or turnip peelings in it – they make it bitter) comes a close second.

---

3 oz/75 g butter, or 4 tbsp oil (sunflower, if possible)

2 medium onions, skinned and chopped

4 good-sized parsnips, peeled and chopped

pared rind of ½ lemon – I use a potato peeler to avoid getting any of the pith

a piece of fresh ginger about 2 in/5 cm long, peeled and chopped

2 pt/1.2 L good chicken stock

juice of ½ lemon

salt and freshly ground black pepper

2 tbsp finely chopped parsley

Melt the butter (or heat the oil) in a large saucepan, and add the chopped onions. Cook for 5 minutes or so, stirring occasionally. Then add the chopped parsnips, the lemon peel and the ginger. Cook for a further 5 minutes, then pour on the stock. With the saucepan half-covered with a lid, simmer gently till the pieces of parsnip are soft. Then cool the soup a little before liquidizing and sieving into a clean bowl or saucepan. Season with lemon juice, salt and pepper to taste. Reheat to serve. I like to stir a couple of tablespoons of finely chopped parsley through the soup just before serving, it does wonders for its appearance!

Fresh asparagus soup

Serves 8

I love to take advantage of asparagus when it comes into the shops, and luckily the season appears to lengthen each year. As with all soups, its strength rests entirely on the stock from which it is made.

I like to chop off the heads of the asparagus and steam them, then serve them in the soup – somehow it seems such a waste to cook and liquidize them along with the rest of the soup.

---

2 oz/50 g butter
2 medium onions, skinned and chopped
1 lb/500 g asparagus, heads removed and set aside, stalks chopped

2 pt/1.2 L good chicken stock
salt and freshly ground black pepper
a squeeze of lemon juice (optional)

Melt the butter and add the chopped onions to the butter in a saucepan. Cook for about 5 minutes, stirring occasionally. Then add the chopped asparagus stalks, cook for a further few minutes before pouring on the stock. Half-cover the pan with a lid, and simmer gently until the pieces of stalk are tender when you stick the point of a knife in one. Meanwhile, steam the heads of the asparagus. Cool the soup a bit before you liquidize, and then sieve it – into a bowl if you intend to keep it in the fridge, or into a clean saucepan if it is for reheating.

Serve the soup with the steamed asparagus heads stirred through, and season to your taste with salt and pepper, and a squeeze of lemon juice if you like.

Cheese and garlic granary bread

Makes 3 1 lb/500 g loaves

We make granary bread each day here at Kinloch for our guests. Quite recently I was having a lovely conversation with one of our guests who was telling me the sort of things about his stay with us that it is pure pleasure to hear, and which you wish you had the entire staff beside you to hear as well, because the impact of compliments seems to lose much in the passing on! But we were discussing bread, and he was telling me what a keen baker he is, and had I ever made cheese bread? He so enthused me that I went straight back to the kitchen and made some. Since then I have embellished it with garlic, dry mustard and a dash of Tabasco as well as so much grated cheese that initially you wonder whether the dough can absorb that much. Don't worry, it can – and still rises too! It is quite delicious, but even more so when sliced thickly and toasted. It would make an ideal accompaniment to the previous two soups, or indeed any of the recipes suggested in this chapter for Sunday night suppers, and is very good served with grilled tomatoes. It freezes as well as other bread does.

½ pt/300 ml hand-hot water
2 tsp sugar
2 oz/50 g dried yeast
1¼ pt/750 ml hot water
1 tbsp salt
2 tbsp demerara sugar

3 lb/1.5 kg granary flour
2 tsp mustard powder
a good dash of Tabasco
10 oz/275 g strong white
 Cheddar cheese, grated
1–2 large garlic cloves,
 chopped finely

Stir together the ½ pt/300 ml warm water with the 2

360

teaspoons of sugar and the dried yeast, and leave it in a warm place until it has trebled in size.

Mix together the 1¼ pt/750 ml hot water with the salt and demerara sugar.

Measure out the flour into a bowl, add the mustard and a dash of Tabasco and leave it in a warm place – the secret of good breadmaking is to keep everything warm.

When the yeast mixture has trebled in frothy volume, stir it and the 1¼ pt/750 ml water, sugar and salt into the flour. Mix well, then turn the dough onto a well-floured surface. Spread it out and spread over its surface the grated cheese and finely chopped garlic. Roll up and knead well until the dough feels less sticky and more elastic – anyone who makes bread regularly will know just what I mean! I knead the whole and count slowly to 200, then divide it in three, and knead each piece to a further count of 50. Put each kneaded loaf-to-be into an oiled 1-lb/500-g loaf tin, and leave the tins in a warm place, covered with a teatowel. How quickly they rise depends on how warm the place is – 15 minutes on an Aga, out of any cold draughts. I find it is better to bake the loaves as they are still 'proving', because they rise a bit more in the cooking. Bake in a hot oven – 425°F/220°C/Gas 7/top right oven in a 4-door Aga – for 25 minutes. Turn out of their tins and cool on a wire rack in a warm place. Cooling the loaves in the warmth prevents them from becoming tough. To slice a loaf warm from the oven, turn it upside-down first.

Cheese, mushroom and bacon soufflé

Serves 8

For 8 people, I would advise making the soufflé in two dishes, each about 6 in/15 cm across. Butter the soufflé dishes, and shake some Parmesan cheese around them. You can make the sauce part of the soufflé in the morning, all ready for the egg whites to be whisked and folded in sometime in the late afternoon.

---

4 oz/100 g butter
1 onion, skinned and
    chopped finely
8 oz/250 g mushrooms,
    wiped, destalked, and
    chopped
3 oz/75 g plain flour
1¼ pt/750 ml milk

6 oz/175 g grated Cheddar
    cheese
salt and freshly ground
    black pepper
a pinch of freshly grated
    nutmeg
8 large eggs, separated
6 rashers smoked bacon,
    grilled till crisp, then
    broken in pieces

Melt the butter in a saucepan, and add the chopped onion; cook for 5 minutes, stirring occasionally. Then add the chopped mushrooms, cook for a minute, and stir in the flour. Cook for a further minute or two, stirring. Gradually add the milk and heat, stirring continuously, till the sauce boils. Let it bubble for a moment, then take the saucepan off the heat and stir in the grated cheese. Season with salt, pepper and nutmeg. Beat in the egg yolks one at a time, beating very well in between each. Stir the broken-up cooked bacon into the thick sauce, and set on one side. About two or three hours before baking, whisk the egg whites till they are very stiff, and, with a large metal spoon, fold them quickly and thoroughly through the sauce. Divide the mixture between the two prepared soufflé dishes, and cover each with clingfilm until ready to cook.

Bake in a hot oven – 425°F/220°C/Gas 7/top right oven in a 4-door Aga – for 40–45 minutes. If you aren't quite ready to serve it, another 5 minutes' cooking time won't hurt, but once you have opened the oven door it must be served immediately! This soufflé is good served with granary bread (see recipe, pages 170–71) and a simple green salad.

Crab soufflé

Serves 8

This is the richest recipe in this chapter, but if you have access to a supply of good crabmeat (you can buy some pretty filthy frozen stuff, so watch out) it is one of the most delicious and luxurious things with which to treat your guests. What I said about soufflé making in my introduction to the *Cheese, mushroom and bacon soufflé* applies of course to this recipe too – it applies to *all* soufflés! The thing to remember about this soufflé is to let the sauce cool completely before you add the crabmeat to it. The flavourings in the sauce complement the crab-meat very well.

---

4 oz/100 g butter
1 garlic clove, skinned and
   chopped finely
3 oz/75 g plain flour
2 tsp mustard powder
1¼ pt/750 ml milk
3 tbsp dry sherry

3 oz/75 g good Cheddar
   cheese, grated
salt and freshly ground
   black pepper
about 2 gratings of nutmeg
6 large eggs, separated
1½ lb/750 g crabmeat,
   either all white, or –
   which I prefer – a
   mixture of brown and
   white

363

Butter two soufflé dishes, each about 6 in/15 cm in diameter.

Melt the butter in a saucepan, and add the chopped garlic. Cook for a minute, then stir in the flour and mustard powder, stir and cook for another couple of minutes, then stir in the milk, stirring continuously till the sauce boils. Let it bubble for a minute, then take the pan off the heat and stir in the sherry, the grated cheese, and the seasonings. Beat in the egg yolks one by one, then let the sauce cool completely – you can do this in the morning for supper that evening, or even the previous day. When the sauce is quite cold, stir in the crabmeat. Two or three hours before serving, whisk the egg whites till stiff and, with a large metal spoon, fold them quickly and thoroughly through the soufflé mixture. Divide between the two buttered dishes and cover each with clingfilm, until ready to cook. Then whip off the clingfilm before baking in a hot oven – 425°F/220°C/Gas 7/top right oven in a 4-door Aga – for 40–45 minutes. Serve immediately. If your guests aren't quite ready to eat when the cooking time is up, leave the soufflés in the oven for a further few minutes – they won't hurt. But once the oven door is opened, they must be served immediately!

Cheese, tomato, bacon and parsley omelettes

Serves 4

I love omelettes but I feel they are really only practical to make for four people, and even then the time spent making and serving them can be halved if you have a non-stick Le Creuset frying pan, in which you can make one big omelette and divide it in two. I once went to a smart lunch party in New York which was an omelette party – there were four chefs skilfully making the most exquisite omelettes, and there were bowls of fillings from which you could choose. I could happily have spent all lunchtime standing and watching them deftly turning out omelettes!

For these omelettes, you can have the cheese grated, the tomatoes prepared, the bacon grilled and broken in bits, the parsley chopped, and all four ingredients mixed together in the morning ready for supper that evening. So the actual putting together of the omelettes doesn't really take a minute.

---

8 eggs
4 tbsp cold water
salt and freshly ground
*   black pepper*
a little butter for greasing
8 oz/250 g good Cheddar
*   cheese, grated*

4 tomatoes, skinned,
*   deseeded and chopped*
8 bacon rashers, grilled till
*   crisp then broken in pieces*
1 tbsp chopped parsley

If you are making individual omelettes, beat together 2 eggs and 1 tablespoon of water. Season with a little salt and pepper. Melt a small bit of butter in the omelette pan and pour in the egg mixture. Let it cook, lifting up the sides of the omelette so that uncooked egg mixture slips beneath the cooked. When the surface has no more runny egg sloshing around, cover with a quarter of the omelette filling. Ease on to a warmed plate, folding it over with the help of a palette knife – it will be quite fatly filled. Repeat the process until all four omelettes are made – I keep the first one warm and have that myself, which makes the serving and eating a bit more together (I keep the second one I make for Godfrey!).

Pipérade with garlic croûtes

Serves 8

This is my favourite Sunday supper dish; it also makes a very good lunch dish, or a first course at dinner. The pepper, onion and garlic mixture can be cooked on Saturday, or on Sunday morning, and reheated before the eggs are scrambled through it. I also like to skin, deseed and slice tomatoes in thin strips to stir into the cooked scrambled eggs, and I fry small triangles of bread in olive oil with lots of garlic, then drain them on several thicknesses of kitchen paper. These can be kept warm for up to 1½ hours.

---

4 tbsp olive oil, plus extra for frying the croûtes
1 garlic clove, skinned
16 triangles of bread, white or brown
2 medium onions, skinned and sliced thinly
3 red and 3 yellow peppers, halved, deseeded and sliced thinly

1 garlic clove, skinned and chopped finely
16 large eggs, beaten together
4 tomatoes, skinned, deseeded and sliced
salt and pepper

Fry the triangles of bread in the extra olive oil, with the whole skinned garlic clove. When the croûtes are golden on both sides, take them out of the oil, drain and keep them warm on several thicknesses of kitchen paper.

Heat the 4 tablespoons of oil in a saucepan, and add the onions, peppers and the finely chopped garlic. Cook over a moderate heat till they are all soft. You can get the pipérade to this stage in the morning. Reheat the mixture

before adding the beaten eggs, and scramble these with
the cooked onion and pepper mixture.

When the eggs are scrambled, stir the sliced tomatoes
through them just before serving. Season to taste with
salt and pepper and serve either piled on an ashet, with
the garlic croûtes all round, or on warmed individual
plates.

Onion and pepper tart

Serves 8

This is *so* good, and very easy too. You can bake the
pastry case several days in advance, and cook the pepper
and onion mixture a day ahead, so that you just need to
beat together the eggs, yolks and cream and bake the tart
just before supper – it really couldn't be easier. I like to
serve it with a mixed green salad.

FOR THE PASTRY

4 oz/100 g chilled butter, cut
   in pieces
6 oz/175 g plain flour
3 tsp icing sugar

salt and pepper
2 tsp mustard powder

FOR THE FILLING

4 tbsp olive oil
5 medium onions, skinned
   and sliced thinly
4 red peppers (or 2 yellow
   and 2 red), halved,
   deseeded and sliced finely

1 large garlic clove, skinned
   and chopped finely
salt and freshly ground
   black pepper
2 large whole eggs, plus
   3 yolks
½ pt/300 ml double cream

Put all the pastry ingredients together in a food processor and whiz till it resembles fine crumbs. Pat round the sides and base of an 8–9 in/20–23 cm flan dish. Put the flan dish into the fridge for at least 30 minutes before baking in a moderate oven – 350°F/180°C/Gas 4/bottom right oven in a 4-door Aga – for 20–25 minutes.

Meanwhile make the filling. Heat the oil in a large saucepan, and add the sliced onions (I know it sounds a lot, but they diminish in size significantly as they cook) and cook over a moderate heat for 7–10 minutes, stirring occasionally, then add the peppers and the garlic. Cook over a moderate heat, giving the mixture the occasional stir, for about 40 minutes, by which time the peppers and onions will be well-cooked and very soft. Season to taste with salt and pepper.

Beat together the eggs, yolks and cream, and season with salt and pepper. Then put the cooked pepper and onion mixture into the cooked pastry case, spreading it evenly. Pour over the egg and cream mixture, and bake in a moderate oven – 350°F/180°C/Gas 4/bottom right oven in a 4-door Aga – for about 20 minutes or until the custard mixture is just firm. You can serve this tart warm or cold. I never know which I prefer!

Avocado, bacon and egg salad

Serves 8

This is delicious on a summer Sunday evening, served with warm *Cheese and garlic granary bread*, (page 360) or rolls. You can prepare virtually all the salad in the morning, with the exception of the avocados; try not to do them too far ahead as they tend to turn brownish.

FOR THE SALAD

1½ average-sized Iceberg
    lettuce, sliced and
    chopped
4 hardboiled eggs, chopped
3 avocado pears, skinned
    and flesh chopped in quite
    large chunks

8 rashers smoked streaky
    bacon, grilled till crisp,
    then broken in pieces
8 tomatoes, skinned,
    deseeded and sliced in
    segments
a handful of chives, snipped
a handful of parsley, torn
    into small sprigs

FOR THE DRESSING

½ tsp salt
½ tsp sugar
a good grinding of black
    pepper
½ tsp mustard powder

1 tbsp wine vinegar
2–3 tbsp oil
1 tsp pesto (optional)

Mix together all the salad ingredients. Mix the dressing ingredients together well – you can keep it in a screw-topped jar. Dress the salad just before serving.

Index

Lemon *continued*
  and orangeade, 223
  and parsley stuffing, 286–7
  Blackcurrant, raspberry and
    lemon súedoise, 352
  Christening cake, 33–4
  cucumber and chive mayonnaise,
    22
  mousse with raspberry sauce,
    250–51
  Parsnip, lemon and ginger soup,
    357–8
  Raspberry and lemon parfait,
    88–9
  Spiced bramble and lemon jelly,
    311–12
Lentil
  Carrot, leek and lentil soup,
    166–7
Light Christmas cake, 271
Lime
  and gin sauce, 148
  Crystallized lime slices, 30
  mousse, 302–3
  Poached fillets of halibut with
    sorrel and lime sauce, 39–41
  Rich lime pie with crystallized
    lime slices, 29–30
  Roast duck with lime and gin
    sauce, 148
  Sorrel and lime sauce, 40–41
Liver
  Chicken liver and pecan pâté with
    cranberry Cumberland jelly,
    275–6

Madeira
  Mushroom and Madeira sauce,
    247–8
  Roast fillet of beef with
    mushroom and Madeira sauce,
    247–8
Marinated mushrooms, 189–90
Marinated pigeon breasts with port
  sauce, 70–71
Marinated pork fillets with orange
  sauce, 183–4
Marmalade gingerbread, 62–3
Marsala
  Mushroom and marsala soup,
    347–8
Marshmallows with chocolate and
  Smarties, 221
Marzipan, 268–9

Mayonnaise
  Curried, 111
  Egg, 199
  Lemon, cucumber and chive, 22
  Pimento, 81–2
  Tomato and dill, 188
Meatballs
  Spicy, 18–19
Melon
  Tomato, melon and applemint
    salad, 23–4
Meringue
  Brown sugar meringues, 209
  Coffee and almond meringue,
    86–7
  Pink and white miniature
    meringues, 219
  Rhubarb meringue tart, 135–6
  Vanilla meringue, 353
  Vanilla meringues with cream,
    and raspberry and blackcurrant
    sauce, 175–6
Mincemeat, 272
Mint
  Pea, pear and mint soup, 164–5
Mixed fish and shellfish in dill sauce
  with rice, 78–80
Mousse
  Blackcurrant and applemint, 53–4
  Curried egg, 181–2
  Horseradish, 186–7
  Lemon mousse with raspberry
    sauce, 250–51
  Lime, 302–3
  Pear and Poire William mousse
    with warm chocolate sauce,
    354–5
Mousseline potatoes recipes, 28,
  158–9
Mrs Hill's Christmas pudding,
  299–300
Mushroom
  and Madeira sauce, 247–8
  and Marsala soup, 347–8
  and rice filo parcels, 234–6
  Asparagus and mushroom gratin,
    103–4
  Cheese, mushroom and bacon
    soufflé, 361–3
  Deep-fried mushrooms with
    tartare sauce, 117–19
  Marinated mushrooms, 189–90
  Roast fillet of beef with
    mushrooms and Madeira sauce,
    247–8

381

A SELECTION OF COOKERY TITLES
AVAILABLE FROM CORGI BOOKS AND BANTAM PRESS

THE PRICES SHOWN BELOW WERE CORRECT AT THE TIME OF GOING TO PRESS. HOWEVER TRANSWORLD PUBLISHERS RESERVE THE RIGHT TO SHOW NEW RETAIL PRICES ON COVERS WHICH MAY DIFFER FROM THOSE PREVIOUSLY ADVERTISED IN THE TEXT OR ELSEWHERE.

☐	13816 9	**A FEAST OF FLAVOURS: NEW VEGETARIAN CUISINE**	*Annie Bell*	£5.99
☐	03785 5	**EVERGREEN (Hardback)**	*Annie Bell*	£16.99
☐	99365 4	**SECRETS FROM AN ITALIAN KITCHEN**	*Anna Del Conte*	£6.99
☐	99444 8	**ENTERTAINING ALL'ITALIANA**	*Anna Del Conte*	£6.99
☐	03816 9	**THE MEDITERRANEAN DIET COOKBOOK (Hardback)**	*Nancy H. Jenkins*	£16.99
☐	03794 4	**RICH TRADITION OF EUROPEAN PEASANT COOKERY (Hardback)**	*Elizabeth Luard*	£12.99
☐	99216 X	**SEASONAL COOKING**	*Claire Macdonald*	£6.99
☐	99288 7	**MORE SEASONAL COOKING**	*Claire Macdonald*	£6.99
☐	99217 8	**SWEET THINGS**	*Claire Macdonald*	£5.99
☐	14209 3	**SUPPERS**	*Claire Macdonald*	£6.99
☐	01595 9	**THE GREENS COOKBOOK (Hardback)**	*Deborah Madison*	£17.99
☐	14305 7	**HOW TO WIN THE WINE GAME**	*Peter Noble and Penny Landeau*	£9.99
☐	02913 5	**FIELDS OF GREENS**	*Annie Somerville*	£17.99

All Transworld titles are available by post from:

Book Service By Post, PO Box 29, Douglas, Isle of Man IM99 1BQ

Credit cards accepted. Please telephone 01624 675137, Fax 01624 670923 or Internet http://www.bookpost.co.uk for details.

Please allow £0.75 per book for post and packing U.K.
Overseas customers allow £1 per book for post and packing.